‘Even as someone who spends an inordinate amount of time studying internet culture, I learnt so much from this book. It's packed with examples, uses compelling evidence and leaves the audience with so many insights.’

Roya Zeitoune, Head of YouTube Culture & Trends, EMEA

‘Rhea cuts through the noise and theory to deliver accurate and game changing insight.’

Joanna Jensen, entrepreneur, author & investor

‘This book is like having access to the best and brightest marketing brains and strategies in the palm of your hand. Whether you have a David or a Goliath marketing budget, this book gives you the know-hows, the know-nots, and everything between to ensure your marketing stops the scroll in its tracks. Rhea's book removes the guesswork from your marketing strategy and provides diverse examples from far and wide, that you can't fail but to learn from. A must read (...and then read again!).’

Jess Littlewood, Chief Community Officer, #SBS Small Business Sunday

‘It is no longer enough to know the 4Ps and other outdated marketing paradigms. This is a new age for marketing where simplicity no longer works. It is easy on the eye and fun to read but it’s not afraid to rubbish the status quo. The book is full of successful campaigns and the lessons to be learnt from studying the reasons behind their success. A must-read for marketing professionals and Masters and Doctoral students.’

Professor John Egan, Regents University, London

‘A highly practical, accessible and usable guide for founders who want to leverage the power of marketing without having the biggest budget. Rhea Freeman demystifies what makes campaigns work, and how to apply those lessons for impact.’

Monique Boddington, Management Practice Associate Professor,
Judge Business School, University of Cambridge

AF819471

‘A warm, practical book that does the thing I always want marketing writing to do: it shows you the working. Rhea doesn’t just admire campaigns from the outside, she finds out how it was done and turns those into ideas a business with any budget can use.’

Joe Glover, Co-Founder of The Marketing Meetup

‘There are lots of small businesses who are eager to grow, and *Big Brand Marketing* is their essential read to making that happen. Rhea breaks down superstar marketing campaigns into practical and digestible chapters, and inspires small businesses to have a bigger influence – on a budget.’

Adam Ferrier, Founder of Thinkerbell & consumer psychologist

BIG BRAND MARKETING

BIG BRAND MARKETING

High impact strategies for small businesses

RHEA FREEMAN

BLOOMSBURY BUSINESS
LONDON • NEW YORK • OXFORD • NEW DELHI • SYDNEY

BLOOMSBURY BUSINESS
Bloomsbury Publishing Plc, 50 Bedford Square, London, WC1B 3DP, UK
Bloomsbury Publishing Inc, 1359 Broadway, New York, NY 10018, USA
Bloomsbury Publishing Ireland Limited, 29 Earlsfort Terrace, Dublin 2, D02 AY28, Ireland

BLOOMSBURY, BLOOMSBURY BUSINESS and the Diana logo are trademarks of Bloomsbury Publishing Plc

First published in Great Britain 2026

Copyright © Rhea Freeman, 2026

Rhea Freeman has asserted her right under the Copyright, Designs and Patents Act, 1988, to be identified as Author of this work.

For legal purposes the Acknowledgements on p. 283 constitute an extension of this copyright page.

Cover design: Louise Dugdale
Cover images © Adobe Stock

All rights reserved. No part of this publication may be: i) reproduced or transmitted in any form, electronic or mechanical, including photocopying, recording or by means of any information storage or retrieval system without prior permission in writing from the publishers; or ii) used or reproduced in any way for the training, development or operation of artificial intelligence (AI) technologies, including generative AI technologies. The rights holders expressly reserve this publication from the text and data mining exception as per Article 4(3) of the Digital Single Market Directive (EU) 2019/790.

Bloomsbury Publishing Plc does not have any control over, or responsibility for, any third-party websites referred to or in this book. All internet addresses given in this book were correct at the time of going to press. The author and publisher regret any inconvenience caused if addresses have changed or sites have ceased to exist, but can accept no responsibility for any such changes.

A catalogue record for this book is available from the British Library.

Library of Congress Cataloging-in-Publication Data

Names: Freeman, Rhea author
Title: Big brand marketing : high impact strategies for small businesses / Rhea Freeman.
Description: London ; New York : Bloomsbury Business, 2026. | Includes bibliographical references and index.
Identifiers: LCCN 2026030394 (print) | LCCN 2026030395 (ebook) | ISBN 9781350592056 paperback | ISBN 9781350592087 epub | ISBN 9781350592070 pdf
Subjects: LCSH: Branding (Marketing) | Small business marketing | Marketing
Classification: LCC HF5415.1255 .F74 2026 (print) | LCC HF5415.1255 (ebook) | DDC 658.8/27–dc23/eng/20260806
LC record available at https://lccn.loc.gov/2026030394
LC ebook record available at https://lccn.loc.gov/2026030395

ISBN: PB: 978-1-3505-9205-6
ePDF: 978-1-3505-9207-0
ePub: 978-1-3505-9208-7

Typeset by Deanta Global Publishing Services, Chennai, India
Printed and bound in Great Britain

For product safety related questions contact productsafety@bloomsbury.com.

To find out more about our authors and books visit www.bloomsbury.com and sign up for our newsletters.

CONTENTS

Introduction

I've been obsessed with marketing for as long as I can remember. How some brands get it, and others really don't. How some can have the best product for a certain job, but their marketing campaigns are so poor – or maybe even non-existent – that it means they'll fail. How others have a seemingly simple product or service, but *really* get it. They get their target audience, they understand what matters to them, they've done the work, created brilliant campaigns to raise awareness (and maybe even a tonne of earned media) and that's driven sales. Having a good product is essential for longevity and loyalty – of course it is – but two products of equal merit could go head to head, and the thing that makes one win over the other, 99 per cent of the time, is the marketing.

It's not just the pretty pictures, the amazing videography, the celebrity endorsement – it starts a long time before that . . . although we don't see all the work that goes in from a consumer standpoint. Through this book, I'll be looking at some incredible marketing campaigns across a range of industries that have leveraged a particular quality, and then I'll speak to the brands, people and agencies behind these to discover the secret sauce. And then I'll be sharing those key steps that made the campaign succeed AND how this can be utilized for all businesses, regardless of budget size.

Of course, if you have nothing but loose change in your pocket, you're less likely to achieve the same exposure as a brand with millions to play with; however, whatever the budget, the theory behind the success can be applied. What's also true is that there are many examples of campaigns with zero budget spent on their reach that organically made a huge impact on the brand's exposure, sales and all the metrics that matter.

But before we delve into these examples, before we extract the DNA, let's set the ground rules, because without these, and without this knowledge, you will struggle to market and, therefore, sell your product effectively. This is a list of assumptions I have made about you, dear reader. Well, maybe not assumptions as such, because if you don't know all of this, that's fine too. These points will be referenced as you read, when we delve into the case studies of the great campaigns we're examining. Regardless of what you know (and what you don't), you'll still get a great deal out of the book.

You'll also find that as you read examples, interviews and we get into the nitty-gritty of it, you'll see these themes recur. It might cause you to think about aspects of your marketing that have evolved (or not) over time that are perhaps misaligned with what you're trying to achieve now. It might make you go back to the drawing board or do some deeper work on some areas. What I'm hoping, in some ways, is that it makes you rethink everything, but not in a way that is built on perceived failure; in an excited way that reignites the fire in you and fills you with inspiration and the desire to embrace and try new things. To be a bit braver, to make sure that the world knows all about you and your brand. The world is busy, people are busy, the noise everywhere is loud and that's why, more than ever, your marketing needs to be special.

I'm going to assume that . . .

- **You know who your target customer is.** Ideally, you'll have a customer avatar or persona that is a fictitious target customer – give them a name, a car, fill in all the gaps in their story because it makes everything else a lot easier! You also know their pain points, the language that they use – in essence, you've done your research. You might have multiple audiences and avatars; that's perfectly acceptable, too, as many brands do. But what you also need to realize is that different audiences require different care. Different topics, styles, language and visuals appeal to them. It's difficult to appeal to everyone all the time unless you do something so bold and wild that it's gathering attention for that purpose. The key is to think about the audience you're trying to capture *in that moment* and make sure you know them better than you know your best friend.

- **You have a good product or service that there's a real need for.** Not a need that you think, one that you know. Yes, you can market a poor product, but you'll end up throwing good money after bad, as no one will be repurchasing, telling their friends (or anyone that will listen!) anything good, and you'll erode any positive reputation that you or your brand may have. Things do go wrong from time to time, and that's when honesty can play a part to get things back on track, but we'll cover that later. From the outset, do your best to make sure what you're offering is worthy of being purchased and enjoyed.
- **You know what makes you and your product or service special and different – your Unique Selling Point/Proposition (USP).** These elements are woven into every marketing activity we do. It will also dictate what actions you take. These will look like a mix of core values, non-negotiables and unique selling points.
- **You have a system that allows you to deliver said product or service.** Or rather, you will have before it's launched, because we're not in the business of not delivering. All your efforts will be wasted if you annoy people – and it's just not fair. (We like fair in this book.)
- **You like your customers (well, most days!).** You want to do the best by them. Being a decent person who cares is an incredibly important marketing strategy. Don't get me wrong, there are some days when 'one of those people' will enter your inbox and you'll think 'I hate it all' – that's not what I'm talking about. There are always people who are sent to try us and test us!
- **You know what you're looking to achieve.** You know what success looks like for you – not everyone else – and your business. You have

a goal (for more on goal-setting, check out my previous book, *You've Got This*), and you understand how to measure progress based on your definition of success.

- **You're up for learning – thinking about things differently and trying new things.** The world changes at an alarming pace – if this book were being written just a few years ago, there wouldn't have been a section on AI. Technology changes, the world moves on, but the key is that we have open minds and learn and adapt as we go. This isn't throwing everything away and starting again; it's looking at what can be improved and the learning needed to do that.
- **You see failure as a learning point, not a reason to stop.** Everyone has failures. Literally everyone. From researching this book, I have seen many amazing examples of strategy that has gone south, marketing campaigns that have fallen flat (or caused offence – sometimes both!), but the thing is, mistakes happen. The key is that we can learn from them so we don't repeat them. Connected to this, you need to be flexible enough to see failure staring you in the eye and move on. The sunk cost fallacy has no place here – we don't just carry on along our route to disaster because we've already started. We stop, pivot and go again with new information.
- **You lean into the data.** As marketers, many of us prefer the creative side of the job, but the data generated from what we do and what we can research should help guide. Don't fear the data; see it as a secret weapon. We'll chat about that in detail later too.

Know that what is in the pages that follow is pitched to you, assuming you know this.

And let's talk about the pages that follow. I had a bold plan to get insight from some of the best, most brilliant campaigns I'd ever seen. Ones that you'd ask your friends if they'd seen over a drink – even friends that aren't wired into marketing. The sort that made the news, as well as made people change their habits or go and buy whatever was being promoted. I wanted to speak to the people involved, to get their input so not only could we explore these campaigns and the strategy behind them from an outside-looking-in perspective, but from the inside too. Because this 360 approach is wildly helpful. I am very, very grateful to all the people, brands, agencies, companies and connectors who have helped make this book what it is. Who understood what I was trying to achieve and got excited. You'll find their names laced throughout the book and mentioned in the acknowledgements page, but I wanted to mention it up front too.

This book and its contents have been designed to inspire, excite and educate. To look at why things work and see how the 'secrets' can be applied to what you're working on too. It's to get those creative juices flowing, to look at different ways to achieve a goal, to support you in making an impact. Regardless of your budget. Yes, there are some campaigns featured in these pages that cost a significant amount of money – but the ideas behind them can be translated to any budget. I promise. Some of the campaigns in this book didn't cost much at all – and importantly, all of them can provide a foundation to help you build something of your very own. It's not about replicating – it's about being inspired – regardless of budget – to create something that excites/educates/informs the customer in a way that stands out against all the noise that we're surrounded by today. To stand out, to stop a scroll, to turn back a page, to pause the TV, to pick off the shelf, to buy. There's a LOT of competition out there, and what marketing aims to do is encourage that transaction. But in order to do this, you need to be different.

You might feel small in the business world. You might see competitors and believe you could never compete. You might read people's social media 'boasts' about their income and think you're never going to make it. Stop right there. There's always going to be someone bigger. There's always going to be someone shouting from the rooftops. You need to silence the noise, focus on you and your business and know that creativity with a hefty side of strategy wins. So, shall we begin? Grab your highlighters, sticky notes, notebook and whatever else you need, and let's get cracking . . .

1

Going viral

The good, bad and ugly of virality

Is it easy to go viral? Many people believe that going viral is the solution to all their marketing problems, but the truth is, it isn't. Or, at least, it's not the only solution.

Let's say you've seen a piece of content go viral for another brand. Or there's a trend that seems easy to jump on. Everyone loves it, people are doing their own parodies, it's everywhere. You decide that THIS is what you need to do, so you get involved with your own version. It could go viral, it could flop. Because someone else had success with a piece of content, it doesn't mean that you will.

Let's say it does go viral. Going viral helps to increase your reach and exposure far beyond what's 'normal' for you – that's how I and many others define it. This could look like hundreds, thousands, even millions of views/comments/interactions. But what if the content has nothing to do with your business and what you do? The people you've found won't know anything about you that's going to move the needle in a productive way. Your ego might love the viral nature of your content, but will it impact the bottom line? Will you make more sales? Get more subscribers? Whatever your measure of success is, will you achieve it? If the answer is no, it's a waste of time.

When virality is a distraction

Martin Huntbach is the co-founder of Vidonary, director of Jammy Digital and former CMO of ScoreApp. Through Jammy Digital, he's worked with a number of business owners, including entrepreneur, author and founder of Dent Global, Daniel Priestley. He recalls a video they did that went viral. 'It was controversial, shared an opinion that a lot of people had, and we published it on a big platform,' says Martin. 'But what did it deliver in terms of leads? Nothing. I would argue a video of 5k views got more leads and customers than this one with 1.5 million. And that's because the 5k one was deep rooted in the methodology we apply (more in Chapter 5). In the end, we saw it as a distraction.'

In some ways, it can be worse than a waste of time or a distraction. In some cases, viral content attracts all manner of undesirable comments. If the overall goal of the content aligns with your business and the increased reach and exposure is worth it, then it's just the price of success. But if it doesn't align with you in any way, and now you're having to manage trolls, the impact could be seen as entirely negative.

Keeping your core in mind

And what if the nature of the content doesn't align with the core values of your brand? We need to know what is essential for us as a brand. What are the values that we are bound by? Some companies have mission statements to sum this up; others have wall art and posters. And if you're a smaller business or a solopreneur, you're likely to know them well. These values that run through your core should never be compromised and certainly not for a viral moment. For example, let's say one of your core values is sustainability. Jumping on a trend that shows wasteful behaviour, even in an amusing way, might gain traction, but could also gain a large amount of backlash, and could well alienate the people who buy from you. The ones that pay the bills. It can also undermine your authenticity and your trustworthiness – going against values and core beliefs can be hugely detrimental.

You might think I'm being overdramatic, and maybe I am, but there have been many examples of brands being cancelled for actions that went against their core values. I think we can all think of situations where companies have made the press (and sustained serious backlash) for being unethical, inappropriate, discriminatory, culturally insensitive or controversial (without good reason) – and let's be clear, on many occasions, that is what the public perceived rather than the intention behind a campaign. I cannot imagine that many companies decide to actively annoy their customers, to be disrespectful or offensive in a way that puts their reputation and business in peril. That would be crazy. And the point is that even the best thought-through campaigns can go wrong and create negative noise because of something that wasn't considered. There have been cases of hashtags that didn't really work, visuals that have been interpreted in an offensive way, and failure to read the room. These things happen to the biggest brands out there. But receiving this kind of pushback when the goal was solely to attract five minutes of fame is a bad use of time and money. Many brands that have endured this kind of misstep have the funds and personnel to rectify the situation – even then, it's tough.

Going back to our second option, if it flops, then you've wasted your time. If it doesn't align with everything above, you could have annoyed the people backing you and buying from you without the potential upside of increased exposure and reach.

And when it works . . .

But there is another side to virality. And that's when a piece of content that aligns with your intended audience, your values and the product takes on a life of its own. That can be magical. There have been many reported cases of businesses going from zero to hero through a piece of content that went viral. It can be a powerful driver. Dr Jonah Berger,[1] Wharton School professor and bestselling author of *Contagious: Why Things Catch On*, explains that viral is often essentially word of mouth, but on a big scale. 'It can be a great way to raise awareness, encourage consideration, and drive conversion,' says Jonah. 'People often trust word of mouth more than they trust traditional advertising, and it can be more targeted, so by turning customers into advocates, businesses can help spread the word.'

One campaign that could be used to define virality is the ALS Ice Bucket Challenge in 2014. There's a lot more about this in the chapter on Big Issues, but there's so much value in the pros and cons of virality that we can learn here; it needed to be shared. Brian Frederick, chief marketing and communications officer for ALS, shares his experience.

Scrutiny

'The ALS Ice Bucket Challenge[2] opened us up to a whole lot of scrutiny, so one of the things I was very clear about was the need to be transparent with how we were spending the money as well as how much we raised,' says Brian. 'This was a change in culture for some, but when you're looking at seventeen million people who uploaded videos, they have a right to know what the impact is. We created a page that was on the website that showed everything – we have a listing of hundreds of research projects and what we'd given to them.'[3]

Even if you don't usually do things a certain way, going viral and the increased eyes and interest that this can gain means that processes need to be examined with a new focus. As Brian says, detailing exactly how donations were spent wasn't something they usually did (the man-hours alone could

[1]https://jonahberger.com/
[2]https://www.als.org/ibc
[3]www.als.org/IBC/commitments

mean something like this isn't viable all the time), but in a move to combat questions that could bring negativity to the cause, it was a considered measure that was taken.

ALS also found it had a few reporters looking to discredit it, to expose potential fraud and show it wasn't as positive as it seemed, so again, transparency won. 'I worked really hard, I even introduced them to scientists,' says Brian. 'We also had people criticize us for the kinds of research we were funding, but without doing the work to really see what we were actually doing! We were also accused of wasting water (which ALS wasn't endorsing as it provided lots of alternatives!). The biggest regret I always had was that this act of showing the progress of the donations and saying thank you didn't get anywhere near the same reach as the challenge itself, so people still don't know the impact they had.'

To show the scale of this virality, the ALS Ice Bucket Challenge featured 440 million people and the videos created gathered 10 billion views. It also raised over $220 million for ALS and attracted over 2 million new donors. Turn to Chapter 7 to find out more.

When Norwich City launched its World Mental Health Day campaign in 2023, it had no idea of the impact it was going to have. At the time of writing, the video has been viewed over 350 million times, won awards, raised awareness of the cause, seen positive sentiment toward the club surge and even the Prince and Princess of Wales reached out.

Case study: Norwich City football club's You Are Not Alone

'The reason for the campaign started in 2022,' says Gavin Beard from Norwich City. 'Every year we have a kit launch and it drives lots of interest and awareness. We went off-site as a team and thought about different concepts and we saw what Roma was doing at the time, which was that each time they signed a new player, they utilized that asset to highlight a missing person. We were inspired by this – we liked how they'd taken a situation that garnered a lot of attention and used the platform for good. For us, the kit launch is the biggest moment from an attention perspective, and we wanted to do something similar.'

The team started to implement this idea in 2022. Norwich City wanted to use its platform to talk about mental health, something that most clubs weren't doing at the time. The team started looking at concepts that would create traction and impact the club's audience, and what they could do to promote key mental health messages in a way that really landed and felt connected and authentic.

Says Gavin:

> For World Mental Health Day 2023, Daniel Williams, who's our marketing manager, came to me and said that there's always a lot of talk around [dying by suicide] being the last person you expect, so we thought about whether we could use this as the start of the idea. This aligned with the data, and it was contextual with the audience at Carrow Road (Norwich City's home ground). We thought about portraying a match day and having one person showing the signs you'd expect from someone with a mental health concern, next to someone you really wouldn't.

The campaign itself[4] was filmed in the team's stadium and shows two men attending a range of matches with the backdrop of an audience (who, fun fact, were the marketing team and others who work full time at the club – even the main actors were local amateur performers, with one being a steward at the stadium!). As the film moves through, the men are seen interacting and responding to various situations across the seasons, with one showing more 'traditional' signs of a mental health issue and one being very animated, happy and engaging. A line comes on the screen saying 'sometimes it can be obvious

---

[4]https://youtu.be/tX8TgVR33KM?si=Obuc25h5pZLfqztA (Search 'Norwich City Check in on Those Around You')

to see when someone is struggling', but the next piece of the film flips the script.

'We wanted to deliver the message that you don't always know, and this was delivered in the last screen with an empty chair, of the person who was "happy",' says Gavin.

Another key aspect of this campaign was that it pushed against preconceptions, as male mental health, especially connected to older men between forty-five and forty-nine, is not really spoken about. Because of this, people might think it's not such a big issue, but the stats disagree.

'The process to create the campaign was pretty quick,' says Gavin. 'We did it in-house. It was a very low-budget production. You could argue it makes it feel more authentic. We tried to deliver something that felt real with real fans. We're proud it was low budget and achieved numbers we couldn't even imagine.'

The campaign went viral and now has over 350 million views. Even today, Norwich City still receives requests for the video to be used in presentations, and it has reached many countries through them offering the file for free to those looking to use it in non-commercial ways.

The work of fame

Virality can add a lot of work though, as Gavin shares. 'We were surprised. We'd done some work in the space previously and our fans were receptive so we thought it would land well, but the impact it had and the pace and momentum that this gathered took us by surprise. When we saw the final cut, we all liked it, but none of us expected the reach.'

The extra exposure led to many more enquiries, so plans were developed around this. 'We had a few personal messages that came to us and we connected them to Samaritans. That was a responsibility we didn't see coming. We were also inundated with requests for the video from people who wanted to use it for presentations and so wanted the original file. It became unmanageable, so we set up a mailbox[5] with an instant response containing the link to where to download the file. Even now, the inbox is active which is mind-blowing really. People all over the world have watched the video, and people from around 60 different countries have requested the video.'

The club also received a lot of charity requests. 'When it came to mental health, many charities involved in the space wanted to work with us. Some were doing it for commercial reasons, some because they wanted to be linked to what we'd done. There was a huge influx, and it became quite challenging for us in terms of which charities had the right interests.'

While Norwich City didn't receive any negativity from the campaign, the biggest challenge was around how it balanced support for other causes that mattered to them – like sustainability and inclusion. It created a challenge around the impact the club was able to make. Due to this, the team created a strategy around what they needed to talk about and the causes they were going to be the most vocal about. This step has been important for the overall marketing strategy as it has delivered clarity.

The science behind the success

We often think of virality as random, but as Dr Jonah Berger says, there's actually a lot of science behind it. 'We've looked at thousands of pieces of online content, tens of thousands of brands, and millions of purchases around the United States and around the world,' says Jonah. 'Again and again, the same six factors come up. In *Contagious*, I put them in a framework called the STEPPS framework. The S stands for social currency (i.e., the better something makes people look, the more likely they are to share it), T stands for triggers (i.e., top of mind means tip of tongue), the E stands for emotion (i.e., the more we care, the more we share), the first P stands for public (i.e., easier to see, easier

---

[5]www.canaries.co.uk/content/mental-health-video-made-available-to-all

to imitate), the second P is for practical value (i.e., useful information), and the last S is for stories (i.e., information often travels under the guise of idle chatter).'

Sometimes, a number of these levers are pulled at the same time to create the response. That's not to say that the level of virality can't still be a surprise, but if the right elements are woven in, the chances of success are increased.

When I spoke to Phil Rumbol, ex marketing director for Cadbury, about the incredible Gorilla campaign that you can read more about in Chapter 20, he shared that while many thought that a gorilla going viral was a fluke, it really wasn't; it was by design and ticked many boxes that allowed it to do this, to have this impact on people and cause them to share and discuss. There was a formula there that worked, something proved when the third campaign in the series, Eyebrows, like Gorilla, gained even more traction online and beyond.

Can slow and steady win?

Another point that was very interesting about the Gorilla campaign, and also another campaign that went viral, Dove Beauty Sketches (see full case study in Chapter 17), was that they pushed against what we think makes a viral campaign – and that's speed. A lot of viral content is fast, short and snappy. From the second the video starts, your eyes and ears are borderline assaulted with sound, movement and action. Neither of these campaigns did this. Both started off in a very calm way – the way the Gorilla advert built was legendary, and Dove's film was three minutes long. So why did this work?

John X Carey, the director of Dove Beauty Sketches, shares some wisdom here: 'Now, virality is largely engineered by algorithms. TikTok made it possible for anyone to go viral, but it rewards very different things: bold thumbnails, big hooks in the first seconds, and content that escalates quickly – closer to a reality show format than a short documentary. The execution of a film like *Dove Real Beauty Sketches*[6] today would need to be reconsidered, because the algorithm doesn't naturally prioritize formats like this anymore. You could still make something with that level of impact, but the approach would have to be rethought entirely – from the thumbnail to the title to how the first five seconds land.'

There was a real emotional pull that allowed it to go viral then. The reason? John believes it was sincerity and authenticity. 'I think it went viral because we sincerely documented people letting go of deep self-esteem issues in real time. That authenticity resonated with viewers, especially women who recognized their own self-doubt in those moments. And summing it all up in such a powerful visual – a woman standing in front of two versions of herself – gave us a simple, striking image that made a complex emotional idea instantly clear.'

How can you make this work for you? Key learnings . . .

- In many cases, virality can be designed into the campaign.
- Going viral without relevance might gain reach, but will it reach the right people? Don't be drawn into making your ego happy without the work.
- Viral content can create negativity – when content starts to take on a life of its own, it will get in front of new people, which can be good, but can be bad too. Think about how you're going to manage this.
- Ensure the content you create is aligned with your brand and its values. The increase in views could be detrimental if the content undermines

[6] www.dove.com/uk/stories/campaigns/real-beauty-sketches.html

your core beliefs and leaves your customers confused and questioning who you are and what you really think.

- If you're tackling a big issue, ensure you've done the research to speak about it in an informed way, and make sure you have the information in place that allows responsible signposting to the right people or organizations.
- When virality strikes, you could become overwhelmed with emails/DMs/orders. Have a plan for how to streamline processes and focus your energy on what moves the needle. Automations can be a good way to do this and don't take long to set up.
- Appreciate that if something goes viral and attracts attention from the mainstream press, more questions could be asked about any claims you've made about the activity you're sharing. If your processes are good and you approach marketing in an ethical way, there's nothing to worry about – but think about how you're going to share this to prevent people from making assumptions.
- If you want to go viral, understand what the algorithms want. This might mean adjusting your delivery to tick more boxes. Algorithms change frequently, so keep your finger on the pulse and try, test and iterate as needed.

2

Humour

Laugh, connect, remember

Humour can be a powerful marketing tool. Whether people are looking for a new product to try, or even a new partner, having a sense of humour can often be a big asset. And yet, there are some brands, some campaigns, some situations in which humour would be wildly inappropriate. Even if you're a brand that doesn't deal with obvious issues that would be at odds with a light-hearted, funny approach, if your brand's personality and tone don't suit humour, then it's usually a good idea to steer clear. You don't want to be the equivalent of the dad joke at a party while the tumbleweed rolls and things get awkward.

What's your vibe?

Brand tone is very important. It should impact every aspect of your communication, every touchpoint with your customer, every marketing activity. Having a clear idea of your brand's tone (or vibe) and how this is communicated is essential, particularly as you start to scale your brand or call on agencies or freelancers to help you. Connected to values, tone is a core part of the equation and there are lots of points to consider. Your brand's tone could be fun, serious, professional, casual, technical, relaxed, formal, funny, inspiring . . . the list goes on.

If you're a law firm, for example, then fun, casual language, imagery and collateral might not be the best fit – unless, of course, you're trying to break the mould and make law fun . . . but then think of the target audience. When looking for a lawyer, what do people want? I've never heard anyone say, 'I love that my lawyer has a wild sense of humour and calls me his mate.' Have you?

If you're a beauty brand that's aimed at teenagers, then it makes a lot more sense to be more casual in your language and use words that people of that age range use and understand. They probably don't want or need the detailed and complex scientific names of everything you're putting into that moisturizer you're marketing – in fact, it could well make them run for the hills.

That said, humour is a vast spectrum, from witty puns and observational humour at one end to the other, where naughty jokes make people blush. There's a lot in the middle. And many brands can and do effectively tap into a little bit of humour in the right situation, at the right time, in the right way, with the right knowledge of their audience and how they will or won't respond. There's an opportunity to test humour in smaller groups – ideally people who are your target audience – to make sure that what you're sharing has the impact you want, and that it really is funny.

Duolingo[1] is one brand that has adopted humour in a space where you wouldn't necessarily expect it. Before this green bird burst all over our phones, learning languages wasn't seen as a fun hobby. In fact, many viewed it as academic, hard, dare I say a little bit boring? But then, Duolingo happened.

'When we shifted away from "mass-appeal" marketing and leaned into humour, it was driven by a simple insight: language learning is hard to sustain unless it feels rewarding and fun,' says Monica Earle, director of public relations and comms at Duolingo. 'We knew our strongest advocates were younger, highly engaged online communities who respond to bold, unexpected content.

[1]www.duolingo.com/

We did a lot of listening, both on social media and through our own learner community, and learned that leaning into Duo's "weird but wholesome" personality resonated most.'

But why did it work so well? Let's take a closer look . . .

Case study: Duolingo

Duolingo broke the mould when it launched in 2012. The company grew through trial and error, but around a clear mission. It prioritized long-term retention because it knew that was how its users would get results. Language isn't learnt in a day; it needs regular practice – something the company was keenly aware of, building a feature for it in the app (the Streak feature).[2] But one of the key aspects that has been huge for Duolingo's success is the focus on fun. The whole product was built on play and gamification to make learning fun and something people really wanted to do, not something that they felt they had to do. The company describes the brand as 'wholesome but unhinged, leaning into what makes fans laugh, even if not everyone gets the joke'. Duo, the company's mascot, reinforces this message through every marketing channel and possible opportunity. In fact, Duo has become such an icon that he's been invited onto red carpets for movie premieres, has become a social media star, and even hosted a fake dating show.

Duolingo doesn't use humour as an afterthought; it's woven into everything it does. As its handbook[3] says: 'It's a world where gigantic, plush owls star in fake Broadway musicals – on ice . . . where no one is safe from the joke (not even the CEO).' The app is full of unexpected things, such as the sentences taught that shun convention and the characters that make the learning experience a lot more engaging. The company appreciates that its competition

---

[2]https://blog.duolingo.com/how-duolingo-streak-builds-habit/
[3]https://blog.duolingo.com/handbook/

isn't just other language apps; it's every app out there. Because of this, the way it teaches has been designed to compete with the other distractions a phone can bring to its users. The old way of teaching a language – asking where the cat is, for example – isn't engaging enough to make people opt for that app over every other available. This is why fun is in everything that happens around Duolingo. It's built into its brand DNA.

Finding its voice wasn't easy and took some time. To start, it went after a broad audience. The issue with this, as so many find, is that marketing aimed at the masses often attracts no one. Or far too few for the costs, time and energy involved. But it takes a lot of bravery to shun broad and double down on niche. It takes even more to do this in a way that the company describes as 'weird'. When you embrace 'weird', some people will be alienated. They won't understand. Humour is subjective but can also draw people toward it – in this case, like a lime green beacon.

The company's mascot owl, Duo, was originally designed to help people practice their new language, and he still does this through the notifications sent through the app to encourage learning – but these aren't simply notifications. You have characters from inside the app telling you that the languages won't learn themselves, you have a dose of passive aggression if you don't do your practice, the app icon even changes over time if you annoy Duo and don't take your lessons! These notifications get the point across at the same time as raising a smile or striking terror into the hearts of those who receive them! The company also uses AI to personalize the messages it sends to users to make them more effective. But the internet moulded Duo into something else. Something fun, quirky, crazy, unexpected, that could be relied on to bring humour into the lives of those who got him. He became bigger than the app.

On April Fool's Day 2024, the world saw the creation of the Duolingo on Ice[4] campaign that enjoyed over 100 million social media impressions.

---

[4]https://youtu.be/lEFRl6Lej_0?si=70EsLzNG_qvY74sW (Search 'Introducing Duolingo on Ice')

In February 2025, Duo faked his own death (the post announcing this had over two million likes on Instagram),[5] got a lot of news coverage and created a whole series of content with characters showing their sadness, and a video of how it happened (a Tesla Cybertruck[6] – even X got in on it!). The company then shared that it was a test and users' app activity had brought him back. In addition to humour (which happened as the campaign unfolded), the shock aspect played a part in this campaign. Risky, but it worked and worked well.

'This was an internal pitch that at first seemed almost *too* bold,' says Monica. 'Duo is a beloved character, so yes, we debated whether "killing him off" might upset people. But we knew that risk was part of the reward. We designed the arc so the humour came through quickly: the Cybertruck gag, the melodramatic reactions, and the reveal that learners could "bring him back" through their activity. The campaign exceeded our expectations in coverage and engagement, becoming a shared cultural joke.'

This bold approach was also seen in the company's five-second Super Bowl ad in 2024 when Duo 'produced' another Duo out of his backside.[7] This might seem (to those who don't know Duo) more than a little random, but this animation was chosen as a result of social listening to find out which of the illustrations used on the app's widget had captured the audience most effectively. This was part of a coordinated campaign that saw four million of the app's users, in the specific regions where the ad ran, receive Duo's perky butt with the message, 'No buts, do a lesson now' at the same moment. And what happened? People took to their socials to share the coordinated effort! The ad showcased the fun, quirky nature of the app – it was beautifully aligned, signalled to their customers and created intrigue for many others.

---

[5] www.instagram.com/p/DF79IjgxfuE/
[6] www.instagram.com/p/DF-peENxg3I/
[7] www.youtube.com/watch?v=QPjgXWm7F6c (Search 'Duolingo Do Your Lesson No Buts')

Duolingo is currently valued in the billions. In May 2025, it shared that it had over ten million paying subscribers, 38 per cent revenue growth and well over thirty million followers across social media.[8]

The magic of humour

But why does humour work? What makes it so effective? Robin Dunbar is a professor of evolutionary psychology at the University of Oxford.[9] He's authored or edited over twenty books, written hundreds of articles in scientific journals and is the 'father' of the theory, Dunbar's number, which suggests the maximum number of people one can maintain relationships with is 150. He says: 'Laughter triggers endorphins in the brain and the endorphin system underpins social bonding in all primates. If you laugh with somebody, you feel much more bonded to them, you feel more trusting and more relaxed in their company. Laughter is the bottom line in sociality.'

Being bonded to someone, or something like a company, can also create comfort, connection and even trust. It has a much greater impact than you might think.

With marketing in mind, research has been conducted to show that humour does aid both awareness and attention.

Humour in marketing extends beyond the initial impact. When something makes us laugh, or even just smirk, we're more likely to engage with it and to share it with our friends. Really good campaigns create a buzz around them; many make it onto the news, and social media is awash with either the campaign itself, the result of the campaign (the product, for example), or memes that are created around it. Viral content is built on this – on shareability – because

---

[8]https://investors.duolingo.com/news-releases/news-release-details/duolingo-adds-record-number-daus-surpasses-10-million-paid

[9]www.psy.ox.ac.uk/people/robin-dunbar

without the shares, the campaign can only travel as far as the spend or the social media reach that accompanies it.

'It's worth thinking about why humour is important for communications in general, and why it is useful for particular brands,' says Jamie Peate, global head of Retail Strategy and head of UK Effectiveness for McCann Worldgroup. He's known for his work across many brands, including Aldi in the UK. 'There are two quotes I always hold in my mind about this; one is from George Bernard Shaw, who said, "if you want to tell people the truth, you'd better make them laugh or they'll kill you,"[10] and I love this, because if you're confronting people with inconvenient truths then a natural thing is to be defensive, so you need to get them to recognize it. This brings us to the second quote from Peter Ustinov, who said, "comedy is simply a funny way of being serious."[11] It cuts to the heart of what we're trying to do with most communications. We want to be noticed, liked and remembered, and we know that things that are naturally entertaining tend to work better than just trying to tell you something. We also know that if you're trying to challenge people and make them think and reflect on themselves a bit, humour is a great way to do this. One of the theories on why humour exists is that it was created to be able to challenge people in a non-confrontational way.'

Let's run through an example of how humour can be used to change public perception and enhance a brand's image. Imagine a brand that has earnt itself a reputation for being cheap – so cheap that those who shop there become 'labelled' as poor and there is even some shame connected to frequenting the establishment. But, what if the reason those products were cheap wasn't because of quality, but due to savings on things you can't see – like logistics etc.? You want to market your brand for quality, to start to dismantle that image and encourage people to try. But how can you start to poke a hole in

---

[10] www.goodreads.com/quotes/14392-if-you-want-to-tell-people-the-truth-make-them
[11] www.goodreads.com/quotes/49156-comedy-is-simply-a-funny-way-of-being-serious

people's beliefs – maybe their snobbish attitudes – in a way that makes them think rather than go on the defensive? Well, humour is the obvious solution. You could showcase people with said attitude trying the products and being delighted by the taste and then putting them in the packaging of more 'prestigious' brands. Or you could see them entering the shop in disguise or moving around the aisles in an 'undercover' way.

Humour can be used in other ways too. If you look at your company and think about what makes you different, what could you lean into there? Sometimes, brands try to cling to the norm and 'fit in' (even when they really don't) but if you embrace what makes you as a brand different, and find the humour in this, it can be magic too. 'Be someone who isn't afraid to be authentic,' says Jamie. 'It's about knowing who you are and owning it. Add humour with how to challenge these norms and it becomes very funny.'

How do you know what kind of humour works? There can be a temptation to jump on any possible trend to get views, but that's not how to develop humour alongside a brand identity, and without being clear on who you are, your messaging can be less amusing and more confusing.

Make the mundane funny

'For the brands we work with, we really look at what we're trying to achieve. An example could be making the mundane funny, or the ordinary extraordinary,' says Jamie. 'We could look at Christmas as a great example here – nothing is normal at that time of year – so could we be a bit "cage rattly", a bit surprising, and disruptive in the right way.'

But it's also about knowing what you're not and what you won't discuss. Some companies steer clear of subjects such as politics or religion, for example. Knowing what is off the table for a brand when it comes to humour can be as, if not more important, than knowing what is up for discussion. Monica Earle from Duolingo supports this point too: 'The key is consistency,' she says. 'Duo's voice – "chaotic, a little unhinged, but always on-mission" – is codified in our brand guidelines.[12] That way, whether it's a TikTok post or a Super Bowl spot, the humour always connects to the mission of making learning more fun and less intimidating.'

Bad jokes?

The truth is that not all humour works. And when it's badly placed, it can do significant damage to a brand. It can make you appear unprofessional, amateurish, untrustworthy, rude. Think about when someone sidles over to you and cracks a wildly inappropriate joke. . . . how do you feel? You don't want people to feel like that about your brand, or product or campaign.

We might fear sharing a 'bad' ad or tone-deaf campaign, but what are we truly afraid of? Is it landing badly or something else? 'What do we really think the danger is with using humour?' asks Jamie. 'Is it not being understood or offending? No. The danger is not being noticed. There's a great stat[13] that says 11 per cent of all ads are remembered, 4 per cent are remembered and liked, 7 per cent are remembered and not liked . . . but that means 89 per cent aren't noticed or remembered at all.'

Sometimes, though, a joke just doesn't work and people just don't engage with it or find it funny – no offence taken, but quickly forgotten. 'We've had social posts that didn't get traction, or small stunts that didn't resonate as widely,' says Monica. 'The important thing is that we treat those as experiments; if something falls flat, we learn from it and move on quickly.'

[12]https://design.duolingo.com/

[13]https://davetrott.co.uk/2008/04/why-do-we-assume-people-have-to-like-adverts/

We always need to come back to the target audience and those core brand values. Is your intended audience going to get it? Is it appropriate? Does it align with the core values of the brand? Is it *actually* funny, or do you just think it is? There's a lot at stake if you get it wrong, but also a lot of ways to try and test. In fact, today, it's never been easier to test more ideas.

The value of testing

Focus groups continue to be a good way to test ideas. This could be on a new campaign, product, design, you name it. Although there is absolutely a place for gathering people together in a physical location and speaking to them face to face, there are also cheaper, faster ways of testing the waters – social media or your own email database. By sending a simple email to a group, you can get a feel for what they think. By creating a community on social media, you can pose questions and gather responses. Reward people for their participation and you're likely to see good engagement too. Alternatively, you can A/B split test on a smaller scale using online ads. Test different ideas and see which gets the response you want before you scale and put more budget behind it. Even the best brands get it wrong – so don't worry about the 'failures'. Think about how you can test and iterate to make sure that when you launch the campaign to the wider world, you're confident that it's pretty damn good, that you haven't missed the mark, and that you and your whole team can get behind it.

The rewards for this are great. We see examples from companies all the time when they really get it right. The audience gets it. They share. More people get to know about it. And before you know it, that company is all over social media, newspapers and even on the news – for the right reasons, of course.

When you get it right, when people get it, the brand becomes more relatable and it can also really humanize a brand. Rather than being a faceless corporation that sells stuff, there's a sense of humour that gives personality that more straight-laced brands simply can't. Humour shows people that a brand is friendly, relatable; it gives a very clear signal to your audience – or 'your people' as I like to say – and the wider community too, because you all get the joke and have the same sense of humour. Humour can create a positive emotional connection – and isn't that really what we all want in every area of our lives? Even the companies we buy from?

One example of relatability from a humour perspective comes from Spotify and the 'Let The Song Play' campaign. Combining Sia's dulcet tones set against an all too familiar situation when we just want to let the song play. . . . and yet we've arrived at our destination. The humour comes from what the people captured in the campaign do in these situations. There's a lot more about this in Chapter 23, where you'll find a case study with insight from the inside.

How can you make this work for you? Key learnings . . .

- Humour can be magical. It can connect, gain trust, make people feel seen and heard and like they belong.
- It has the potential to do significant damage to a brand if the tone is wrong, it's offensive or tone-deaf. Know what you won't joke about.
- All humour has to align with your brand's core values to make a positive impact for the overall brand. You might win fans and followers if it doesn't, but it won't be building on your foundations.
- Keep your target audience in mind all the time. And don't make jokes at the expense of your customers in a way that would be seen as bad taste.
- Test your humour and your ideas on a smaller group of your target audience if you're unsure/just starting out. The more you do, the better you'll understand what works and what doesn't.

- Remember, it's not frivolous – there's real evidence to show that using humour in marketing can make campaigns more memorable and deliver real, tangible results.
- Consider utilizing social listening – this can be a great way to understand what people are discussing at any given time, which can allow for campaigns using humour to be more timely and relevant.

3

Let's work together

Strategic collaborations: Grow reach and reputation

What if there was a way to extend your reach, increase exposure, and even enhance your brand's perception in a way that didn't have to cost you a penny? Well, look no further, you're in the right place.

Working with the right companies as part of your marketing strategy, to help amplify your message, delight your target audience and/or get in front of more people is a brilliant marketing strategy when it's done well.

So why isn't everyone doing it? It's too easy to see your business in competition with everyone when that simply isn't the case. Yes, your direct competitors are your real competition – that is, if they sell exactly what you do and have the same target audience. But if a brand has a similar audience but the product isn't the same, you don't necessarily need to be sworn enemies! Yes, you might be in competition over the same people, but if you offer products or services that work together, it's not really competition, is it? It's complementary.

There are lots of different examples of collaborations when it comes to marketing. It could be a joint promotion or competition; it could be something as simple as an offer card that gets shipped alongside your orders. It could be working with a host of brands on products that support a big launch or campaign you're running to not only help you but to also help them get involved in the fun. Maybe it's even creating a product together or with someone else's IP under licence. There are so many different options out there.

But before you start asking everyone to work with you, understand that rules need to be in place, whatever type of collaboration you're thinking of entering into. And before you even get to that part, you need to think really hard about who you want to collaborate with.

Know the 'rules'

Once again, we need to start at our brand values. What is core to our brand's very being? Essentially, what won't we compromise for what could be a quick win, extra reach and maybe a nice ego boost too? It is essential to be clear on this. Collaborations that are well thought through and align well can have value that extends on and on. The new audience you attract is relevant and gets you. The brand/s you're working with will help to amplify your message because you align with theirs. The brand/s you're collaborating with are proud to be associated with you – as you are with them – and are very happy to shout about it too. Like finding the perfect partner, you need to do the groundwork and know what your non-negotiables are before you start deciding what dog you're going to adopt together . . .

Let's start at the top. What should we be looking for in our perfect (brand) partner?

Perfect partner checklist

- **Tone.** How do they address their audience? If their tone doesn't mirror yours, it's not necessarily a problem, but if they're very informal and you're very professional, what you create together could be rather jarring.

- **Audience**. Would your audience be interested in what they do – and vice versa? This works on many different levels. One is the fundamentals – like core beliefs and values – but also the demographics are important to understand. If your brand is all about women, then collaborating with a brand that's all about men could work in certain circumstances, but the overlap is going to be less.
- **Brand values**. Yes, they have been mentioned more than once in this book already, but knowing yours and knowing theirs is fundamental. If these are in direct conflict, see it as a warning sign. Not only could it reduce/prevent the success of any campaign, you could also find your current audience wondering what is wrong with you, and if you pick really badly, you could find yourself at the end of some nasty comments too.
- **Like-minded.** This might sound like a softer one, but it's still important and has to do with the person you'll be dealing with as part of the collaboration as well as the overall brand. Do they approach business, life, and customers the same way that you do? If your brand prides itself on a high level of customer service and the other brand appears not to care in the slightest, is that acceptable? Equally, if you're really excited about the collaboration and have started to put together a detailed plan and they really don't seem all that bothered, is that a red flag? And will this cause you problems further down the line?
- **Complement, don't compete.** Although you want your brand and its offering to align with the brand you want to work with, you don't want them to do the same thing. As an example, if you're an eco-friendly deodorant company, you could work with a make-up brand, but you wouldn't work with another deodorant brand. That would just be weird and very confusing . . .
- **You're in it together**. Knowing that the other brand understands that you're both responsible for the success of the collaboration is a big

one. If they think they're doing you a favour by just giving you some product and that's the end of their involvement, it is unlikely to fulfil its potential.

You might find that with your specific product or service you have more on your must-haves list than above. If you have a bricks-and-mortar business, like a café, for example, collaborating with a brand at the other end of the country is unlikely to be as effective as working with a complementary business a few doors away.

The next step

Let's say we've found our perfect partner – or partners – and we're starting to work on the nuts and bolts of how we can work together. A great place to start is to look at what success means. You might want to increase your social media following, they might want to grow their mailing list, and someone else could want to work on a co-branded product. Each of these requires a very different strategy. Generally, greater success is seen when only one call to action is implemented at a time. Asking someone to like your page, sign up to your mailing list and then go to a website to buy a product is a lot. Especially if they're not a relative or best friend!

The goal can be as simple as increasing social media reach – and competitions can be a very effective and easy way to do this (subject to a lot of caveats – competitions don't guarantee success!). Or it can be as complex as designing a product together. It doesn't matter what the goal is, what matters is that all participants are on the same page.

When you know your goal, you can then reverse engineer the steps to get there. It's important to ensure that everyone is clear on what needs to happen and, importantly, who is responsible for each step. The timeline is important too. Whatever kind of collaboration you're looking to run, you'll need a launch date and to launch you'll need to make sure your assets/content/videography/

photography/copy/ads are done before that date. Allocate fairly and work with all parties to ensure everyone's skillset is being used to its full potential, that no one feels overwhelmed, and that there's a place where everything can be put when completed and accessed by all – such as a shared file.

The devil is in the detail

Then look ahead to the campaign itself and when and how each piece of the puzzle will unfold. Be as detailed as you can. Life is busy, and in addition to collaborating with you, the people you're working with will have numerous other things going on. It's very easy to drop a ball. A detailed plan doesn't mean mistakes won't be made, but it increases the chances of success at the same time as managing expectations. I've observed collaborations before when one brand has thrown everything (and the kitchen sink) at its success and the other brand hasn't. This means one brand – or the person responsible for the campaign – feels hard done by because they have done all the work. The thing is, the other brand might not care, or may not have prioritized the collaboration, or failed to realize what the other brand expected. We see this time and time again when vague measures are given. 'I'll share a few times' can mean very different things to different people.

If you're looking to put some budget behind your activity, this also needs to be discussed in advance and agreed, as does the length of the campaign. Did I mention that details matter?!

What can a good collaboration do for a brand?

When you get it right, a good collaboration can make a huge difference. It can:

- Expose you to new audiences at a low cost.

- Increase your reach for minimal cost.
- Improve your brand awareness.
- Create a buzz with the potential to really supercharge your exposure and reach if you get this right.
- Give you more ideas. If you're a small business or solopreneur, the chances are you do most of your work on your own. This means that you only bring what you know and your worldview to the party. When you start to expand your network, people bring different perspectives, ideas and experience to the table, and this can open a lot of new opportunities.
- Help you create better content. Whether this is because you've pooled your budgets, there are more hands-on-deck, or the brands you're working with have experimented more than you have or have better kit. Linking to the previous point, different ideas help us to experiment more and test new things, and testing is what leads to improvement.
- Increase engagement. More eyeballs, more brands and more buzz generally lead to increased engagement. Depending on what you do, you could also get another organic engagement boost from that. A competition that requires engagement will help.
- Enhance your credibility. Another reason why a like-minded brand works. If they're well known and people have trust in them, it does no harm to either party to be associated with someone else who shares the same public perception.
- Help you achieve your goals! Whether this is mailing list growth, social media followers or straight-up sales – when the collaboration is built on solid ground, a lot is possible.

GoPro has and continues to work on some brilliant collaborations, most notably with Red Bull.[1] It's easy to see why this one works. Both brands appeal

---

[1]https://gopro.com/en/gb/news/gopro-and-red-bull-form-exclusive-global-partnership

to audiences that enjoy extreme sports and excitement, so there's a big overlap – but it's more than that. Both of the brands are premium, quality, clear and definite in their messaging and product, and if you look at the content that both produce, there's a very clear alignment in the quality behind the output too.

'You just kind of know what and who will vibe with your brand,' says Rick Loughery, senior vice president for GoPro. 'Look at their audiences, are they complementary? Is there opportunity for your content and message to resonate with their audience? What value will your brand (and the content) bring to their audience? And vice versa.'

When influencer and company founder Lorna Andrews had the chance to collaborate with ELEMIS, she saw it as a great opportunity to promote her brand, LA Space, to ELEMIS' audience, in a way that benefited everyone.

'I'd been working with ELEMIS as an influencer for a long time, so when we looked at doing something with LA Space rather than me, it was all about aligning brands,' says Lorna. 'It was positioning LA Space into an arena with a juggernaut of a skincare brand, and it went really well (2,000 kits sold in five days). It's all about elevating the brand, and I knew my community loved them too. It made total sense, and it was so easy. They let me choose products, the bag was made with our own print, it just worked so well.'

Different perspectives and fresh stories

This isn't the only collaboration Lorna has done, but as an influencer, she uses these slightly differently. 'It's something to talk about that's new and fresh, because for people that follow me, they know all about me, so I'm always looking for stories,' Lorna continues. 'When I started talking about LA Space, it was a new story to tell, something that isn't so me-centric. There's money to be made, but sometimes it's not about that. Sometimes it's tapping into an aspirational element of my brand to keep it interesting. With the wine (Lorna collaborated with wine company Lady A and launched a new wine called GHOST by Lady A, which linked to the name of Lorna's house), it reminded people that I like wine, they like wine and that we had a shared interest. Also, the fact I did it was aspirational. And the product was good – I would never want to launch anything that was rubbish.'

Collaborations can, as Lorna says above, give you something different to talk about, or at least tackle a subject that rolls around each year in a new and exciting way. Take Christmas. We know it is a regular event, but instead of a brand saying, 'It's Christmas, buy my stuff', that same brand could approach Christmas marketing from a different perspective. It could create content that entertains and engages to raise brand awareness before saying what's available to buy. In this way, collaborations can be used to add more value to an audience. Audiences consume content at an alarming rate, and sometimes collaborations appear – even from the biggest brands – that aren't so much about selling a product, but to share a different perspective, to create a talking point and to give people something new to view/listen/learn about.

There are many examples to call on that can show the potential rewards a good collaboration can have. When we look to big business, it can be overwhelming when we start to think about what we could do and how much it could cost. The thing is, collaborations can cost you nothing. Zero. Zilch. If you want to share content or expertise, that's just about allocating time to hop on a live stream or broadcast with someone, or write copy for a blog or newsletter, for example. If you want to do a competition, it could just be the cost of the product. Of course, the sky is the limit and there have been some incredible collaborations in recent years.

The cookie brand Oreo has been part of some truly awesome collaborations over the years, including Lady Gaga, Xbox, Spotify – and even Batman. James Whatley, a senior strategist who worked on this collaboration with Mondelez (the company that owns the Oreo brand) during his time at Digitas UK, shares the Oreo + Xbox Cheat Cookies story.

Case study: Oreo + Xbox Cheat Cookies

Oreo teamed up with Xbox to create a multi-award-winning campaign in 2023.[2] It brought together nostalgia and millennial entertainment passions to create a collaboration that was more than just skin deep, creating a buzz online and delighting both audiences. But what did they do, why did they do it, and why did it work?

'The Xbox campaign was called Cheat Cookies,' says James Whatley. 'We'd experimented with musical notes embossed on the cookies for Gaga and Spotify, and with the previous Batman campaign we had more embossments, but we wanted to take it further, we wanted to do even more embossments *and* we wanted to make them scannable. The mix of product and tech was a hard hurdle to clear. But then the team found a way and we were told we could have six different embossments. That, combined with our ambitions for the brand and business led us to cheat codes – well, cheat cookies.'

This was something different, interesting (and delicious!), but what really set this campaign apart was the depth of collaboration that was achieved. It's clear that not only did both Oreo and Xbox really want to work together, they went beyond the obvious. The cookies and the cheat codes created with them unlocked exclusive game content across the AAA Xbox titles: Forza Horizon 5, Halo Infinite and Sea of Thieves.

Says James:

> You got your pack of Oreos and you could arrange and rearrange your embossed cookies in different sequences before scanning to unlock the benefits, like a wrap for your Pagani Zonda or unique sails for your boat in Sea of Thieves.

To date, the campaign has won over 100 awards for strategy, creativity and effectiveness.

So, what was the secret sauce? James says that everything aligned.

---

[2]https://news.xbox.com/en-us/2023/01/09/oreo-xbox-prizes-halo-forza-sea-of-thieves/

'We had the road to getting the embossment right, the perfect partner who just got it, and as Oreo's brand was "Stay Playful", it was the perfect fit as Xbox believes play should be everywhere and is for everyone. The unifying elements just came together, and everyone was so invested and so bought in.

'When you look at a campaign holistically, it is rooted in the product truth, and linked all the way through the brand. The playfulness is there. It's there for secrets being easy for people to unlock, for cheat codes being part of culture, to older millennials having that nostalgia for cheat codes (something that doesn't really exist in modern gaming today), to Xbox showing up and making it real. From product to brand, everything was through the roof.'

When the film *Wicked* launched in 2024, it wasn't just about the movie – it was about the collaborations,[3] and how these entered every area of our lives. From colour-changing cakes to sparkly drinks. Fun-themed bath products using *Wicked's* iconic colours to handbags too, these careful partnerships ensured that *Wicked* was never far from our mind . . . and parts of it came to live in our houses as well. It's reported by NBCUniversal that *Wicked* had over 400[4] partnerships at play during the first film's launch. You don't need to go for 400, but this ensured that a broad audience was captured.

Case study: *Wicked* + Vera Bradley

When a company's vision is to unlock joy and ignite conversations through colour and artistry, and it does this through a collection of stunning bags and associated accessories to empower and support women, you just know it is going to be the perfect collaboration partner, don't you? From *Harry Potter* to *Star Wars*, NFL to Disney, American luggage and handbag brand

[3]www.nbcuniversal.com/article/global-lineup-wicked-product-collaborations-will-defy-gravity-fall
[4]https://variety.com/2024/film/features/wicked-marketing-campaign-brand-partnerships-1236222100/

Vera Bradley has partnered with many an iconic brand, and *Wicked* is no exception.

The Wicked Collection in 2025[5] utilized the emerald green tones of Elphaba, alongside the pinks and peaches of Glinda, on bags, pyjamas and other associated products. But why did Vera Bradley see the perfect partnership in something a little wicked?

'*Wicked* is such a beloved cultural phenomenon that has inspired so many with its themes of friendship and individuality – values that resonate strongly with the Vera Bradley brand,' says Melinda Paraie, chief brand officer for Vera Bradley. 'We've always believed in creating products that empower our customers to express their own unique style, and this collection allowed us to take that a step further by tapping into the magic and excitement of *Wicked: For Good*. The whimsical, vibrant energy of *Wicked* beautifully complements the playful, colourful aesthetic that Vera Bradley is known for, and we saw this as an opportunity to bring fans of the story something truly special – whether they're heading to the theatre for the upcoming movie, or just want a bit of that magic in their everyday lives.'

To develop this collection and ensure it worked for *Wicked* and Vera Bradley's customers, the design team immersed themselves in the world of *Wicked*, creating two ranges with bespoke prints for Glinda and Elphaba. The ranges also complement each other, showing true alignment with *Wicked's* iconic 'pink and green go together' moment.

The results of this collaboration illustrate how well these kinds of partnerships can work, when the effort goes in and the attention to detail is there. 'We were so thrilled with the results and feedback from the collection – we saw incredible enthusiasm across channels, from our retail partners to our fan community,' says Melinda. 'The collection garnered strong earned media

---

[5]https://verabradley.com/collections/wicked-collection

coverage, including *Rolling Stone*,[6] *Town & Country*,[7] *Refinery29*,[8] and *The Business of Fashion*,[9] which helped drive both awareness and engagement.

'From a sales perspective, the collection surpassed expectations, exceeding our original sales volume goals. The Large Original Duffel in the Wickedly Beautiful pattern quickly emerged as a fan favourite. The strong results reinforced how deeply the collection resonated with both long-time Vera Bradley loyalists and *Wicked* fans alike. More importantly, it connected emotionally with our consumers – and that's always the biggest success metric for us.'

Why did this collaboration work so well? It's the connection, the respect and finding common ground in all things at a company level. Without this, the range would lack the depth that allowed it to truly resonate with its desired audience. 'Both teams should feel inspired by what the other brings to the table,' says Melinda. 'From there, authenticity and storytelling are key. Consumers can tell when a collaboration is thoughtful versus purely transactional. And finally, go all in – take the time to develop something truly special, from the creative concept to the customer experience. When both brands invest fully, the results speak for themselves.'

Collaborations can be deep or shallow, and budgets can be huge or non-existent, and that's the beauty of them – no one size fits all and they're completely customizable.

How can you make this work for you? Key learnings . . .

- Collaborations can have huge value if you get them right.

---

[6]www.rollingstone.com/product-recommendations/lifestyle/best-wicked-merch-collabs-1235161888/
[7]www.townandcountrymag.com/leisure/arts-and-culture/g62546379/shop-wicked-movie-merch-collabs/
[8]www.refinery29.com/en-us/wicked-movie-brand-collaborations
[9]www.businessoffashion.com/articles/marketing-pr/with-wicked-fashion-tests-the-limits-of-the-barbie-model/

- Shared values and mutual respect for partners provide two key elements in any successful collaboration.
- Do the work on your potential partners and really dig into the detail – are they the perfect match for you?
- Be clear from goal to execution so everyone can do the right thing at the right time.
- Ensure that everyone is on board. You don't want to be the one doing all the work when no one else cares.
- In a good collaboration, everyone should win.
- Look beyond the obvious. Small collaborations can be great and achieve goals, but for those who harness creativity and do something different, surprising, deep or even a bit disruptive, they can achieve a lot more.
- Don't see everyone as competition. Look for those who support and complement the product or service that you sell.
- Create shared assets and a place where all parties can access them. It shouldn't be about trying to catch out the other parties; it should be about every person or brand doing everything they can to set themselves and each other up for success.
- Ensure you've considered the legal side – the terms and conditions – or any restrictions that your collaboration can have. This might be geographical or age-related if products are being sent, the entry mechanism to a competition, or any number of other things. Don't waste your efforts because you didn't bother with the small print.

4

Partnerships and sponsorships

Alignment drives big gains

Why do brands partner and sponsor? Whether it's the local market, a professional sports team or event, or maybe something even bigger, there's no shortage of opportunities available, but the truth is, they don't all work all that well.

Partnership or sponsorship?

You might wonder what the difference is between partnership and sponsorship. In my mind, it's the depth of the opportunity and the way the brands work together. Sponsorship is more hands-off – one brand is paying another to promote it. But for partnerships, there's a lot more to it. Although they're different, they share similarities in some areas; hence, they're both covered here.

Sponsorships and partnerships inhabit a sliding scale. Some might involve a few hundred pounds to have your logo somewhere at an event, or as naming rights on a small award, all the way up to serious money when big teams are supported and branded, and everywhere their players are, so is that key logo. And then there are partnerships that achieve a lot more, with deeper integrations with the party that is being sponsored and its marketing plans.

What makes sponsorships and partnerships work well?

- **Alignment**. As with collaborations, influencers and celebrities, the alignment has to be there.
- **Research**. Ensure that the research is done in whatever you're looking to sponsor to make sure it makes sense.
- **Check the values**, the beliefs and how these measure up to yours.
- **Audience**. You might get loads of exposure, but if it's getting your brand in front of people who will never have any interest in what you're doing, it's not a great use of time or money.
- **Value.** What are you really going to get from it, and will this generate what you want? Having your logo on a page full of 'sponsors' tucked in the back of an event programme is unlikely to generate anything. But if as part of your deal you are also able to market to the event's mailing list, have some social media posts, and maybe even something at the event that people can get involved with, it might become a lot more interesting.
- **What's the plan?** Ask how the association is going to be promoted – for example, how is the event going to tell people what's going on? What's the marketing plan, and how can you achieve the maximum benefit for all concerned?

Let's take a closer look at one example – when speed and skincare worked together on something groundbreaking.

ELEMIS and Aston Martin Aramco Formula One™ Team started working together in 2025, launching an incredible partnership, not just in terms of the depth, but in its innovation – beauty and Formula 1®. Crazy, right? As discussed in Chapter 9 on challenging preconceptions, both companies pushed against this to create something that generated a whole lot of earned media as well as new fans and followers for ELEMIS, Aston Martin and F1®.

Case study: ELEMIS + Aston Martin Aramco F1® Team

Formula 1® was known for many years as male-dominated, although the demographic had started to shift. And when these shifts happen, it's down to the brave to embrace them. Early adopters break new ground and take a risk, but when it pays off, the impact for the first is always far greater than that of those who follow along. ELEMIS did this with Aston Martin Aramco Formula One™ Team, creating a partnership that was the first of its kind, redefining beauty's role within sport and culture, and encouraging a lot more women to get involved in the sport.

'As Formula 1® continues to evolve into a global cultural platform, we saw a unique opportunity to connect ELEMIS with Formula 1®'s rapidly growing female fanbase, which now makes up over 41 per cent[1] of the global audience,' says Amy Mansell, global chief partnerships officer – ELEMIS. 'Together with Aston Martin, we're demonstrating how two leaders in their respective fields can unite to shift perceptions, empower others, and deliver elevated lifestyle experiences both on and off the track.'

The partnership isn't a logo on a car part; it goes far, far deeper than that, and that's where the real magic happens. 'In our home market we launched

---

[1] www.reuters.com/sports/formula1/f1-enjoying-surge-support-middle-east-nielsen-data-shows-2024-12-03/

high-impact activations including our custom-built Airstream, The ELEMIS Skin Spa, which toured the UK and Ireland delivering treatments and product education in partnership with leading spas and retailers,'[2] says Amy. 'Across the globe we delivered wellness moments in the Paddock Club, a trackside spa suite for Aston Martin F1®, and on board the team's yacht at the Monaco Grand Prix, with over 1,000 VIPs experiencing ELEMIS facials and massages to date.

'We also co-created four ELEMIS x Aston Martin skincare collections,[3] launched at the Monaco Grand Prix with global distribution. Plus an exclusive Harrods collection assortment targeting their high-net-worth customers with our Ultra Smart Pro-Collagen range. This is just the beginning, and we see much more potential from product innovation to luxury wellness experiences.'

Through developing the partnership in this way, the alignment and connection deepen and both can leverage their connection beyond the key moment, such as the Grand Prix itself, although having that presence there reinforces the messages and provides another important touchpoint.

What's great is that this campaign has generated very impressive results – at the time of writing, ELEMIS has been working with Aston Martin Aramco Formula One™ Team for just nine months. 'The partnership has grown beyond visibility; it's become a true platform for impact; one we're fully committed to evolving and expanding in the future. Success, for me, is measured in impact,' says Amy. 'One message I received really stuck with me. A female F1® fan reached out to say thank you for showing up in a space that hasn't always felt like it was built for her. As a mother of a young daughter, that hit home. If we can keep breaking down those barriers, keep elevating underrepresented voices, and continue to challenge outdated perceptions, that's the kind of legacy I want this partnership to have.'

From Aston Martin Aramco Formula One™ Team's point of view, ELEMIS supported its desire to engage a broader fan base and encourage more women

---

[2]www.astonmartin.com/en-gb/our-world/news/2025/7/10/elemis-and-aston-martin-announce-multi-year-partnership

[3]https://uk.elemis.com/aston-martin-f1

into the sport, riding on the increased interest thanks to *Drive to Survive*, the F1® movie, and the increase in interest in America too. 'Through the lens of Aston Martin F1®, ELEMIS is able to tell two great stories. Firstly, a technical story which links to product and there's no better platform in world sport than Formula 1® for a technical showcase – but also a story of female empowerment,' says Rob Bloom, chief marketing officer at Aston Martin Aramco Formula One™ Team. 'Since relaunching Aston Martin back into F1® in 2021, we have invested in a substantive programme of activity around our Make A Mark social impact strategy, and I think ELEMIS recognized the authenticity of our approach and the opportunity to enhance our ESG programme.'

A further example of this authenticity comes in the form of Jessica Hawkins,[4] head of F1® Academy for the Team, James Bond stunt driver, and in 2023 the first woman in more than five years to drive a Formula One™ car (which was, of course, an Aston Martin AMR21). Jessica helped to show Aston Martin's true commitment to changing the game and also provided a great way for ELEMIS to activate its partnership.

When we think about partnerships and sponsorships, we often think it's all about getting in front of more people, but it isn't just this. Truly impactful campaigns resonate on a deeper level and tap into something cultural as they connect to a passionate global community. These become something that unites, excites and enriches people's lives as they broaden their horizons.

'For non-luxury or lifestyle brands, there is still an opportunity to identify cultural moments that overlap with your brand values and your audience, then it's how you activate creatively,' says Amy. 'Whether that's through partnerships, experiences or content, the goal is to move the dial through emotional connection.

'For luxury brands too, these moments also present powerful entry points into new and emerging markets,' says Amy. 'At ELEMIS, we've made our presence known at high-profile global events like the Monaco Grand Prix, where we

[4]www.astonmartinf1.com/en-GB/driver/jessica-hawkins

delivered a first-of-its-kind spa experience aboard the Aston Martin F1® Team's luxury yacht. Each time we activate and spotlight our partnership, our mission is the same: to push the boundaries of performance and innovation on a global stage.'

Staying with the sport theme, Adobe, the brand known for its incredible software that supports creatives, went slightly outside what you might expect when it partnered with the Football Association to become the sponsor of the Women's FA Cup. This wasn't just a 'logo in a prominent place' kind of partnership; it was one that supported and empowered the over 500 grassroots clubs that entered the competition by providing them with content creation tools to help promote themselves and the sport in a much more professional and engaging way.

Case study: Adobe + Women's FA Cup

What does graphic design software have to do with football? On the surface, not all that much, but the key is the audience, and that was a perfect fit for Adobe, which was looking to engage with a younger audience. It undertook research and awareness studies and found that although Adobe was a well-known brand, the perception metrics were high for 'professional', 'complex' and 'expensive'. Adobe does provide creative tools that have the immense power and precision that a creative professional requires, but it also has tools like Adobe Express, which are easy to use, free and allow anyone to create standout content. This partnership was designed to help increase awareness of Adobe Express and change perceptions of Adobe.

'We saw the Adobe Women's FA Cup as a great opportunity,' says Simon Morris, VP Marketing for Adobe. 'It's a prestigious competition, but it starts out in the grassroots, in the communities, in hundreds of smaller clubs. When we did some research, we found that what was holding these clubs back in terms of content creation was lack of skills, time, and money, so we could see an opportunity to help.'

As part of the partnership, Adobe provided all FA Clubs with free access to Adobe Express as well as digital training, empowering them to create high-impact content quickly and easily. Clubs could now produce professional social media graphics, matchday programmes, websites, branding kits and more – helping them build a consistent and compelling brand identity while sharing the stories of their players, fans and local communities.

'The reason the partnership got so much industry recognition was that it wasn't just a branding label, we were empowering clubs, fans and players to tell their stories and, in doing so, inspiring more girls and women to get into sport.'

So why did it work so well? It's all about passion. 'Ultimately it's about tapping into the passion points of current or future customers,' says Simon. Adobe has used this strategy before, finding opportunities across fashion, music and art, areas that the company knows are interesting to its customers. 'Women's sport is a passion point that tends to attract a younger audience, including families, it's packed full of creativity and it's on a great trajectory.'

The partnership has extended even further, utilizing broader online activations such as encouraging people to design their favourite crest using an AI prompt, or partnering with the Premier League, which sees twelve million people play the fantasy side with Adobe Express. 'We see our partnerships as fantastic story telling opportunities,' says Simon. 'It's about showing up with real purpose. It's not just about brand visibility.'

How can you make this work for you? Key learnings . . .

- It's not just about visibility; it can be far more.
- Ensure the alignment is there. Through sponsorship or a partnership, two brands are bound together, so make sure you're happy with whom you're bound to!

- Make sure the audience you want to get to is a good fit – don't assume, do the research, look at the stats and do all you can to increase your chances of success.
- Have a clear marketing plan. Know the minimum you will receive for your investment. There might be additional scope in the future, but agree what you can expect as well as by when, and what (if any) assets the other party needs to do this.
- Look for ways to activate the partnership that utilize the strengths and connections of both parties. Add to the customer experience, deliver value in a different way utilizing the links created – do something different to amplify the message.
- Think about ways you can provide value beyond the obvious. You might do things at the key event you're working with, but can you enhance and prolong the exposure and experience through online opportunities too?
- What other ways can you help each other? Or help the other's audience beyond the expected?
- Look beyond the obvious. Use research to identify new trends and opportunities that allow you to buck a trend and push against the norm. Those who go first in new areas – with the research to back it up – are more likely to gain a lot of earned media as well as kudos for their actions.
- Whatever partnership or sponsorship you're looking at, ensure that you feel proud to celebrate and shout about it too. Even if it's the other brand's 'job' to promote you, it could be an excellent opportunity for you to create content and reveal more about your beliefs and passions to your audience.

5

Leading the way

Founder-led content: A secret weapon

Founder-led content is a big deal and continues to be an excellent marketing strategy, whatever the size of the business. Founder-led isn't just for big brands; it works brilliantly for start-ups, side hustles and businesses of all sizes. And the great thing is, it can cost you nothing to get started.

When I think about great examples of founder-led marketing, I don't have to think too hard as there are many. Steven Bartlett, founder of Diary of a CEO; Trinny Woodall, founder of Trinny London; Gary Vaynerchuk, aka Gary Vee, who has written many a good book and heads up Vaynermedia; Sara Blakely of Spanx; Daniel Priestley of Dent Global; and many other businesses come to mind. Even Jeremy Clarkson has used the founder-first approach to launch a farm shop, a pub, drive change, support an industry and grow a beer brand too.

And all of this just because the founder got in front of the camera at the most basic level. There's a popular saying, attributed to Bob Burg, a well-known speaker, author of *Endless Referrals* and co-author of *The Go-Giver*, that says: 'All things being equal, people will do business with, and refer business to, those people they know, like, and trust.' When thinking about founder-first content, the founder is looking to grow that know, like and trust factor. The way this is done is through something Bob refers to as pull. 'Pull is an attraction,' says Bob. 'Successful influencers first attract people to themselves and only then their ideas. The essence of influence is pull.'

So why does it work? Being British, I hear many fellow Brits use any excuse you can think of not to 'get their face on board'. Whether we think it's arrogant, no one would be interested in what we have to say, that we really aren't that interesting, or any number of other excuses, I get all of that. But the fact is, it works. When we embrace founder-first for marketing and harness the power of the personal brand, a lot can happen:

- The brand isn't faceless; it has a face. Yours! This will help people connect to your brand, whatever its size.
- Connection can be created.
- Customers and potential customers can see the brand as relatable (depending on the content shared – more of that later!).
- It provides the perfect platform for storytelling about the brand, the people behind it, the products, the growth. People connect with stories a lot better than facts and figures, and through storytelling, we capture people's imagination too.
- Embrace founder-first from the start and you can take people along on your journey. You'll find people who follow you watching this – to celebrate the highs, to commiserate on the lows.
- It can build trust.
- It gives your brand a point of difference – you! You might not have the only product or service in an industry, but you'll be the only you!
- It taps into people's nosiness. When brands get to a certain size and founders are known, people Google them to find out everything about them.
- Many other opportunities can open up – whether this is public speaking, business deals and plenty more too.

Lean into your personal brand

Embracing this side of marketing relies on founders fully leaning into personal brands and the power that they have. There will be times when you wonder what the point is. You'll tell yourself that no one is interested/watching/listening. But the thing is, founder first is not a one-hit wonder. It's not one campaign or ad or video and you're done. It's there all the time. Slowly building and building.

Lorna Andrews, better known as Lorna Luxe,[1] is the founder behind clothing brand LA Space[2] and beauty brand 98.[3] Her following on Instagram alone is over 1.5 million. She's an influencer in her own right (and has built a great business as an influencer), but she's also the founder behind her brands. Below, she talks about the benefits, but from the angle of leveraging an existing following and connecting a brand to that.

'The story is already told when you're a founder-led brand,' says Lorna. 'When I launched LA Space, I'd be on social media and had built my following over the last ten years, so people knew what I liked wearing. Because I'd always done fashion, it made sense for me to launch a fashion brand.' Lorna built on the trust and credibility that she'd nurtured with her audience to give her own company the best platform. But there's a balance to be had, particularly when you've worked hard to establish a personal brand.

'What I have done very differently is I haven't made my brands (LA Space and 98) front and centre of my personal brand. Most other founder-led brands, they are that founder and that's what they talk about each day. The future will tell me if I made the right choice, but I never want to feel that people just think they're being sold to.'

With 98, Lorna is part of a team of four, all bringing something different to the party. In addition to customer service and the fulfilment infrastructure

---

[1]www.instagram.com/lorna/
[2]www.laspace.co.uk/
[3]https://no98beauty.com/

she's built with LA Space, she's bringing her personal brand too. 'The hair mask we launched the brand with is just part of the story, but I knew I needed to enter the market with something that was true to me – people that follow me know this,' says Lorna. 'We know where we want to be but we aren't brazen enough to just launch with something that we want. The community have put me here and it has to sit well with that. No amount of money will jeopardize that and make me risk my audience as they're the most valuable thing we have. Putting my name to it has really helped. We have also worked with a PR agency to get that story out there which I can then add my spin on, because with 98, I couldn't just keep talking about alopecia all the time as it gets a bit boring!'

How do you start?

So, let's dive into how we start a personal brand . . .

As with any brand, it's a good idea to lay the ground rules. Some believe that to do a personal brand well, you have to share every aspect of your life, but I don't believe this. I do believe you need to show a balanced view but if, for example, you don't want your children included as part of your personal brand, I think that's more than acceptable. And I have seen many people create very successful personal brands without them needing to share every part of themselves.

What I will say, though, is that what you do share should be authentic, honest and transparent. When you show up, you're authentically you. Whatever that looks like.

It can be tempting to go down the path of always showing up perfectly polished and only sharing the highs, and I can absolutely see the appeal from the founder's side, but from the consumer's side, it's a lot less engaging. What I've seen on numerous occasions is that the magic happens when the founder shows up in a truly honest way. They're not preened, filtered, smoothed and made up to within an inch of their life.

When we consider personal brand, we need to think about the overall objective of the exercise and why we're doing it. You might think it's obvious – to make sales – but it has to be deeper than this to work. Yes, you do want to show what you're doing for work, let people behind the scenes of your brand, and share what you're excited about and what they can buy, but to build a connection, it needs to be more than this. There's also the possibility to extend this beyond the obvious, into the realm of 'celebrity' – which can really further your brand and business when you're invited to special events or get involved in things that matter. You also have the option of becoming a thought leader in your field, which is something that I see as a sign that you've built your personal brand the right way. If your message and your brand's messages are woven so deeply within you that they come out in what you do, the reinforcement of this over time will mean that people see you as a leader in the field.

And don't we all want that? Do you want to buy your moisturizer from someone who shares the behind the scenes, the science, the testing, the results and everything they have learnt, or someone that says, 'buy this, it's good'? Which person do you think gets invited to speak at beauty events? It's the first person, isn't it?

It's not hard to start – it can be as easy as opening a social media account where you know your target audience spends the most time. As you grow, you might want to scale to more platforms, but starting in one place can help you hone your craft before you set about adapting it to other places. Then you need to think about what you're doing and how you're doing it. Popular content on social media for founders includes things like:

- **A day in the life** – take people behind the scenes of you (the founder), your team, the products you're using, etc.

- **Get ready with** – a great way to show vulnerability as most people turn up bare-faced to this, but also relatable, interesting and even educational when pitched correctly.
- **Design with** – perfect for brands that make a physical product – share glimpses as you go, or even track the journey so when the product is released, this can be used as part of the marketing campaign.
- **Thoughts on . . .** potentially controversial, but if aligned and you, as the founder, feel passionate enough, this kind of content can gain traction.
- **Here's how I . . .** think about what you're known for, what you're good at and what people are interested in – what can you teach people that could help them on their way, increase people's trust in you, and cement you as an authentic person, maybe even a thought leader too?
- **Highs and lows** – part of being honest and authentic is sharing the not-so-great parts. This could be that your trousers ripped on your way to work, or that your speech flopped. Keep in mind, you don't have to share everything – you still need to protect yourself and your mental health.
- **Ask me anything** – an easy way to find out what people want to know about you, create content that is likely to be well received, and also show that you care about your community.

Martin Huntbach, who we met in Chapter 1, works with many entrepreneurs through his business Jammy Digital.[4] One of these is Daniel Priestley. Martin has condensed his strategy for helping founders to shine into a brilliant model made up of three parts, which he's used to make a massive impact with a lot of people and their businesses too. Here, he shares more about his work helping Daniel grow his presence online and the impact that has had for him as an individual and his businesses too.

---

[4]https://jammydigital.com/

Case study: Martin Huntbach and Daniel Priestley

If you don't know Daniel Priestley, you can thank me later when you follow him in all the places and have purchased all his books! He's the entrepreneur behind Dent Global[5] (and many other businesses, including one called Vidonary that he's co-founded with Martin), author of some of my favourite books, including *Key Person of Influence* and *Oversubscribed* (in addition to many others), and has featured on some of the biggest podcasts in the world, including Diary of a CEO. Daniel has been good at what he does from a business point of view for some time, but he wasn't showing up in a founder-led way, with the supporting strategy behind it.

'Daniel had had fame for such a long time, but his content wasn't performing,' says Martin. 'Sometimes you think that you just need more followers or a bigger audience, and you can think that when you get that, you just need to put out more content, but he had those followers, he just wasn't consistently putting out content that spoke to his audience.' As with so many people when they're under pressure and feel like they're on the content treadmill, Martin says that there wasn't a real plan behind the posting, and this meant that some content got views, some didn't; it wasn't consistent, and it wasn't strategic.

It's easy to think the approach should just be to get in front of as many people as possible, but that's not the case when it comes to business, and often doesn't align with an overall plan, processes and strategy. Martin says that, many times, there's a fame versus fortune argument, particularly when it comes to founder-led content. 'You can have someone who has millions of followers, who interviews people on the street and gives away money and has lots of fame,' says Martin. 'It's easy to think you want that, and when someone comes to us with this, we ask, "Do you want fame or fortune?" every single time. Do

[5]www.dent.global/

you want the fame and the kudos, or do you want to get predicable leads and sales every week?'

This approach works. As Martin shared, 'With Daniel, 95 per cent of leads used to be through Facebook ads, and now 60–70 per cent are organic,' says Martin. 'Views have shot up but more importantly, leads have tripled. The leads are more trained because they've seen Daniel organically, and because they know so much, when they speak to the sales team they are working to convince the sales team that they should be a customer rather than sales having to sell. We've found this across all the businesses as well.'

It works for sales, but it also works well when it comes to the further development of a personal brand. When founders take the founder-led approach, it doesn't just help close to home. Opportunities further afield can open up that align well with everything the founder and his or her business are hoping to achieve, getting in front of a target audience, enhancing credibility by working with others, etc.

Daniel provides another great example here, which can be traced back to leading from the front and developing a founder-led strategy.

'When Daniel went on the Diary of a CEO (DOAC) podcast with Steven Bartlett first in 2024, one of the things he said was that he'd seen Daniel's content online and that was why he wanted him on the podcast.'

Just to show how significant this one opportunity alone was, in 2024, DOAC was Europe's no. 1 podcast and the fastest growing globally with one billion views[6] and listens across its publishing platforms. The YouTube channel[7] has 16 million subscribers (as of April 2026). Daniel's first podcast video on DOAC[8] sat at four million views at the time of writing – and that's just on YouTube – that doesn't include Apple, Spotify and all the other platforms. Daniel himself did a video explaining how he got onto the show six times (to date!) and how he believes appearing on the show has made him

---

[6]https://stevenbartlett.com/the-diary-of-a-ceo-hits-1-billion-streams/

[7]www.youtube.com/TheDiaryOfACEO (Search 'Diary of a CEO YouTube')

[8]www.youtube.com/watch?v=u0o3IlsEQbI&t=6635s (Search 'DOAC Money Making Expert')

$10 million.[9] 'That was enough for me to think does millions of views matter or is it consistency?' says Martin. 'He's written loads of books, but if he's not putting content online, there's no proof he can speak eloquently for any length of time, so I think it was really nice that one of the reasons Steven had him on the podcast was because of this consistent approach.'

Is it hard to work out what stories to tell? Martin has a simple plan that looks at the past, present and future, and builds content around that. 'In the past area, we look at anything back in time, from where we are now to earliest memories, there are things that have happened to you, assets, experiences and we can soak up that as one pillar for content. Then we have the present – what's happening in the news and the world and the conversations you're having now. This can be an area that people rely on too much. It's where people create content from and there's no planning. Then there's the future, which is based on what your goals are for your business – what are you launching, what narrative do you want to lay out. You can imagine how much content you can make there.'

This approach also has the ability to help future-proof founders, because if you look at anyone in the public eye, you can see that nine times out of ten, they're not in or with the business that they started with. This can also fuel people's worry about being too linked to their business and what that might do when it comes to the time to think about selling it or moving on. 'Some people think that it impacts the ability to sell the business if they become that key person of influence,' says Martin. 'But as Daniel says, you need to get it to a point with your founder-led growth before you start to think about acquisition and moving on. Ferrari and Disney started with a founder who was passionate.' And that's how most people need to treat their brand.

Says Martin:

> Thinking of Daniel, if we went into his content plan and said, OK, he talks about family, watches, entrepreneurship and travelling – this would allow

---

[9]www.youtube.com/watch?v=FW2-QA73Vuw&t=20s (Search 'How I Made 10 Million from DOAC')

> us to fill our content calendar easily. But what's going to have the most strength – it's the true values he has, the deep-rooted beliefs he has and what he wants to see in the world. None of this is necessarily related to one individual business; it's related to the mission for his life for entrepreneurs to stand out, scale up, and make a big impact on the world. And you need to look at it from a bigger picture. It's not about filling a calendar; it's about building a personality online that allows people to grow and their businesses too.

Utilizing founder-led content, allowing people to get to know you and to relate to you also means that when you say something – whether this is something you're passionate about or a new product or service you want to launch - people listen. When Daniel launched a new platform, Vidonary, with Martin in 2025, they got 2,800 people on the waitlist in a few days for a very specific app. At this point, the app didn't exist. But because of Daniel's consistency and the equity he'd built up in his personal brand too, when something launched, people trusted in him and trusted in the product too.

'Transformative'

Georgie Holt, CEO of FlightStory[10] and co-founder of FlightStudio, the company responsible for Diary of a CEO in addition to many other chart-topping podcasts, illustrates the value of this approach in what it can add to a company's bottom line, and the salaries available for those who build personal brands. 'The type of salaries that companies are willing to pay for someone to come into their business and build their CEO's personal brand tells you everything you need to know about how important that is right now,' says Georgie. 'It can be transformative on share price, business valuation, impact,

[10]www.flightstory.com/

growth, it will drive every single metric of your company if you have a strong founder.'

Sharing this kind of content might seem strange but think about it from a marketing point of view – you're ticking so many boxes when it comes to how people make decisions about not just who they follow and spend their time watching, but who they buy from too. There are also other advantages to this kind of marketing, and one of these is instant feedback.

The power of founder-led in action

Let's walk through an example. Someone you follow and whom you feel like you know, like and trust shares something they're working on, an idea they have or maybe a problem they think they've uncovered. As a keen follower, you'll probably comment. You could agree with them, you could say you love it but . . . you could say that you haven't found that particular issue, but you've found something similar. What if the founder asks for an opinion on a post, or a live – 'what colour do you like the most – the blue or the pink?'. The brand doesn't know which to launch first as all the testing they have done shows a dead heat . . . so how do you decide? You could go to a focus group and to your online community – all good things – but for instant feedback, the founder could just ask it on social, and boom, you have some feedback to do with what you will. You could even ask for pre-orders if you're unsure about a product, sharing that when you reach x in number, you'll push the button.

Of course, we've focused on social media above because social media has huge power when it comes to building influence. 'People often ask if you can cultivate meaningful know, like and trust relationships via social media, and the answer is a definite yes,' says Bob Burg. 'You do this through bringing value to every touchpoint.'

Through developing this, through adding value, cultivating those know, like and trust factors, founders can work their way into all forms of marketing and can be a powerful force, particularly if the effort has been put in to build up that personal brand as it only strengthens its impact. We tend to view people we watch on social media as friends – they're even called that on Facebook. Friends listen to each other's advice and there's a connection there that can also happen when there are screens between you.

The downside to 'fame'

Founder-first marketing isn't all sunshine and roses, and it can have its downsides. The first part is that the founder is putting themselves in the firing line, as the spokesperson for the brand, all the wins and all the woes. If there's been an issue with an order, some think, 'No, I won't go down the customer service route, I'll just message my "friend" x.' If something bigger goes wrong, annoyance can be targeted squarely at the founder when the chances are it wasn't their fault – or at least not theirs alone.

As we talked about earlier, being clear on who your target audience is matters, but what that can do is repel people too. If they're repelled and move away to find brands and people who suit them better, then all you've lost is an unloyal follower who never really understood you. But there are some people who have too much time on their hands and use this to post negative content and even troll those they don't agree with. And it doesn't even have to be about a contentious issue. People can turn a preference for oat milk versus cow's milk into something to start a hate campaign about. But on the flip side, these people were never going to be your customers and that's what block, report, hide and delete are for.

Georgie, from FlightStory and FlightStudio, works with creators. Georgie believes that you can't mitigate against potential negativity, but she views it very differently. 'Quite honestly, you have to have so much belief in your purpose, vision and mission that any negativity doesn't matter,' says Georgie. 'Steve (Bartlett) says the cost of embarrassment is the cost of entry, and if you believe in what you're building, it doesn't matter. This is just the opportunity cost. It's the cost of entry if you want to build something spectacular and world changing.'

Oversharing?

There's a fine line between sharing and oversharing, and this is something I stress over and over again when working with clients. Everyone has a different idea of what is fine to share and what isn't. Some people will share themselves weeping in a corner with mascara running down their face because they've had a horrible day, and others won't. Personally, I wouldn't, but that doesn't mean I wouldn't address that day when I'd given myself some breathing room and space to process. Some will take to social media and call out those who have upset them. Some will share medical problems/poke fun at their spouse – I'm not saying what is right or wrong, but I am saying that you have to know what you're happy with and decide this when you're not under emotional stress. Like emailing someone immediately when they have *really* annoyed you, it's sometimes better to revisit situations when you've had a nap, a snack and can see things more clearly. Sure, you can delete what you said in the heat of the moment, but it could have done a lot of damage to you and your brand in the meantime, and people do screenshot and share.

And then there's copying – and wow, is there a fair amount of that around! Many brands and people are copied – some obviously and blatantly, and some more subtly. And some services and products that look the same have been designed in isolation and it really is just coincidence. You might feel that sharing every step of your journey online – even if it's for the greater good of your personal brand and for the brand part of your marketing strategy – is opening you up to being copied. But that's where you need to think about what you're sharing and how much detail you're going into, as well as timing. Timing matters. You might share going to a factory and looking through fabric choices and colour options – you don't have to give the details of the factory, the exact composition of the fabric, and what you're using the fabric for – you don't even have to share the ones you're using, do you? But it's part of the journey! You could share the design process with people sitting around a table, sketching furiously, chatting etc., but you don't have to share the actual sketches, the audio or anything that could make you vulnerable. You're in charge.

One final thought – what if, as well as having your founder front and centre, other members of your team were encouraged to build brands too? This is something that is actively done at FlightStory. That's how much Georgie and the leadership team believe in the power of personal brand. 'We are in a new world,' says Georgie. 'Anyone who isn't willing to do it themselves has to deeply question their motives and incentives for building a company – because do you really believe and are you willing to put everything including your personal brand on the line for it? And if you're not – who is? Anyone who's not thinking about this is costing their business money.

'To this point, FlightStory really supports the team to develop their personal brand too, to help elevate the brand and the individuals within it. As a founder, you might need to build in public and build theirs too.'

How can you make this work for you? Key learnings . . .

- Anyone can do it – the cost to enter the arena is zero.
- There are positives and negatives, but in most cases the negatives can be reduced . . . or you need to change your mindset, so you just don't care.
- Utilizing founder-first helps to enhance connection and trust.
- Being your authentic self online will attract people, and it will repel people too, but that's fine. Your people will be drawn to you and your business like a magnet.

- Raw and authentic can be seriously powerful.
- Sometimes, you just need to press publish. Not everything will land as expected, but you can't test until you start, and starting begins with publishing that first piece of content.
- By not investing in founder-first content, you're costing your business significant money.
- By putting yourself out there as a founder and creating content that resonates and interests your followers, you have the chance to grow your personal brand and your business brand simultaneously, which will have benefits for both if you do it right.

6

Own the media

Be the source

Some brands give a nod to what's available to them in terms of media – whether this is social media, websites, apps, videography, photography or audio. The 'nod' means they might dabble, but they don't fully commit in terms of thoughts, time or budget. In some more niche industries, social media was branded as a 'fad' until shockingly recently, and this left those brands who believed social media was a short-lived phase in the wake of those who were quick to catch on . . . and I've not seen that many make up this lost ground. Of course, social media is just one part of the media mix, but when talking about owning the media, I'm looking at brands that didn't wait for permission or to be asked to be part of something; they just started and then learned how to leave a huge dent in the space.

Brands that 'own' the media go that extra step. They don't advertise for an 'intern' or school leaver to do their content/marketing/social; they hire professionals because they understand the value and the impact it has on their business. In some cases, those without the space or budget to hire upskilled themselves – they watched the videos, they bought the courses, they got the kit, they tried, failed, tried again and they honed their craft. This isn't to say that there aren't incredible interns and school leavers who do an amazing job of social media content and media in general, but the point is that there was a time – and for some that time is still here – where this side of marketing was seen as an afterthought, then a necessary evil, and this led to a 'what's the cheapest way to do this?' thought process. Content creators, marketers, editors, designers and social media managers weren't selected for their skill; they were hired for their price tag.

This was historically, and even more so today, short-sighted. It shows a total lack of understanding about the size of the opportunity and the gains that can be made that deliver an excellent return on investment when compared to traditional options. But some brands see media differently, and that's where the interesting stuff happens – those who see it as essential. These people change the game and continue to push the boundaries.

Let's look at what this definition means, or at least means in the context of this book. You could say it's content marketing, but I think it's more than that. Brands who really own the media aren't relying on traditional media to run their story or showcase their founder. They're not posting random stuff on social media because they feel they have to, but really don't care that much, and deep down believe that their brand is 'better' than social media or that it's not relevant to them. They don't have 'build mailing list' on their to-do list, which never becomes a priority. They're taking control of how their messages, beliefs and passions get to their audience. They're making podcasts, investing in high-quality video production, understanding the places their audience like to frequent and making sure they're creating content that is native to that platform (and they're doing this for all the platforms they have highlighted). They're actively building their mailing lists and subscriptions so when they have something to share, they're not reliant on an algorithm when it comes to who sees it. They're working on nurture sequences and automations to deliver content and value. They're making sure they have their own website and maybe even an app, and not just a 'shove it up, it's better than nothing' kind of website, but one that really gives value and keeps people engaged. They're creating original content that they are the source of. They make a place to go to hear from them. And why would people care? Because they've established themselves as *the* place to go for this content. To truly own the media, you need to be more than a company selling a product or service; you have to be a brand that cares about more than that, that people really care about and have trust in. Without this, you might have the best video producer in the business, but if you're missing that essential something that people care about, it won't really catch on. You can't just throw money at the situation; you need to fully understand it.

The time is now

The opportunity has never been so great as it is today. Podcasts are easy to create (by which I mean, the tech and equipment are readily available at a reasonable cost) and host, and people are used to listening to their favourite people instead of the radio. The stats around social media, including YouTube, continue to be staggering. The way that people consume media and information is changing, and that provides a lot of opportunity.

This might well sound expensive, and of course it can be, but when you look at the costs associated with 'renting' space – ads, for example – it can work out as a very cost-effective way to grow your brand.

Humour me. Let's say you want to promote a product and you have a budget of £1,000 to do this. Perhaps the most obvious plan would be advertising. You promote that product and have a link to click or a code to scan to buy the product. This could well be successful and achieve that immediate goal, but if you haven't captured those people's details, let alone a deeper interest in you, when the next product comes out, you'll need to start from scratch. If you had the same budget and approached it differently, looking at how to create content and capture those people, you might not get that initial spike, but it's arguably a strategy that creates longevity in customers, can ensure greater lifetime value, can last for long beyond the duration of the campaign, and should allow you a direct channel to share messages with these people when you want to.

Long-term strategy

That's not to say owning the media in this way is a silver bullet. Sometimes it's important to worry about the here and now, those sales that need to come in within the next week that make the difference. Owning the media isn't a short-term strategy; it takes time to build, money to produce and sometimes the greater value can be from the PR perspective in the short term. It can allow people to get to know, like and trust you, to allow you to build your equity with them and your brand before you make the big ask. It is how communities are formed. How movements happen. How people can reduce ad spend and increase leads on a longer-term basis (as per Daniel Priestley's example in Chapter 5). However, it takes dedication, patience and a clear idea of why you want to adopt this strategy and the value you bring to the audience that's beyond your product or service.

One of the things that can overwhelm people is the sheer amount of choice out there. There are so many places you could be – and you need multiple pieces of content for all of them. But Martin Huntbach has some advice on this, which he's seen with the work he does across a range of clients. 'I think people have this opinion that it's difficult to cut through on some platforms when there's so much noise, and it stops people in their tracks, and that's because all you see is content. You don't see the very small percentage of people that are on the platform creating content. Like LinkedIn, the numbers are extreme – for instance, if you post on LinkedIn once a week, you're probably in the 1 per cent of people who have accounts on LinkedIn.' We see the activity, but we don't see where this activity comes from, and in the case of LinkedIn, it's not people posting, it's the people consuming the content, and this provides massive opportunity. With LinkedIn as an example, when you start to delve into the metrics that can move the needle for a brand or individual, there are lots of reports based on research showing that if you post between two and five times a week – so not every day, not multiple times a day – the impact on reach and engagement is significant. The point that Martin is making, which is eye-opening when you start to explore it, is that most people are consumers of content rather than creators. By posting valuable, useful insight, you can cut through the noise, and then this can scale.

'We do seven posts a week on Dan's profile, but if you can find three posts a week, say, and do it for long enough, you'll see a huge difference,' says Martin. 'The illusion is that you need to be everywhere and post every day on all platforms and this is overwhelming . . . and it's simply not the case. People need to post enough to get consistent data and then plan.' It can still feel overwhelming to create even a small amount of content for all the places that you want to be, but one of the approaches that Martin advises is what he calls 'bar stool energy' – that is, don't think of having to put on a show, just speak and start from sharing that right there. 'Say something as it happens, it just has to be honest, the more you do this, the more you'll be able to expand and predictably grow,' says Martin. 'When we started working with Daniel we didn't do 100 pieces of content a week, we moved up to that based on being consistent. I remember having a conversation where Dan said he wanted to post more on LinkedIn but it wasn't his favourite, but as we saw it, it was the easiest and the most profitable.'

Martin advocates slow growth when it comes to truly owning the media and being in all the places, simply because of the time it takes to be consistent on the platforms you need to, and then get the data on these to help inform your strategy and ensure you perform well. 'When you have this you'll never run dry of ideas,' says Martin. 'There are new conversations happening in Daniel's life every day, new books he's read he has got ideas from, there's always something to add.' Martin makes another really good point about this approach, and that's that by stepping into this, by thinking about creating content that serves the community and grows an audience, it can significantly reduce a company's ad spend too. But the time – surely that's a significant cost? Well, yes and no. In Martin and Daniel's situation, the pair spend a day a month together filming the content and that's then edited into numerous pieces of content across the different platforms. Of course, there's a time and cost to editing, and that can't be overlooked, but when you see it working down the system and the gains that can be achieved, it becomes very cost-effective.

All the data

One of the positives about 'owning the media' is that you as the brand get a lot of data that you can then use to market better. Using this data from all these points (i.e., if you interpret and listen!) is huge. But it's more than this. The data allows you to market better, which we'll explore a lot more in the chapter on data.

Beverage brand Liquid Death is a company that has taken the 'own the media' concept to a whole new level. Not only does it produce its own content in-house, but it also works with other companies that want a little bit of that Liquid Death magic woven into their marketing, too.

Case study: Liquid Death

Liquid Death[1] is no ordinary beverage brand. Not in how it presents itself, the content it shares, its target audience . . . well, anything really! One area it has excelled in is its dedication to media. This has allowed the brand to grow at an incredible rate and also enabled the company to keep its advertising costs (in the most traditional sense) really low. Stephen Nilsen, aka Stix, is the former VP of Cult Indoctrination, aka Lifestyle Marketing, at Liquid Death, and explains more about how the company has owned the media from the very beginning.

'Mike (Cessario) has got some amazing people in place who can act really fast and are given a wide berth that allows them to make the call,' says Stix.

[1]https://liquiddeath.com/

'The value in this is huge. We put out content a lot of brands wouldn't. To be able to act fast, to help people know that they're being heard, one easy way is reposting relevant content. You must be nimble and act quickly as a lot of these trends are fleeting. With bigger brands it can take so long for people to make a decision. When you have that genuine love as a brand, when customers can see you're listening, it all helps. We had some great content from normal people too – some brands focus on the person that's going to win this award or that award, and that can be a financial rabbit hole to go down.'

Owning the media doesn't have to be with company-generated content alone. If the alignment is there and your audience really gets the brand, user-generated content (UGC) can be hugely valuable too. And sometimes, through sharing this content, the ripple effect can cause a further impact.

'We get earned media coverage too because of the impact of the above. It's fun to see the reaction from people – even on places like LinkedIn – when people see their content reposted and they're excited. It's listening to what's going on out there too.'

This strategy works so well for Liquid Death because the content isn't a hard sell. It's not a buy this or buy that; it's a very different approach that has brand building and nurturing the audience for engagement very high on the agenda. 'People don't feel they're being sold to – it's more "what is going to happen now?" but the goal for content started with making people smile. Humour and comedy are never going to be out of style. Liquid Death has got to the point where when they post something, people stop what they're doing to watch it.'

Before working at Liquid Death, Stix also worked for Red Bull, a company that is a real machine when it comes to the content and media side. 'When I started, it was when Felix Baumgartner had just crossed the English Channel, aka "The Channel Crossing"[2] with a fixed wing and it blew up everywhere in the media. We were always looking for that. Red Bull also branded its athletes in a way that the media couldn't crop out the branding, so they're getting

[2]www.redbull.com/gb-en/felix-baumgartner-english-channel-flight

earned media too. They're fantastic at doing these moments in a Red Bull way, so you know it's them. They've become masters. They did Stratos where they built their own space capsule! They have created these moments.'

Taking owning the media to the next level, Stix recalls his last project at Red Bull, Project X,[3] where pro snowboarder Shaun White was built a private halfpipe in the backcountry of Colorado. The idea was that this build would allow Shaun to create and perfect new tricks in the run-up to the Olympics – and Red Bull would record it all. Shaun went on to win in Vancouver 2010 . . . and the footage captured from the entire project was turned into an NBC documentary. That's some dedication to owning the media – creating a set and documenting the journey at a high enough quality, in such a professional way, that it can be turned into a documentary on a big network.

Pushing boundaries and trying new things

Anthony Smith is the director of Trailers for Steven Bartlett at Diary of a CEO (DOAC) and is completely self-taught. His skills are incredible and have been a big part in helping the podcast scale to the size that it has with his engaging hooks and captivating trailers that disrupt the feed and make people click through. One of the things that sets Anthony and DOAC apart is their ability to truly own the media . . . in ways that have never been done before. When the podcast started, the team agreed that it could be much bigger than a podcast, but the industry urged them to stay in their lane. Trailers for podcasts weren't a thing. And making it into a long-form piece of video content? In a documentary style?! Not at all! But this opened a lot of opportunities as DOAC went outside the box. 'Steve brought together people from different industries and said: "how would you make it a show"?,' says Anthony. 'So, we looked at different elements from other spaces and did something very different.'

---

[3]www.redbull.com/gb-en/galleries/shaun-white-project-x-best-pictures

Many people think of the media as old media – TV being a key example. But this space is struggling to compete with brands that take owning the media seriously. 'I was speaking to a guy from the TV industry, and he asked me why I thought TV was falling behind,' says Anthony. 'I said that a massive part of it was the time constraints that they have unjustifiably put on themselves. Netflix is a great example of this. They asked how they could halve the amount of time it took to create a TV show. The producers explained why they needed the time to write, and Netflix looked at how they could streamline the process while empowering the writers and creating something exceptional. The same with filming. They went and really looked at what they were doing and how to save time. Now, with things like YouTube and content taking over, the competition is fierce.'

But times have also changed with tech being available to everyone. And as Anthony says, it's never been easier to do a good job and get better. 'All you need is an iPhone and to teach yourself the basics of video editing and you can create content that can really make a difference,' says Anthony. Being self-taught, Anthony strongly believes that it's a dedication to learning, a passion and a strong work ethic that has got him to where he is, because the 'stuff' people need as they grow, such as software, is now inexpensive, and uploading to platforms like YouTube is free, so there's nothing to stop people from embracing these possibilities.

What does the future look like? Stats show that traditional media is falling behind, providing huge opportunities for those willing to seize them. We could see a lot more brands truly owning that space and creating incredible content as a result. Rachel Hardy is the director of communications for FlightStory and has had an extensive career in TV and the celebrity world. She believes we're likely to see a lot more of this. 'We're going to see a lot more brands commissioning content from entertainment and documentaries to reality shows. They may product place in this content or it may be a brand piece,' says Rachel. 'There has been a huge focus on owning IP and now we've realized the value is in owning the audience. Brands were renting audiences from media, then they were renting audiences from talent, now everyone wants to own their audience on their own platform, and they'll do this by creating and commissioning engaging content.' We're already seeing examples of this, and over a relatively short space of time, the quality of the media has really gone through the roof . . . it's an exciting time if you're thinking of embracing the media as your own.'

The companies above have shown incredible examples of their commitment to owning the media, scaling internal teams to create true masterpieces that have been used to scale personal brands, podcasts, products and plenty more besides. But I also wanted to share a slightly different take – a brand that not only utilizes the media incredibly well but also has created tools that allow anyone to get started and begin to grow their brand without a team, large financial outlay or in-depth knowledge. And how does this company tell people about the amazing things available? You guessed it – through owning the media.

Knowing how to own the media in different places, for different people

Adobe's audience is as varied as the range of products it's so well known for. This could provide a challenge for any brand when communicating to such a diverse audience, but Adobe doesn't see this as a problem as it's developed a clear content strategy, making sure that what it's sharing with the world lands well with the right people, as Simon Morris, VP Marketing for Adobe explains: 'From a social media perspective, we have a content framework that we have broken down into engage, entertain, inspire and inform,' says Simon. 'Different types of content get a better response on different channels. For example, we see entertainment content doing well on TikTok, but on YouTube, it's the longer form content we use to inform the audience. It's tailoring it to the channel and audience.' If you look at Adobe's YouTube, you can see how different the content is, with technical videos aligning to key products, experts talking people through specific creative tasks and how to achieve the best results, customer stories . . . and that's just on the Adobe Express channel.[4] There are other channels for different products too – the Photoshop[5] one, full of technical, detailed tutorial-style videos to help support its users, has around 850k followers and uploads a lot of content to achieve its objectives.

With multiple platforms and multiple products, Adobe completely understands the demands when it comes to content, and it knows its customers feel that pressure too . . . and the beauty is, through its ability to create content, it's supporting its audience in a way that will help them solve a real problem. 'We have seen an explosion of channels and platforms and consequently brands need to have the tools to produce content at scale,' says Simon. 'We've seen the democratization of content through tools like Firefly and Adobe Express, giving people of any skill level the ability to bring their stories to life, quickly and easily. For brands, we're seeing the need to develop on brand content at scale. We know that if brands want to optimize their performance media, there needs to be a lot of variants that allow them to refresh their content frequently to achieve the results wanted. The amount of content needed to serve the different platforms, try, test and optimize is enormous.'

To take its messaging to the next level, to engage a specific area of the audience, Adobe decided to join forces with business influencer Grace Beverley on a campaign around International Women's Day. The video series wasn't about how to use the products in Adobe's portfolio; it went a lot deeper than that.

Case study: Grace Beverly and Adobe's Conversations with Female Founders

Grace Beverley is the founder of TALA, Shreddy and The Productivity Method, as well as being a prolific content creator, podcaster and influencer.

---

4 www.youtube.com/c/AdobeExpress (Search 'Adobe Express YouTube')

5 www.youtube.com/@Photoshop (Search 'Adobe Photoshop YouTube')

When Adobe wanted to create something different for International Women's Day, it started with the data that showed one-fifth of female business owners felt they faced unequal access to opportunities compared to men. How could it help support women with this? Well, calling on a highly relatable, popular female founder and working with her to create a video series was the idea they chose.

'The partnership with Grace for the Conversations with Female Founders series[6] was created in the context of International Women's Day,' says Simon. 'We asked, how do we create a series that is aimed at empowering small business owners, particularly women entrepreneurs? We worked with Grace on a six-part series on YouTube to provide tools, inspiration and confidence to help them. Grace hosted the series that featured candid conversations with some of the UK's most inspiring female founders, and it was really purpose-driven storytelling.' The content ran across multiple channels and Adobe saw incredible engagement. 'We measured engagement rates – 280k engagements, 8.7 million interactions and the three-second view through rate was almost 50 per cent versus 6 per cent industry benchmark,' said Simon. In 2025, this campaign also won the Creator Campaign of the Year award at the ITV bCreator Awards.[7]

How can you make this work for you? Key learnings . . .

- The outlay to utilize this strategy doesn't need to be huge. With the technology you have on your phone, a video editing app and some online tutorials, you can make a good start.

---

[6]www.youtube.com/playlist?list=PLqxJbfyK9yZcgiUXV1vcjJ2Ua0HkD5o1- (Search 'Adobe Conversations with Female Founders YouTube')

[7]www.bcreator.co.uk/winners-2025/

- Traditional media – in general terms – isn't achieving the reach it used to, and the price tag continues to be significant. Through developing your own high-quality content, you have the ability to reach a lot of people on a modest budget.
- Owning the media and developing quality assets, automations and the accompanying strategy is a long game. You're unlikely to see overnight results, but those results are more likely to reap long-term rewards.
- By ensuring your systems are linked, you can use your content strategy to grow an owned audience, which is incredibly valuable for marketing. For example, adding an opt-in that delivers a freebie such as a PDF template or mini course can be a great way to grow your own list.
- Many people think the noise on social media comes from all the content being posted, but that's not the case everywhere. Look at key platforms to understand where there is the opportunity to become a trusted voice.
- You don't necessarily need to post multiple times a day to gain traction – post enough to start getting the data in to inform your strategy around frequency, placements and topics.
- It's not about volume; it's about the quality of the content you create and whether what you're sharing will tick any of the boxes you need it to. It should always have a purpose and a point.
- Depending on your brand, you could consider utilizing customer-supplied content too.
- If you want to make a big impact, look at ways to do things differently. Challenge those norms, ask why, look beyond your industry; it's risky, but the rewards can be great for those who lead.

- There are so many tools available to help you own the media that you don't need to be an editing rockstar to use them effectively. If you don't have the budget to hire in, find software to get you started.
- Don't do everything to start with. Just because the opportunity is there, it doesn't mean you should do everything at the same time. This is likely to lead to overwhelm, burnout and substandard work. Focus on one part of the puzzle at a time.

7

Big issues

Emotive topics can matter to brands

Connecting a brand to a big issue can be risky. If you do it well, your campaign can help to amplify the voice of something your brand cares and feels passionate about. It can also help you shine in a positive way, helping people see you in a different light, growing your relatability and appeal and helping people to know, like and trust you. If the issue is big enough, you have the potential for your brand to reach new heights and even become a thought leader in the field you're campaigning for. But, and it's a big but, getting behind big issues can backfire in a dramatic fashion. There are lots of reasons why this can happen, which we'll dive into, but just know that grabbing onto a passing issue your company doesn't really believe in is unlikely to be a good idea.

Some of the 'easiest' big issues I've seen brands cling to are awareness days/weeks/months. These are periods of time during which (usually) the charity connected to the issue, which can often be health-related, rallies the troops to share stories, information and promote awareness around the cause. An example that does this well, I believe, is Breast Cancer Awareness Month – which happens every October. This month brings together the colour pink with campaigns around awareness, fundraising, research news, inspiration, stories and plenty more. A lot of good happens in those thirty-one days. I also see lots of brands get behind it, to help share the message, to connect it to their brand in a genuine and authentic way (often through telling stories connected to people who work for/with them) and even raise money for key charities where a percentage of profits from certain items (often connected to the colour pink) get donated. This is powerful. I have also seen companies just jump on the back of awareness days and show no connection whatsoever (but still hang on them for additional exposure). I remember one I saw a while ago that – essentially – said 'it's breast cancer awareness month, these are some products we've made, you should buy them'. To this day, I think this was one of the most random, lazy and disrespectful posts I've ever seen. The thing is, when tackling a big issue, it's emotive. People will know someone who has experienced the issue connected to a health-related awareness day – they might personally be going through it now – and to show a lack of empathy won't just make people turn off from the messaging, it could also make people move away from the brand too.

Between me and you, that post changed my view of the brand in a dramatic and wholly negative way.

But there are a great many brands that haven't just aligned with big issues; they've started movements to highlight cultural issues that directly impact their customers. This is bigger than the brand and the product, but it can still connect beautifully with the target audience. In fact, without that connection, it could just appear a bit random.

One company that has (in my opinion at least) provided us all with a high-level masterclass on aligning brand with big issues is Dove. Not only has it created a big impact, educated literally millions of people around the world, but it has been positive for the bottom line too.

Case study: Dove – Campaign for Real Beauty

Dove is known for its personal and hair care products, simple and beautiful branding and, of course, its Campaign for Real Beauty, which challenges society, media and the beauty industry to change its representation of women. This isn't a campaign that was deployed for a season and then forgotten about. In fact, in 2024, the campaign marked its twentieth anniversary by releasing *The Real State of Beauty: A Global Report*.[1] The study spoke to 33,000 people across twenty countries, making it the biggest of its kind by a beauty brand, looking at the reality of beauty and the pressures that people face today.

The Campaign for Real Beauty launched in 2004, starting with billboards that set about destroying beauty myths, showcasing real women and asking whether passers-by thought they were 'wrinkled or wonderful' as an example. The same year saw the launch of the Dove Self-Esteem Project, which provides academically validated resources to develop and increase body confidence and self-esteem in young people.[2] It also shared campaigns aligned to this purpose with a focus on social media and has partnered with UNICEF, WAGGGS and Youth Board. It aims to reach over 250 million people by 2030.

In 2005, following the successful launch of the Campaign for Real Beauty the year before, Dove continued to spotlight everyday women in its advertisements before 2006 debuted a video called 'Evolution'.[3] This was hugely impactful, lifting the lid on what really happens behind the scenes on beauty shoots – using timelapse to show a woman go from an ordinary model via significant hair and makeup to photography, before the image is edited with features adjusted and distorted to show the final image, made into a fictitious billboard, that bears little resemblance to the person at the start.

But Dove didn't stop there. If anything, it was just getting started. In 2013 came Real Beauty Sketches (see Chapter 17 for the case study on that amazing campaign), while 2021 saw Reverse Selfie,[4] which challenged digital distortion, spotlighting the negative effects of social media on body image among girls. In 2023, The Cost of Beauty campaign examined the impact

---

[1]www.dove.com/uk/stories/campaigns/global-state-of-beauty.html
[2]www.dove.com/uk/stories/about-dove/dove-self-esteem-project.html
[3]www.dove.com/ca/en/stories/campaigns/evolution.html
[4]www.dove.com/nz/stories/campaigns/confidence.html

of narrow beauty stereotypes on the mental health of women and girls, before 2024 saw the brand renew its vow to champion real beauty, with a commitment to never using AI[5] to create or distort women's images through the #KeepBeautyReal campaign.

The thing that's so brilliant is that there is no mention of any product in these campaigns. It was about the target audience, the customers, the future customers, who knew that Dove saw them and understood what they were dealing with. For over twenty years, Dove has stood out from the crowd, openly challenging unrealistic beauty, providing diverse representation and educating around this too. The brand has also conducted several studies to support the campaigns it does.

But not to boost sales, to boost self-esteem.

The *Real State of Beauty: A Global Report* (2024)[6] explored how thoughts and feelings around beauty compared to 2004, to see the impact of the work that had been done, what was still to do and also assess the changing pressures of 2004/2016 versus 2024, as so much had altered in a relatively short space of time.

Not content with that, in 2019 Dove took a further step towards fulfilling its commitment to create more inclusive beauty standards and increase representation, with its #ShowUs campaign.[7] The campaign saw Dove partner with Getty Images and Girlgaze to create a library featuring more than 10,000 images of women and non-binary individuals. #ShowUs calls on media and advertising industries to use the library and set a new standard for representation and more inclusive beauty.

You can probably guess, I'm quite a fan. The campaign and its iterations year on year aren't surface level. Each new release cut through the marketing noise and left lasting memories with those who saw it.

---

[5]www.dove.com/uk/stories/campaigns/keep-beauty-real.html
[6]www.dove.com/uk/stories/campaigns/global-state-of-beauty.html
[7]www.dove.com/uk/stories/campaigns/showus.html

So, why does it work? It's not about the product. You could argue – and some have – that it's just a marketing ploy . . . but I don't believe it is. The body of work, the money spent, the research is too great for that. Is it good for brand perception and brand awareness? Absolutely, but I think it's important to remember that doing good and supporting a brand and its reputation don't have to be mutually exclusive. They can work together.

For me, the research is one of the cornerstones for the success of this. The campaign wasn't based on someone's idea – Dove put money into it to understand more about its audience (potential and current) to see the scope of the issue. When it understood this, it listened to what was going on in the world, used data and insight to apply it to what people were experiencing and created culturally relevant campaigns. The earned media was huge – but why wouldn't it be? Every piece of the campaign has been relatable to a lot of the population, brave in its approach, emotive, thought-provoking . . . it has tapped into so many attributes that help a campaign to go viral for all the right reasons.[8]

Does everyone think Dove just wants to do good? No – but does it matter? What Dove *is* doing is helping people feel more confident, address concerns, show people that they aren't alone in how they feel, that it sees and understands its customers – and it's providing resources to help those people in the above categories inspire and influence others too. Dove is doing good. It has the numbers (137 million people supported to be precise!) in addition to the anecdotal evidence.[9,10]

It also works because of the quality of the result. With each campaign, the message is clear, but it is a joy to watch in the longest form and has then been adapted as needed into different formats. And these variations are works of art too. They're engaging because they're great.

---

[8]www.dove.com/us/en/dove-self-esteem-project/our-mission/expert-partners.html
[9]www.dove.com/uk/dove-self-esteem-project.html
[10]www.hbs.edu/faculty/Pages/item.aspx?num=56459

The long-term dedication to this campaign also reinforces the brand's commitment to its customers and to challenging the status quo.

This has had significant benefits for the brand too, with seriously impressive stats around, for one, the speed of Dove's growth from a monetary point of view (it's reported that the campaign drove over a decade of consecutive growth, delivering $6 billion to Unilever, Dove's parent company in 2023).[11] The level of customer retention and brand loyalty it sees is also very impressive. And why wouldn't it? Don't we want to buy from organizations that get us?

A very different take on big issues – but one that's useful to consider too – was the Ice Bucket Challenge that took the world by storm in 2014.[12] This didn't start as a big brand campaign; in fact, it was just three people living with ALS – Anthony Senerchia, Pete Frates and Pat Quinn – who started the phenomenon by accident. They wanted to raise awareness for the cause, but how do you 'market' a cause that's truly devastating? It turns out, the sweet spot really is a mixture of fun and reality.

When the ALS Ice Bucket Challenge gathered steam, Brian Frederick, chief marketing and communications officer, was brought in to handle what was a 'good crisis', because overnight everything started to change.

'One of the first things I did was to say that for every press release we put out or anything else we do, it needs to be the ALS Ice Bucket Challenge – not just the Ice Bucket Challenge – to frame it around ALS to get that brand recognition in the public mind,' says Brian. For the first few weeks, everyone taking the challenge was connected to ALS, but then pro athletes, celebrities and politicians got involved too. Once the team saw it had momentum, they started using how much money the challenge had raised as the main reason to contact the media and keep ALS in the spotlight.

Unlike a brand connecting itself to a campaign it doesn't have a connection to, what we saw with the ALS Ice Bucket Challenge was quite

[11]www.unilever.com/news/news-search/2024/20-years-on-dove-and-the-future-of-real-beauty/
[12]www.als.org/ibc-how-it-started

the opposite. People who didn't have a connection to ALS were jumping on the trend, but the charity capitalized on this in a positive way. 'In terms of why everyone did it, the news was awful all the time, there was a heat wave around the world, and this was something fun and positive. Facebook also made it easy to upload to its platform, and everyone suddenly had an iPhone that allowed people to take quality videos easily,' says Brian. 'It did a great job of raising awareness of ALS globally, but not about ALS and the truly devastating part of it. I think that's also one of the reasons why it was successful though. It wasn't putting the horrific nature of the disease at the forefront, it was just fun and family in the backyard, but we've tried to educate people since then.'

With many of these big issues, ALS being a key one, the true nature of the condition or situation can be very uncomfortable for people to see, in some cases triggering. While it's important to keep the main 'thing' as the main thing, this must be balanced with what's likely to have an impact and spread in a positive way, to help raise awareness to provide the space to educate afterwards.

Says Brian: 'With ALS, it's a rare disease, so it's all about widening that circle, and highlighting the devastating nature of the disease is not the best way to do it. Some people feel we need to be showing the horrific side, but in my experience, people donate to causes they feel good about. For us, it's about how to highlight the inspirational and amazing nature of the people with ALS and their caregivers too – by making this more relatable and common. Because caregivers are common across multiple diseases. But the fun is what drives fundraising.'

Project Revoice

In 2018, ALS managed to make waves with one project that came about through the Ice Bucket Challenge. Pat Quinn, the co-founder of the challenge, lost his own voice in 2017 due to ALS, but the association created Project Revoice. The video[13] showing the journey was moving, sharing the reality of living with ALS, the impact of the challenge, shared messages from loved family members and explained that losing the ability to speak had been particularly hard for Pat. At this time, the voice provided through the technology used was computerized, but the team was able to work with a company called Lyrebird and put Pat's voice into his own computer, and the first moment that this was shared with his friends and family was captured on camera. This won the 2018 Cannes Lion Grand Prix for good and was the second time ALS had won this award as it was won in 2015 for the original ALS Ice Bucket Challenge.

If you haven't seen this video, I would urge you to have a look.

Authenticity wins

One of the questions with big issues is when a brand should get involved, and Brian offers some great advice here too: 'It's no secret that authenticity is the most important factor,' says Brian. 'Story telling around the people in need or who are benefiting from that support I think is the most important thing. For us, Pat and Pete were at the heart of the Challenge. It's important to find the people in need and feature them. Let them tell their story. It took many conversations to find out what was interesting and compelling, you have to explore the relationships and find the goal.

'A brand can also look at their own people. Someone on their team or working with them. And if their colleagues get behind them, that's the sort of thing that a consumer can see – that a company is doing the right thing and supporting their people. It makes people think they want to buy from them. It should be grounded in who you're serving and connecting with them.'

---

[13] www.youtube.com/watch?v=Dcg0rKG5WlU (Search 'Project Revoice ALS Founder Video')

Brands for a cause

Let's look at another big issue – child labour. You might expect me to say this became a key issue for a company that made a change, but you'd be wrong. Tony's Chocolonely was actually created based on the desire to address this issue in the world of cocoa.

The company was founded in 2005 after a group of three journalists started investigating exploitation in the cocoa industry after learning about child labour and modern slavery. It turned out that wasn't 'new' info – in fact, the big chocolate companies had signed up to a pledge to remove all child labour by 2005.[14] Unimpressed with the results, Tony's was founded by these three journalists, one of whom was Teun Van de Keuken, to prove that another way wasn't just possible; it made financial sense for everyone too.

'At Tony's, we're an impact company that makes chocolate, not the other way around,' says Sadira E. Furlow, chief of Global Brand and Communication. 'Our mission – ending exploitation in cocoa – hasn't wavered in twenty years. From the moment our first bright red bars hit the shelves, every decision we've made has been guided by that goal.'

But the thing about Tony's is that this mission isn't just for them. It's bigger than them. It's not about how it looks on the outside or being better than the rest. So fundamental is their belief that Tony's Chocolonely opened up their sourcing model by launching Tony's Open Chain,[15] a global industry initiative which invites cocoa-using companies to join Tony's mission by becoming Mission Allies. In doing so, they commit to adopting Tony's 5 Sourcing Principles[16] and the Child Labour Monitoring and Remediation System.[17] This isn't a marketing ploy; in fact, Tony's proudly partners and shares the

[14]www.cocoainitiative.org/knowledge-hub/resources/harkin-engel-protocol
[15]www.tonysopenchain.com
[16]https://uk.tonyschocolonely.com/pages/tonys-5-sourcing-principles
[17]https://uk.tonyschocolonely.com/pages/clmrs

companies that they are working alongside. The company's 2023/2024 annual FAIR report (AFR)[18] stated:

> In 2019, we came to the realization that if we were serious about industry-wide change and accelerating the positive impact for cocoa farming families, going at it alone and being choco-lonely just wasn't going to cut it. We had to face the bittersweet reality that, even though we believed in our model, we weren't going to be able to prove quickly enough that it could be effective at large scale.

So, how can one market to the end user around big belief? Do they even care? Well, it turns out that people do, and there are plenty of ways to weave the message into the day-to-day, without making people feel 'bad' for previous choices. Education is a key part. There are some great ways that Tony's does this. First off is the name. Tony's Chocolonely was created through combining a translation of one of the founder's names (Tony=Teun) and a feeling of being the only one who cared about this plight – hence lonely. Next up is the design of the bar itself. When you unwrap a bar of Tony's Chocolonely, you'll notice that it isn't divided into uniform squares; it's all unequally divided to represent the divisions within the cocoa industry. In 2021, the company also left an advent calendar window empty to illustrate this point further.[19] This created quite a stir on social and beyond, further highlighting the cause. The company also created an iconic – and let's be honest, controversial – campaign with Sweet Solution.

Case study: Tony's Chocolonely Sweet Solution

Tony's reminded the world that, in 2005, there should have been an end to all illegal labour in the cocoa chain thanks to the Harkin Engel Protocol.[20] The

---

[18]https://uk.tonyschocolonely.com/pages/annual-fair-report
[19]www.bbc.co.uk/news/business-59636955
[20]www.cocoainitiative.org/knowledge-hub/resources/harkin-engel-protocol

company then explained that this wasn't the case, and later that the process used to source cocoa was to be made open, to allow other brands to source 100 per cent traceable cocoa beans via Tony's Open Chain, to allow other brands to join their mission to end exploitation in the cocoa industry. This is all well and good, and no doubt useful . . . but is it headline-grabbing? Maybe not. So, in 2021, twenty years after the industry said it would end illegal child labour, Tony's launched its first 'Sweet Solution'[21] where the team created four limited-edition wrappers, inspired by some of the chocolate bars from leading brands, to help encourage these manufacturers to take positive steps in addressing injustices in the system. Under the wrapper, the bars themselves also had more than a little nod to the chocolate bars they were hinting at, to carry on the message as people took their first bite. To go even further, Tony's donated all profits from these limited-edition bars to an NGO called 100WEEKS that helps to support women in escaping extreme poverty. The first campaign hit the Netherlands, United Kingdom and the United States, and then there was a second campaign in 2024 in Germany and Austria. This was dubbed Tony's 'Faire Alternative'.

'With Sweet Solutions, we wanted to do more than raise awareness – we wanted to lead by example,' says Sadira. 'By reimagining even competitors' fan favourites, we showed it's possible to make chocolate in an ethical way. It's not enough to call out the problem; we have to demonstrate solutions, even if that makes some uncomfortable. For us, it's an open invitation to the industry: together, let's build a better, more equitable cocoa industry.'

The 2024 campaign didn't come without its problems, including a legal challenge[22] from one of the companies that had seen similarities to their own brand in Tony's campaign. If anything, however, this added more fuel to the fire with Tony's removing the colour from that bar, with a little note explaining it wanted to pay farmers, not lawyers.

---

[21]https://nl.tonyschocolonely.com/blogs/press-releases/tonys-chocolonelys-sweet-solution-look-alike-bars-are-back-for-good

[22]www.instagram.com/p/C3pberzMt3i/?hl=en

And you know what's really interesting about all of this? Until recently, the company hadn't spent any money on conventional marketing, also known as paid media. Its missions, its branding, its customers, the quality of its products and its campaigns that grabbed attention and headlines promoted the brand to the point it crossed the €100 million revenue mark.

As Tony's example proves, you can be a bit controversial or unusual in your approach to addressing big issues and create a huge impact. The key is that it has to really matter. As mentioned earlier, don't decide to use something that matters to people as a marketing opportunity when it means nothing to you. That's exploiting a cause for a quick gain . . . but the chances are when people realize this, it'll do a lot of harm.

Tokenism

As per the case study in Chapter 1, we know that Norwich City used mental health as the focus of one of its marketing campaigns, with the content in 2023 going viral. Looking to integrate a 'big issue' or emotive subject into marketing can be dangerous ground, but by getting that support, they helped to mitigate any risk. Gavin Beard, head of Marketing at Norwich City, gives advice: 'The key thing is, you can't be tokenistic, you can't be leveraging a moment to benefit your brand, at the heart of everything we've done is to make a positive difference,' says Gavin. 'There has been no commercial element to this, no commercial KPIs, and we've done it to support our community, for our duty of care, to use our platform to support our fans. We've also seen that with the right due diligence you can deliver that impact. We've been really careful throughout as we didn't want to get it wrong – and it would be so easy to get this wrong. To me, it highlights that football is the centre of a community. Our fans might not follow Samaritans on Twitter, but they follow us, and so we felt it was our duty to leverage our platform to talk about big topics, but without the support of Samaritans, we wouldn't have felt comfortable doing so. It's dangerous to get it wrong.'

As long as the foundations are in place and the big issue really matters, the options for how you convey this are endless.

Enter Liquid Death. This completely unconventional beverage brand has pushed against everything expected for a company selling the product it does and gained fans, followers, fame . . . and is now valued at over $1.4 billion.[23] Liquid Death is serious about business, water, tea and sustainability . . . but how it conveys these messages, well, they have a little fun and they push the boundaries. The messaging taps into the darker part of the brand's name using 'Death To Plastic' as a battle cry. One campaign that jumps out is the 'Liquid Death Recycled Plastic Surgery Centre'[24] that used the knowledge that, as plastic was costly to recycle, a lot of it ended up in landfill and oceans. So, what could this useless plastic be used for? Well . . . not plastic surgery, but the campaign was a great way to deliver the facts, with comedian Whitney Cummings. It was funny, informative, a little dark . . . and highly effective.

Let's explore another cheeky campaign or two with Stephen Nilsen, better known as Stix, Liquid Death's former vice president of Cult Indoctrination (or Lifestyle Marketing).

Case study: Liquid Death and Loving Homes for Plastic

'The sad part is, every brand is being pushed to be sustainable, and some are just checking a box,' says Stix. 'One of the lightbulbs for Mike (Cessario, founder of Liquid Death), was that the US Postal Service will mail anything

[23]www.thegrocer.co.uk/news/liquid-death-hits-unicorn-14bn-valuation-as-it-raises-67m-for-npd-drive/689242.article#

[24]https://youtu.be/mJz7JOfwriA?si=Eo-r_gk-o_GaH2G6 (Search 'Liquid Death Recycled Plastic Surgery Center with Whitney Cummings')

with enough postage. So Mike had an idea that the biggest soda companies in the world say they're sustainable but they aren't really, so there was a campaign "Loving Homes For Plastic"[25] with these prepaid labels, and if you found the brand's rubbish on the ground, you could put on a pre-paid label and it would go back to the respective brands' mailrooms.'

With every order, pre-paid postage stickers were sent out to make it easy for people to post the plastic back that they found. It was launched on World Earth Day and raised awareness around the fact that the larger companies sell billions of plastic bottles a year. The conclusion Liquid Death drew from this was that the companies must really love plastic . . . hence the campaign.

At a different time, Liquid Death embraced another, very different angle, connected to sustainability. 'One of the members of my marketing team was an adult actress and she helped direct the "Don't F The Planet" campaign, and the woman that's featured in it is an adult film star. Yes, it was taboo, but these things are here to stay and it worked.'

These campaigns are fun and certainly grab people's attention (and headlines), but underneath it all, it's a core value for the brand. The product is sold in infinitely recyclable aluminium cans; it supports the 5 Gyres charity, which focuses on cleaning up plastic pollution through a donation of profits, and it's even partnered with events to share more sustainable options in places where a lot of drinks are provided in plastic containers.

How can you make this work for you? Key learnings . . .

- Do your research – understand what you're talking about and how to talk about it correctly.

---

[25]https://youtu.be/wAyblZNRt70?si=20GCQpBFrtYOmBS4 (Search 'Loving Homes for Plastic (A Liquid Death Initiative)')

- You cannot be tokenistic – don't hook onto a big issue purely for commercial gain; it has to be deeper than that. Think about why it matters to you and your brand. Is it a personal connection? Something that matters to your team? Think about the real reason you're doing it.
- Going after every awareness day, for example, isn't the best plan – focus on ones that you can make a difference with.
- Look at how you can do things differently to grab attention for the cause. As a side effect, your brand will gain reach too, but it needs to be about the big issue, not about you.
- Don't be afraid to signpost – ensure you have resources available and a plan around how to support people impacted by what you're sharing; you have a duty of care when big issues are tackled.
- Even if the issue is serious, you can be creative around how to engage your fans.

8

Product placement
Alignment reaps big rewards

From a subtly placed drink can on a desk in a short-form video to the car used by one of the world's most famous spies, product placement is everywhere, even when we don't necessarily notice it.

Aligning brands and specific products with shows, creators, fictional characters, events and influencers isn't new, but the way in which we incorporate brands has changed. And the options available have expanded, too.

You might consider films and TV the place to start. Think about some blockbusters and the brands woven into the narrative. The Aston Martins in *James Bond*. The Audis in *Marvel*. The Ray-Bans in *Top Gun*. Manolo Blahniks in *Sex and the City*. There are many examples of products in key places that have helped to solidify, elevate or support a brand's reputation at the same time as the character leveraging that brand's standing to cement that status.

Can you imagine Maverick rocking some plastic-framed star sunglasses instead? Or Tony Stark climbing into a clapped-out hatchback with the doors in different colours? How about Carrie Bradshaw sporting a pair of black faux leather flats? And equally, brands aligning with characters that really didn't fit their vibe? It wouldn't work.

Case study: Audi

Audi is a brand that nails product placements with great examples in films – *Marvel, 50 Shades, iRobot, The Intern* . . . the list goes on. Different models are selected for the roles, like pairing an actor with the right part. Of course, this isn't by accident, and neither are the places that Audi supports the use of its legendary brand and everything connected to it. Benjamin Honal from Audi Product Placement shares his insight: 'We follow a clear and structured process when deciding where our brand is integrated. Every placement is aligned with our company and communication goals focusing on authentic, organic integration into the storyline and association with strong, innovative characters. We focus on film projects where our vehicle integration contributes meaningfully to the narrative, that fits our brand values and resonates with our target audience. All opportunities are carefully reviewed based on a global principle to ensure a consistent overall brand appearance across all placements. Together with our global markets, local product placement agencies, we evaluate each opportunity for strategic fit, authenticity, and audience relevance.'

The assessment of each opportunity is thorough, from script evaluation to who's going to drive the vehicle and in what scenes, for what reason. 'By ensuring our presence is relevant to the story we maximize the probability of being featured in impactful moments in key scenes across cinematic and serial productions,' says Benjamin. 'At the same time, we fully respect the creative freedom of our partners, the filmmakers.'

When it comes to placing the right car in the right role, authentic integration sits at the top of Audi's list. By assessing the script, the car is selected, down to the colour, interior and even the technology in the vehicle, before the team works with production to ensure they can get the angles they need to create the best result too.

The positive effects of these placements are significant, but this is because of the planning, the alignment and the collaboration with the film teams that enable the car to be seen in the best light as it enhances the story. Audi continuously monitors all product integrations using quantitative and qualitative criteria.

'Qualitative factors include visibility, logo integration and verbal mentions while quantitative measures relate to the performance of the production – audience size, target demographics, platform and airing time,' said Benjamin. 'Combining these dimensions allows us to determine a clear media value for a specific product placement and assess its overall effectiveness for the brand.'

In addition to the data, research is also conducted on brand perception, analysing awareness, image shifts and uplift effects. And there are the direct consumer responses too. 'For instance, customers specifically requesting and ordering vehicle colours seen in popular series or films,' says Benjamin. 'We also saw noticeable traffic increases on specific product pages following a major release even without any additional marketing activities. Nice and motivating stories but also tangible signs of impact complement scientific evidence and externally validated evaluations confirming the effectiveness of product placements in both the short and long term.'

Case study: Champagne Bollinger + Bond

Long-term partnerships provide opportunities for greater depth. A brilliant example of this is seen with arguably the world's most famous fictional spy, 007 James Bond and luxury Champagne Bollinger. This is a great example of a partnership that spans decades and over fourteen films, and has extended beyond the set to develop products and experiences.

One of the key attributes of Bond and Bollinger is the enduring nature of the partnership. Victoria Carfantan is the director of Champagne Bollinger UK & Global Partnerships and shares the value of commitment. 'Longevity brings authenticity and depth,' says Victoria. 'Over time, the collaboration has evolved from simple on-screen visibility into a shared narrative that has become part of Champagne Bollinger's DNA. The partnership infuses the House with a sense of excitement and offers a unique platform for storytelling, one that complements the heritage and refinement of a prestigious, family-owned Maison like Bollinger.'

Alignment is mentioned many times throughout this book, and for anyone who knows the iconic Bond and Champagne Bollinger brands, it's easy to see that the alignment is there – luxury, style, high-end. But going deeper, why do the two brands work so well together? The legendary alliance began in 1979 with *Moonraker*, although Champagne Bollinger was first mentioned in the book *Diamonds Are Forever* in 1956. 'Since then, the partnership has blossomed into a unique and historic collaboration spanning nearly half a century,' says Victoria. 'There's a commitment to elegance, craftsmanship and timeless sophistication. Champagne Bollinger partnership works because it fits organically.'

Champagne Bollinger and James Bond have taken this collaboration a step further, reaching far beyond the screen. This helps to cement the connection, provide additional links between the brands and share opportunities for fans of both to enjoy. Over the years, there have been special limited-edition releases (such as the Special Cuvée 007 Limited Edition launched at the end of 2025), and immersive experiences such as The 007 bar in Burlington Arcade, Mayfair. 'We have collaborated on global events that celebrate both brands' shared sense of style and adventure,' says Victoria. 'It's about building touchpoints that allow consumers to engage with the story – not just watch it. When we unveiled the Special Cuvée Limited Edition, it was housed in a sleek, black collector's box that embodies the elegance and intrigue of the brand. Inspired by the hypnotic circles of the franchise's iconic opening sequence, the front of the box features a striking gold gun barrel motif with one of, if not the, most recognizable silhouette in the world at its centre, a cinematic emblem instantly recognized by fans across the globe. Every detail was considered with this, down to the branding on the neck collar.'

What a brilliant example of product placement extending beyond the screen to deepen the connection. As we can see above, the attention to detail that makes this partnership really resonate is second to none. The alignment is perfection; the obvious respect for the brands and audiences is evident, and the innovative ways of showing the connection delight all concerned.

Beyond the silver screen

Product placement isn't just for movies; it has traditionally been found in TV too. If we think of product placement as a way of integrating products seamlessly into content, then it opens up new avenues with influencers, podcasters and celebrities with strong social media platforms to place products in what they do as well.

Just like any form of collaboration or partnership, product placement needs to be carefully considered. Sometimes, particularly when it comes to influencers and even celebrities moving more into that space, the brand is not always in control of who decides to use and share their product. But when they do have a say in the matter, it takes some thought.

Brands want their products to be seen in a positive, aspirational way. They need to keep that target audience in mind and think about what kind of shows they watch, whom they follow or whom they listen to. They need to think about how the product will be integrated. They need to think about the quality of the production and whether that aligns with the brand's messaging. They also need to consider conflicts in terms of other products being integrated into the same content or – with celebrities and influencers in mind – the person.

There have never been more options to get your product placed, and although this can be really good, it can also lead to some issues, particularly when we move more towards content creators and away from TV/film. How do you know you're going to get the reach and exposure you need? How do you know the product will be featured in the way you want? How can you be sure the audience will even care? And what kind of cost is involved?

Rachel Hardy is the director of communications at FlightStory and has worked extensively in TV. She says that the shift between old media and new media has led to more integrated product placement. 'When I worked in TV, editorial and sponsorship sat very separately, and product placement could be really clunky as well,' says Rachel. 'The creator economy changed the game. Ads are content, so our editorial and commercial team at FlightStory work closely together. The ads are approached with the same level of care and passion as our editorial content.'

The brands that are placed within FlightStory's media – with Diary of a CEO (DOAC) as an example – matter too. With the best creators having worked hard to build personal brands, their integrity needs to be protected, but also, the alignment simply won't be beneficial for the brand in any meaningful way without this work. 'With DOAC, we're really selective,' says Rachel. 'The commercial team really considers all the brands that come on board – we need to know that the brand and their product align with our talent. The ads come from that place of authenticity. Here, we're entirely aligned, because of our integrity, when our talent talks about a product and endorses it, it's so much more powerful than a random can of something sat on a table.'

Sometimes, product placements show up in different ways in the same space, using the opportunity to increase understanding around specific aspects of what you do. Aston Martin utilizes product placement in Formula 1®. In addition to having a team, one of the road cars is also used as a safety car at some of the Grand Prix. What's interesting is that this product placement is used to add another level to the perception of the brand. Aston Martin has an established position in the market as an ultra-luxury brand, famed for beautiful products and cultural extensions outside of the automotive space. The challenge for the brand is to also ensure that the high-performance story cuts through, for which there is no better platform than Formula 1®. 'Having an Aston Martin road car as the F1® Safety Car, visibly positioned alongside the highest performing cars in the world, is great association in front of a huge global audience,' says Rob Bloom, chief marketing officer for Aston Martin Aramco Formula One™ Team. 'Importantly, we can back this up with the product itself and double down through our broader marketing campaigns on the road car side that lean into the performance story.'

Product placement is a great way to tell a story and, when supported with additional marketing content, can be a hugely valuable tool in a marketer's kit.

Having been wooed by Audi, Aston Martin and Champagne Bollinger, and admired what they've been able to achieve, you might be asking if a small brand can utilize this marketing strategy. And the simple answer is yes. It is true that you're unlikely to get your product into the hands of a superhero for free, but you can make a big impact with smaller, highly engaged audiences on the influencer side, identifying very targeted opportunities where your product could work, looking at the 'talent' over the programmes, and being tenacious too. Here are some ideas to explore . . .

- Follow people online – whether this is through 'normal' social media or longer form platforms that host videos, live streams and video podcasts. Do any of these creators align with you and your values and have opportunities in their content that provide the perfect place for your product? Video podcasts are becoming more popular and provide a host of opportunities if the alignment is there – as do the creators who make them. If you do the research and find out more about them, their pain points, the things they talk about and their passions, there could be the opportunity to gift an item with the hope of it being featured.
- Even if your budget is non-existent, you could propose a percentage of each sale tracked back to the placement through affiliate links, for example.

- Are there any TV shows that fit your niche? With more channels comes more programmes, and more opportunities. As an example, there's been a surge in shows tapping into hobbies and crafts in recent years. If you have a product that fits this niche, do your research and find out who to contact.
- Instead of going for the shows, you could target the talent and/or their stylists. Follow them on social media, understand their style and needs, research who they work with and start to build a relationship with them.

How can you make this work for you? Key learnings . . .

- Product placement can be a great tool in a marketer's toolkit. It has the ability to create significant traction, particularly when run in alignment with supporting elements in an integrated campaign.
- To ensure product placement is effective, the alignment has to be perfect. That brand must be placed in a way that is fitting for it to enhance its reputation and perception. Put more focus on the quality alignment rather than just the potential reach and exposure.
- Think of your objective. With Aston Martin, for example, it wanted to remind people of the performance credentials of its road cars.
- How can you measure the positive effects of the product placement? Some brands have data-led ways to judge success, and for others it's more anecdotal. Think about how you're going to do it so you can see if it's worked well, allowing you to do more, or less, moving forward.
- Work closely with the other parties. You might want your product in a specific place, but if it doesn't align fully with their plans, or there

would be a more authentic placement based on their experience, consider this too. Use their experience as well as yours.

- Don't push for placement that you really want for your ego, but if you take a step back, it doesn't work. There are thousands of opportunities out there; you don't need to push in places where it won't work.

9

Challenging preconceptions

Defy the norm, show your values

Challenging preconceptions is a space that's not all that crowded – get it right and you'll be celebrated, go viral, win awards and attract earned media coverage that far exceeds your spend. But get it wrong, and at best your brand will flop, as will your campaign . . . and depending on the preconception you're challenging, it could get even worse than that!

When thinking about preconceptions in this context, it's all about challenging the accepted norm in a way that is almost jarring *but* has to be accurate to allow that impact to have a positive effect at the end. It's easy to say something wild or challenge what is expected in your marketing, but without substance behind it? It's not going to go anywhere.

Water

Let's start with water. Babbling brooks, white mountain tops, snow, health, athletes, models – what other words would you add if you were brainstorming key elements that need to be woven into the marketing of a water brand ? I can see it now, can you? This is what is normal for a water brand – and this isn't a criticism. We know that it is good for us, we know it's calorie-free, essential to life, we know the benefits of drinking the right amount (and the negatives when we don't). People want to be, and look, healthy – it all makes sense. But what if drinking water didn't have to mean those things?

When we create campaigns and messages around our brands, we draw some people in, and we repel some people too. Some people will like and get you, and for some people your beautiful campaign leaves them cold. And that's good, that's how you find your people.

Let's push against this and make water something a whole lot darker. 'Mike (Cessario) just said, "Why is everything that has fun in marketing the worst for you" – nothing that is super healthy is doing anything cool,' says Stephen Nilsen aka Stix, former VP of Cult Indoctrination at Liquid Death. 'The mantra was let's make drinking water and sustainability fifty times more cool. It's important to look where people don't go. The people who don't get love from brands.' And so they did. The name alone pushes against life-giving water, and this is complemented by the skull logo, the gothic font, the names of the individual drinks (Slaughter Berry, Green Guillotine, Cherry Obituary, to name but a few), and the bold colours used. The presentation also pushed against the norm, shunning plastic bottles in place of cans, and not just any cans, cans that were chosen to look like beer cans from afar. Liquid Death wanted to make being sober cool too, giving people who wanted to avoid alcohol the option of blending in with the crowd. 'That placebo effect of having that can in your hand, it's a genius of Mike, and if you read the side of the can it's so funny too,' says Stix. 'In the early days it became almost an accessory. Every single successful brand changes your life in some way. The ones that are here to stay change lives. It purposely looks like a beer brand.'

These deliberate choices attracted Liquid Death's fans, investors and team too. It also created the opportunity to work with some true icons, from Ozzy Osbourne to Metallica, Tony Hawk to Martha Stewart, Travis Barker to Spinal Tap . . . and that's just a snapshot. The brand works in different ways to any other beverage brand out there. It's funny, sells merch (that people want to wear), pushes boundaries and has a 'Country Club' online. It's pushed against preconceptions and won. The company has a value of over a billion dollars, has over seven million followers on Instagram, and the same on TikTok . . . and keeps creating an impact on its tribe, its profits, its community and sustainability too.

Challenging preconceptions around a company and what people believe about it can be brave, particularly with companies that have been around for a while. With older brands, people will have opinions about them and what they stand for. But the thing is, as times change, what the audience wants and even the leadership evolves, so can what the brand is all about. One of the brave parts about this is that if you want to change people's preconceptions, you have to fully lean into and be receptive to what these are. And then decide how to tackle them, to encourage people to look at you and your product or service with fresh eyes.

Luca Lorenzini is from SMALL, a creative agency in New York. The agency executed a campaign for an Italian client, called Misura. In the past, this brand was well known for its low-calorie, healthy snacks that were maybe not the most delicious. However, over the years, the company and its products have evolved in line with demand and now, they're pretty tasty! To promote this new era and reposition itself in people's minds, it needed to acknowledge what its reputation was. It did this visually. The first part of the campaign saw people being given snacks and being asked what brand they were. When they were told, they began to question other things that that person had told them as they didn't believe they'd been told the truth about the delicious product they were eating. These questions ranged from whether they were actually related to whether they really loved them. Because the company challenged the preconception head-on, the campaign worked, with great results reported from the first stage.

Health

If I asked you to think about someone with Down Syndrome, what words would you use to describe them? I know it's quite a question for a marketing book, but think about it. We all have opinions and preconceptions about so many things in life, and Down Syndrome is no exception. What CoorDown, a non-profit dedicated to people with Down Syndrome, did in 2024, was to challenge these preconceptions head-on, launching a video and associated assets on World Down Syndrome Day. And it went viral.

Case study: Assume That I Can

Assume That I Can[1] took the world by storm when it launched, quickly gaining over 150 million views in a week. The campaign was shared by Down Syndrome charities all over the world simultaneously. Celebrities retweeted; everyone was talking about it online and on the news; it really did go wild. It did a lot to help challenge the preconceptions that people have around those with Down Syndrome too.

The idea came from when Luca Lorenzini and his partner Luca Pannese saw Marta Sodano, an Italian lady with Down Syndrome, address the UN in New York. She was talking about the prejudices people faced, how if you don't believe people can do things, they're not given the opportunity, and that means they never will. This was the seed that started the process. 'Each year, we work with CoorDown to create a campaign to mark the awareness day, and this speech got us thinking,' says Luca. 'We did the research and it was very real. People in the community felt the same way. The campaign was born in twenty-four hours. We wrote the text, Martina Fuga (president of CoorDown) loved it, and she said we could do it. But the idea is only half of the process, we had to produce it well, and luckily we found great production partners and then we started casting. We saw ten seconds of Madison Tevlin in action, and we knew the key role in the campaign had to be filled by her.'

---

[1]https://youtu.be/9HpLhxMFJR8?si=0hLgljJs12nT2506 (Search 'Assume That I Can CoorDown')

The video begins[2] with a simple focus on Madison saying, 'Hey, bartender, you assume that I can't drink a margherita, so you don't serve me a margherita' before the actress is handed an orange drink with a straw, and so it continues across a range of different situations showing how assumptions can become reality if left unchecked. Then, the video steps up a gear and the idea of assumptions becoming reality flips to assuming the actress can drink, live on their own, etc. She swears, she dances, she drinks and the final line is 'Assume that I can, so maybe I will.'

It was a brave campaign, but it worked, and Luca says that's because it was set on strong foundations. 'Always involve the community you're talking to. The first insight came from someone with Down Syndrome,' says Luca. 'The first draft was checked by people with and the parents of people with Down Syndrome. We wanted to make sure we weren't putting words in their mouth that weren't acceptable or believable. It's a risk if you don't involve the community. Sometimes we believe we know what other people think but that's often not the case. It happens across everything – people of different nationalities too. Be humble and test the thinking with the right people. This can just be speaking to people, it doesn't have to cost a lot of money.'

Some of the language and imagery used in this campaign caused pushback, but that was very much part of the work in challenging preconceptions. 'There's always a risk, but what's important is that we believe in what we said,' says Luca. 'Some people attacked it because we talked about alcohol and sex, and the actress swears, and a lot of people said you could have expressed it without using those words . . . but would it have had the impact? No. It also pushed against some people's preconceptions that people with Down Syndrome are like little children. You can't just do it for shock, the meaning has to be deeper or else it just won't land.'

---

[2]https://youtu.be/9HpLhxMFJR8?si=pBiSgKkpeDyCTCYS (Search 'Assume That I Can CoorDown')

Using data that signals change

There are some sports and activities we think of as male, and some that we think of as female – or at least, that's the common thinking. In general, many see football as male, fashion as female . . . you get the idea. That's not to say that any of this is right, but it's what many people believe.

Most people would put Formula 1® in the male category. Why? It's how it's been historically. The field is dominated by male drivers and the imagery surrounding the events and the teams features a whole lot of men. Cars and horsepower are traditionally seen as male interests. But there have been a series of events that have started to change the way the sport is viewed, and brands that are listening can make it work. If the opportunity is there and the research supports it, there's a chance for a brand that's seen as appealing to more women than men to get into a space where there's limited competition. And that's exactly what ELEMIS did with its partnership of Aston Martin Aramco Formula One™ Team. A full breakdown of how this partnership worked is explored in Chapter 4. It seems like an interesting move for a skincare brand to get involved with Formula 1, and it challenges preconceptions from traditional avenues for skincare when it comes to partnerships and event support, as much as it challenges the racing team to work alongside this and go beyond to deliver a partnership that means something.

Does ELEMIS and Aston Martin F1®'s partnership challenge preconceptions around 'normal' F1® partnerships? It does, but the data shows that in 2024, between 40 and 41 per cent of F1® fans were female,[3] Gen Z women were the fastest growing demographic of F1® fans and Formula 1 itself started to address the lack of women in the sport through its F1® Academy,[4] giving a firm foundation to challenge a long-held belief.

---

[3] www.forbes.com/sites/maurybrown/2024/12/03/formula-1-now-sees-750-million-fans-due-to-growth-with-women-and-middle-east-demo/
[4] www.f1academy.com/

Interestingly, when Aston Martin entered the world of Formula 1® in 2021, it did so in a way that challenged the preconceptions connected with the sport too. The team always knew it needed to be about more than cars, and there was a lot of brand equity from the 100-year legacy of Aston Martin to help them do this.

Case study: Aston Martin Aramco Formula One™ team

When Aston Martin's Formula 1® team began, there was a lot resting on its shoulders from a brand point of view. Aston Martin is a classic brand, but there's a lot more to it than that. The Formula 1® team had to honour the heritage, magnify the brand's performance, while challenging preconceptions of the sport and coming up with different ways to get more people involved at different levels – partners as well as sport fans.

'Our brand is one that endures. It continues to reinvent itself, attract new fans and stay relevant as times evolve. Aston Martin has always gone beyond its core category; it's more than an automotive brand,' says Rob Bloom, chief marketing officer of Aston Martin Aramco Formula One™ Team. 'When it came to Formula 1®, our goal was to harness the power of this iconic brand and align it with where the sport is today – engaging a newer, younger audience and building a modern Formula 1® team that does things differently.' And it did. As a consequence of this new approach, it's attracted partners like ELEMIS (read the full story of this partnership in Chapter 4), Glenfiddich, Hugo Boss and more. 'Different brands are increasingly attracted to the sport due to its global appeal and diverse demographic audience,' says Rob. 'Our brand already exists in culture, lifestyle and luxury, which is a perfect fit for high end brands.'

Although premium and accessible don't normally sit hand in hand, the way that Aston Martin F1® has managed the brand and the activations around this has allowed the aspirational nature of what it does to draw people in. 'The way we show up and connect with fans all over the world in different ways has allowed us to move away from the traditional arm's length approach of Formula 1®,' says Rob. 'By balancing tech with lifestyle and cultural collaborations, we make sure everyone has the opportunity to engage with the sport in a way that reflects their own interests.'

Aston Martin Formula One™ Team has done this in diverse ways, from branded team apparel available to buy to I/AM events and more. 'I/AM is our fan membership programme,' says Rob. 'It's an invitation for fans and partners to come and co-create our story with us. It's a symbol of togetherness and recognizing that we're more powerful when everyone is with us on the journey.' In 2025, the team put on an I/AM event with partners Glenfiddich called 'Paddock After Dark'. This took place in Austin around the time of the US Grand Prix, held around a thirty-minute drive from the downtown venue. In addition to an Aston Martin road car, a Formula 1® car and whisky, there was also a DJ to encourage people to enjoy and experience Formula 1® in a different way.

Furthering this, the team has created touchpoints far from the track too, but all to complement its highly strategic approach regarding audience engagement. 'We did a matcha pop-up in Covent Garden, tapping into the matcha culture that's thriving on TikTok as a way to engage new fans and spark their interest in Formula 1®,' says Rob. 'We even created a nail gel perfectly matched to the Aston Martin 2025 Formula 1® car colour after spotting the trend taking off on TikTok.' This product, created with Glaize, tapped into the #nailtok trend that had amassed tens of billions of views. In addition to the perfect green gels, the kits also contained stickers that mirrored some of the car's details and came in a custom box too. These are just a few examples, but the approach has caused the team to think about the role they all play in the sport and provided an opportunity to write a new chapter for Aston Martin and for Formula 1® too.

How can you make this work for you? Key learnings . . .

- If you're going to challenge a preconception, do the work to ensure you understand the situation at the deepest level.
- Keep in mind that while challenging preconceptions can be great, if your campaign is pushing against the status quo, maybe even calling people out on behaviour, you might also gain a few haters.
- Challenging preconceptions requires bravery. To stand out, to make a difference, to make a statement, a brand needs to be brave and unapologetic. It won't work if your challenge is wishy-washy!
- Use evidence and research to back up your campaign – this can add a lot more clout to what you're doing and also increases the likelihood of more earned media as there's a story there too.

10

Going hard

Going all in creates a groundswell

Marketing can be mundane. People can just go through the motions and create campaigns that *should* work – and then just hope that's the case. None of the examples in this book are average in any way, and while many could well sit in the 'going hard' category, I've decided to really dissect some examples that didn't just exceed the norm; they re-wrote the rule book on what was possible. 'Going hard' isn't easy, and it's not for the faint-hearted. It relies on thinking differently, research, pushing barriers and testing things that people will think you're mad to even contemplate. It means your brand needs to go over and above in terms of time, effort, thought, exploring possibilities and, to use a cliché, thinking outside the box. Big budgets help when you want to go hard, but there's no denying that, by understanding the theory behind these feats, you can see the patterns and how and why they work. And from this point, you can look at how you can apply the same methodology to whatever you want to do.

Case study: The LEGO Group – She Built That

In 2025, the LEGO Group carried out a survey around the term 'building', and what people thought of it. Of the over 32,000 people surveyed across twenty-one countries,[1] it was revealed that the term 'building' was perceived as a male activity, that 70 per cent of young women didn't see themselves as someone who was good at building things, and that 72 per cent of parents felt there was a lack of female role models who build the world. More than this, children attributed major inventions to men, when many of the inventions shared in the survey were pioneered by women. LEGO addressed this problem in many ways with its brilliant 'She Built That' campaign, which sits in this section because of how the LEGO Group tackled it.

The campaign was truly multi-faceted, from reimagining the 1980s Run DMC hit to the company's work with *TIME Magazine*. Let's look at a few of these in detail:

- The song 'It's Like That' became 'She Built That',[2] a song that was all about empowering girls, building confidence and addressing preconceptions. The lyrics were changed and sung by the Global Girl Crew with the video showing girls from a range of backgrounds dancing, singing and creating with LEGO.
- Sets were handpicked to create a selection online that leveraged what girls were more interested in to help encourage building.
- Online workshops[3] with female celebrities such as Nadine Coyle and Diane Buswell were shared, showing prominent, highly regarded successful women building with LEGO.

[1]www.lego.com/en-us/aboutus/news/2025/may/she-built-that-2025
[2]https://youtu.be/Q4Tintbg0lo?si=4NikYVakig65oFtw (Search 'She Built That LEGO Music Video')
[3]www.lego.com/en-gb/she-built-that

- A two-day immersive pop-up in Southbank, London, brought together 350 girls to build, play, dance and get creative (which was captured for social and beyond, obviously).
- Further in-store and other activations happened all over the world, attracting media coverage in addition to hundreds of female builders excited to learn more and build. As an example, in New York, a series of events was held with inspiring women across a range of activities.
- Support was provided online to help parents nurture girls' creativity.
- Four LEGO plaques[4] were taken to iconic London landmarks that women were integral in the creation of. Tapping into the idea of blue plaques on buildings, this supported the fact that a great many women are, in fact, amazing builders.
- A partnership with *TIME Magazine* saw the first 'Girls of the Year' list.[5] Following in the footsteps of the well-known 'Women of the Year', this list highlighted ten girls making a real difference to the world. To accompany this, there was a LEGO-themed cover, and a digital version too, which was animated and depicted each of the girls as a LEGO mini figure.[6]
- The earned media from this campaign was significant.
- Influencers were utilized on social media, using the She Built That audio, to show LEGO creativity in action – some of these racked up many millions of views.
- Some of the shops stocking LEGO also got involved with discounts or in-store promotions to further reinforce the message.
- The social media reach through user-generated content was also significant – #SheBuiltThat allowed people to share their builds too.

---

[4]https://blocksmag.com/the-lego-group-launches-she-built-that-campaign/
[5]https://time.com/7309462/time-and-the-lego-group-partner-to-celebrate-extraordinary-girls/
[6]www.lego.com/en-us/aboutus/news/2025/august/time-girl-of-the-year

To my mind, this campaign knocked it out of the park for a few reasons. There was obviously a good budget here, but the key threads running throughout provide a lot of points to consider:

- The idea started with research. It wasn't a 'we think that', it was a study that created results showing a trend. If you're looking to make a point or to validate a campaign with a mission, do the work!
- There were a lot of opportunities for people to get involved in a hands-on way. Through immersive experiences such as pop-ups all over the world, as well as in-store activations, people could have an experience with LEGO in a non-sales way. Allowing people to experience and touch things and feel a human connection has a whole lot of power.
- The campaign was bigger than the LEGO Group – it was about a movement of helping to empower and inspire young girls. This helps people to get enthused about a subject because they're not being sold to; they're learning and helping to empower a future generation. A lot of people want to get behind that.
- It went outside – the plaques idea made adults as well as children think, and the delivery was superb as blue plaques in the UK are well known and understood. Tapping into culture with a twist can be very effective.
- Utilizing influencers as well as encouraging community engagement through #SheBuiltThat further amplified the message in native ways.
- The *TIME* collaboration brought the campaign to another audience, and the whole premise attracted a lot of earned media coverage as it was so different. The addition of the digital cover was next level as it provided interest and engagement for those who hadn't purchased the magazine and was very shareable. Looking beyond the obvious, at what already exists, and the adjustments that could be made can create a lot of interest.

- The audio. Creating a specific audio and video was an extra step. Using something that was nostalgic for many parents was a clever element too. The audio then allowed people to create content and share online with the track designed for the campaign, further reinforcing the messaging.

Going hard can focus on individual campaigns, or be something that is adopted as a way of operating across a company. The below is a great example of the latter.

Constantly experimenting

The Diary of a CEO (DOAC) podcast and everything connected with it were at the front of my mind when I started to think about this chapter. The podcast's success is just off the scale, and when you start to look at it, it's no surprise. The team is constantly experimenting and gathering data across all the metrics that matter to hone what they do, to make their efforts even more effective. The energy and skill put into how they operate, at every stage, is incredible. But if you'd done the work – the experimentation and data gathering – that DOAC and the team pride themselves on, you might also be more willing to push those boundaries and put more time, money and energy into the areas that generate the results. Georgie Holt, CEO of FlightStory, is very clear on why DOAC's approach works, but also how even when – to most people – they have dominated the space, they're onto the next opportunity. 'We lead with a culture of experimentation,' says Georgie. 'So you start with a hypothesis and then you have to test that relentlessly and use an experimental method – not changing everything all at once, focusing on one distribution engine or content channel, committing to a cadence of delivering something every day on that channel, and testing it. It isn't going to be an overnight success. Steven and DOAC have taken seven years to achieve what they have done. Steven has been in this mode since he was seventeen. It doesn't happen overnight. There's an amazing graph at DOAC that shows compounding consistency over time. It's the obsession to try, then do it, and getting those data signals back. There's no magic answer – it's testing different things on different channels and doing research, understanding the customer. We have a mantra in our business which is "kill the guess work". We have so much at our fingertips that allows us to get the data. It's a romantic idea to believe we have the answers and we know – we have to use the data. It makes you grow.'

It also gives you the confidence to know that all that work, that obsession, that content creation, is worth it.

Case study: Diary of a CEO

To illustrate Georgie's point above, I wanted to share a bit more about the DOAC brand and what it has achieved up to 2025.

Steven Bartlett launched the Diary of a CEO podcast in 2017. It started off as audio only, as most podcasts continue to be, but in 2019 was ahead of the curve in publishing podcasts as long-form, highly produced videos to YouTube too. Originally, DOAC focused on interviewing prominent UK entrepreneurs, but this brief started to grow to include experts and stars from all over the world who had value to share that he believed his audience would benefit from.

DOAC grew (and grew), becoming the biggest European podcast in 2024, and the second largest on a global scale on YouTube. In November 2023, it was Apple's number 1 UK show,[7] and in the 2023 Spotify Wrapped it ranked ninth globally. In 2024,[8] DOAC shared that the show is downloaded or viewed fifty million times a month, with each episode seeing around three million downloads. In January 2025, it celebrated reaching one billion views and

[7]https://stevenbartlett.com/apple-confirms-the-diary-of-a-ceo-is-the-uks-1-podcast-of-2024/
[8]www.flightstory.com/stories/doac-hits-1-billion-streams

listens across Apple, Spotify and YouTube, the first UK-produced podcast to do this. As of April 2026 , the DOAC YouTube channel had over 16 million subscribers, on Instagram it had 3.1 million followers and 1.4 million followers on Facebook too.

These results are amazing, but also show what a dedication to going hard can achieve.

Sometimes, brands find themselves in a scenario where they're trying all the things all at the same time – and sometimes this is because 'their friend said' they should be doing X or featuring on Y. This is guessing. And this can leave you spread thin, doing all the things, with no data to show for what is – if we're being honest – a mediocre attempt in lots of places. This isn't a criticism; a lot of people do it. But that doesn't mean it works.

The content machine

We can all appreciate the demand for content that falls on every brand out there, but how about having to combine twenty-four events with drivers, team members, partners, sponsors and the legacy of a truly iconic brand in a sport that has a huge audience all over the world? And a growing audience in areas it's not had that resonance with before? That's what Aston Martin Aramco Formula One™ Team has done across its platforms, with incredible results. And how did it achieve this? Well, developing its own in-house creation company definitely helped . . .

'We consider the season as one long movie, and we unpack the story across the year,' says Rob Bloom, chief marketing officer for Aston Martin Aramco Formula One™ Team. 'Aston Martin carries an expectation to show up with a sense of craft and sophistication. Our challenge is that our story plays out 365 days a year, which means creating a huge volume of content for ourselves and our partners. From the outset, we've been building a world-class content and media production company in-house – the AMR Creative Studio.' Rob shared that the studio has attracted the best talent from inside and outside sport, all with the objective of packaging the Aston Martin Formula 1® story in interesting and different ways. 'There's no shortage of content on social media,' he added. 'So, when Aston Martin appears in your feed, it has to feel intentional, stylish, and worth your attention.'

This dedication to quality, content, and stories has created an incredible online following with figures well in excess of fifteen million followers/fans across Instagram, X, Facebook, LinkedIn, TikTok and YouTube, through which channels the team generates over 750 million annual video views of its team and partner content.

How can you make this work for you? Key learnings . . .

- Going hard takes dedication, a real passion for excellence and not resting on your laurels.
- Combining a mix of media, ideas and activations can be a way to go hard around a specific campaign when you want to make a big impact in a short window. Working with others in different ways can also amplify this by leveraging the ways that they excel in their field.
- It's relentless and needs a well-thought-through strategy to ensure that the delivery doesn't burn out those doing it. For brands looking to really dominate, it should be seen as more of a marathon, not a sprint . . . and certainly not a marathon run at sprint pace as that can't be maintained for months or years.
- Constant assessment of success metrics is needed to ensure the efforts are creating the rewards.
- Some brands employ in-house creative teams to keep up with demand and also ensure it's all on brand and of the correct quality. This

might not be achievable for all businesses, but finding ways to ensure consistent quality is something that is. There are many tools available to help.

- Look for new creative ways to share what you're doing and experiment with new ideas that make sense to you.
- Plan, plan and then do some more planning. You cannot apply a scattergun approach to this – the impact will be diluted whether you're looking to utilize this strategy in the long- or short-term.

11

Going 360

Multi-platform = something for everyone

Many campaigns are multi-platform – including plenty of the ones shared in this book – because to be truly effective in marketing, you need to meet people where they are more than once. It was previously thought that seven was the magic number (although some sources say eight), but now some reports suggest up to fifty touchpoints are needed for a cold lead. So, it doesn't matter how amazing your ad is in that magazine – the messaging, the brand, the product or service needs to be put in front of your target customer more than once. Nowadays, there's no shortage of ways to make these connections, from organic social media to earned media, digital ads to social media ads, paid media to collaborations – the list is practically endless, but the work needs to be done to stack up these touchpoints.

More than just getting those points in, the cohesion between all the elements needs to ensure that each touchpoint, in whatever format, is another tick in the box. It needs to link to the brand, be easily recognizable, have the same vibe and tone – it needs to be connected by an invisible thread. If these parts are disparate, it won't feel like part of one campaign, or even one brand. It won't help you achieve your objective.

This doesn't mean you can't be creative with how you stack up those touchpoints – quite the opposite. I would argue that touchpoints that keep people engaged for longer are worth more than a fleeting ad impression – more than one touchpoint's worth achieved if you will. That's not to say that different campaign aspects with different objectives don't all add value, because they can.

One piece of marketing that I really think was a masterclass in utilizing multi-platforms was the Season 2 launch of *The Marvellous Mrs Maisel*. This Amazon Prime Original Series put together and executed an incredible experiential piece of marketing,[1] but it also utilized deep collaborations in innovative and immersive ways, in addition to its own platforms and so much more to ensure that Mrs Maisel was in front of her target audience, consistently, in a way that engaged and delighted the people Amazon wanted to get in front of. Charlene Charity is vice president of integrated strategy and brand experience at Digitas, and ex-head of Brand Marketing for Amazon Europe. She shares how Mrs Maisel and *Stylist* created something unforgettable across multiple platforms.

Case study: The Marvellous Mrs Maisel

Mrs Maisel Season 2 launched in December 2018, but following the data, and the online chatter, Charlene felt that Season 1 hadn't got in front of the people it needed to, so she asked for a budget to ensure that Mrs Maisel found her audience. She wanted to do it in a way that really gained traction and love for the show. 'It was a multi-channel approach and we had a reasonable budget too,' says Charlene. 'I sat down with the media team and I felt that it warranted something more. The show was very 1950s and the target audience was women aged twenty-five to forty-five,

---

[1]https://experience12.com/projects/prime-marvellous/

so *Stylist* seemed like the perfect partner. It was pre-lockdown, so people were in the office, and *Stylist* was a regular publication that you'd pick up and it had great kudos. Given the target audience, it felt like the perfect partner.'

Stylist offers many advertising options, but Charlene felt that to give Mrs Maisel a fitting launch, more could be done in a way that everyone benefited. 'I wanted to do something over and above a backpage ad, so we got *Stylist* in and had a good conversation and they set aside a brainstorming session.'

Stylist found brilliant, engaging ways to integrate Mrs Maisel into the publication. 'Multi-platform must be a coordinated effort. In *Stylist*, there was an advertorial, but we wanted to make it feel super relevant,' says Charlene. '*Stylist* has a really popular feature called Stylist picks – a smorgasbord of things the team love – there's always a theme. We did a reverse takeover. So you turned the magazine upside down and backwards and there was a Mrs Maisel cover – the reason we'd done this was because as part of the publicity shoot to promote the series we did a "Vogue" style cover shoot, so it looked very stylized. Then in the front, when you opened up the magazine we had the top picks, and they were all Maisel or 1950s-inspired, which felt super in keeping with the magazine and the show. All the products were available on Amazon, which further worked with the brand. It felt authentic to the publication itself too.'

This all culminated in the event held to celebrate the launch, and *Stylist* was involved here too. From running competitions for tickets to having copies of the magazine next to the overhead dryers in the salon, and even securing the three comedians – Sindhu Vee, Josie Long and Rose Matafeo – who were at the event.

Of course, Mrs Maisel utilized Amazon's incredible platform as well. 'We were able to target display ads to the right target audience via the website and Amazon Prime,' says Charlene. 'It felt really well connected.'

The biggest question of all – did it work? Charlene shares that it was the most successful second-season launch ever at that time. And more than just enjoying Season 2, more people watched the first and second seasons, so by promoting the second season, Amazon was able to reengage the target audience with both.

As the case study above demonstrates so well, multi-platform doesn't have to be confined to places accessed via a phone or computer, and some really powerful things can happen when new and old media, physical and digital combine, adding extra dimensions to a campaign.

Case study: 'OK Google' launch

One of the most detailed and public uses of community and UGC I've ever seen was Google's 'OK Google' Google App launch.[2] Instead of looking at all the features of the app, which could have overwhelmed users, it took a different approach and looked at what real people who used Google's services wanted to know, showing human curiosity across all ages. Noel Yeo is a creative director and writer who worked on the 'OK Google' campaign and shares more about the approach taken and how this utilized community in the best way.

'Google, at least back then, was somewhat allergic to regular advertising, and so its ask would be for communications that felt less manufactured,' says Noel. 'That often meant using found footage and then we would build assets on top of them, like those Google queries you see.'

The video assets developed were incredibly effective. Some were fun, some tugged on the heartstrings and all were relatable because real people were shown. But Google's campaign didn't stop with these short videos. It partnered with *The New York Times* and *The Washington Post* and had a banner ad that showed relevant questions relating to the news below. These relatable questions, which were perfect for the target audience, generated click-throughs that were 2.5 times greater than the industry standard rate. Printed

---

[2]https://noelyeo.com/Ok-Google-Launch

ads were shared showing questions asked in specific situations too. And then they took it a step further by utilizing Out Of Home (OOH) advertising that gamified the process of using the app, all around New York. Questions were hidden all over the city with bespoke artwork, printed crockery, neon lettering and much more to share the question that New Yorkers could ask to uncover a fascinating fact. Not only did this involve the community from a consumer perspective, but it also highlighted businesses that could be/were customers of Google.

'The Out Of Home campaign started because one thing we were always cognisant of was that Google wanted to encourage people to not look at their screens,' says Noel.

'Yes, Google actually wanted you to not look at Google! The idea was that whatever question you had in mind, you could just ask, and Google, as this somewhat sentient omnipresent being, would be able to answer. This led us to insert questions in different parts of the city, trying to stoke wonder and curiosity as you navigate through it.'

Blending new and traditional media

Utilization of printed media can be a great way to support online content, even today. With the campaign above, it was utilized to support and promote what was already happening online and beyond, and below, it all started off as a teaser for what was to come.

The Cadbury Gorilla is known for that iconic 2007 video,[3] but the campaign was multi-platform and designed to evolve across different spaces to keep this going. The more in-depth case study is in Chapter 20, but I had to include it here too. Before the campaign launched, Cadbury took out ads in *The Evening*

[3]https://youtu.be/Rs2z7OA3XKI?si=1n-qr78YH2NJMmcw (Search 'Cadbury's Gorilla Playing Drums Advert')

Standard and *Metro* saying that something was happening at 9.00 pm that Friday night. It teased with a picture of a gorilla, assuring people that he'd been waiting for this moment his whole life. All would be revealed on Channel 4, during the live *Big Brother* final, at that time a real cultural, water-cooler moment. At 9.00 pm, the ad hit, and the marketing director at the time, Phil Rumbol, watched the response online from his laptop. The video made its way onto YouTube (where it gathered real momentum) and accrued a lot of earned media as the press went wild for it. But it didn't stop there. 'There were also remixes with different music over the film,' says Phil. 'Then, for the Rugby World Cup in October, we took spots in the coverage of the matches and changed the skin on the drum to support the England team, which we know went down really well with fans. It was treating it like a cultural moment. It's harder to generate that level of organic virality now, but looking to weave marketing into popular culture rather than a commercial intrusion is still powerful.'

Not thrusting a brand down people's throats can be a powerful marketing ploy, creating more intrigue, interest and engagement. This can be utilized across different platforms too.

As you'll read about in Chapter 21, the 'That Place' campaign also utilized multi-platform.[4] Like the Cadbury campaign, the brand wasn't obvious, but there were strong clues, such as the company's iconic yellow and red colour palette, Mindy Kaling in a yellow dress, the beige colour of the uniforms, even if the branding was pixelated. This was one of the elements that made the campaign transcend multi-platforms and still feel very connected, as Nate Able, creative and art director, shared: 'What mattered most from our side was making it memorable and having all the parts hang together and add up to something bigger,' he says. 'The thread that tied everything together was the intrigue – hinting at "that place" but never actually naming McDonald's. Every piece carried that same line: "That place where Coke tastes so good." That consistency of voice helped it hang together.

[4]https://www.nate-able.com/that-place

'On top of that, we leaned into consistent visual cues. So whether you saw a billboard, a TV spot, or a digital placement, it all added up to one cohesive idea.' Being connected across multiple places doesn't always need to be with a logo, but it's important to have a thread that connects everything together.

Distribution and accessibility

Some things seem designed for one space – such as a podcast, for example. You might assume that this online product is limited to the digital world through podcast platforms, websites, mailing lists, etc. Diary of a CEO (DOAC) is different. This chart-topping podcast hosted and produced by Steven Bartlett and his team has taken to the cinemas for specific episodes, staged live events and offered VIP and meet-and-greet options at events. But why go to this level of effort and push into different places? Georgie Holt, CEO of FlightStory, explains why this multi-platform approach is essential to DOAC's mission. 'With distribution, it's decentralized,' says Georgie. 'The idea and the mission we have is that wherever there's a screen, you should be able to find our content, because our mission is so strong and we believe it should be accessible everywhere. The team has relentlessly focused on creating a world-class podcast, I'd say the best in the world, and they continually strive for more experimentation to elevate the product, so we come back to distribution and how we can get it everywhere. Translation is the next focus for us – we focused on Spanish first and in two months this became 6 per cent of our audience for DOAC from 0.2 per cent.'

Getting it right in the different places

Anthony Smith, DOAC's director of trailers (a role that sees him direct the trailers to promote the podcast across all platforms as well as train trailer editors), is heavily involved in ensuring the promotion of the podcast across a range of digital platforms. Like many of us, he's seen mistakes happen with brands working across multiple platforms, and the significant negative impact it can have. 'It's so easy to have your audience click out of an asset, so you need to hook people and do everything in your power to keep them,' says Anthony. 'Every platform has its preferred ratios. Every trailer we share needs to feel like it was built for that ratio. We don't want the audience to feel like we don't care.' DOAC takes this commitment to native content to the next level. The team designs the text so each word can be repositioned on its own, giving ultimate control over how every piece of text sits over the video as well as when it comes onto the screen. The type of shots captured allows for different ratios and space for wording too, giving more opportunities to create impactful and different content across all platforms, regardless of the preferred ratio.

'There are different personalities on different platforms too. We sometimes do alternate hooks for YouTube versus social. We know YouTube viewers are more likely in it for the long haul, for example.' Although some of the above sounds very technical, in essence, it's very simple – know where the content is being posted and change the ratios. It's a level of detail that makes people feel like you care about them, because you're showing the platforms and the audience a level of respect. Concepts can work across platforms, but the detail needs to be adjusted.

How can you make this work for you? Key learnings . . .

- There needs to be a thread connecting all elements together, so a multi-platform campaign feels like it's all part of the same thing.
- The thread doesn't have to be your logo placed in every scene; the connections can be more subtle – like a colour or even a font that people know as your brand – such as Cadbury's purple.

- Your audience is the key to working out where to show up. Understand where the attention is and prioritize those areas first.
- Think outside the box – how could you create real impact as you add to your touchpoints?
- Ensure that each place a customer encounters you is tailored specifically for the medium. Resizing assets can ensure your image or video appears in a 'native' way wherever it's seen (many apps allow a version of resizing to happen inside them).
- In addition to resizing assets, would some benefit from a redesign or a repositioning of elements, based on the platform?
- More platforms create more opportunities, exposure to different people and the opportunity to cater for different preferences.
- You don't have to go it alone – collaborations and partnerships can also be a great way to utilize multi-platform.
- Different platforms have different audiences that can be more or less invested in what they're being shown. In addition to changing the ratio of the asset, you could also explore different hooks based on what you know about the people in that place.

12

Working with influencers to show values and boost reach

Influencers remain a fundamental part of the marketing mix today. If this book had been written a few years ago, we wouldn't have thought of them in the same way, as they were few and far between.

Today, the term influencer has been adopted by those building their own brands on social media as content creators. As their followings grow, so does this influence and so does their potential value to a brand trying to get access to their audience. Of course, there are a lot of caveats.

Working with influencers works if a set of criteria is met. As with collaborations, you have to do the work to make sure that the following is genuine, engaged, that the creator is adding value and their audience cares about what they're saying. I also think ensuring tone, alignment and values are vital to a positive partnership.

Why does it work?

Why does this marketing strategy work? Essentially, we listen to people we know, like and trust, as we talked about in Chapter 5 on founder-led marketing. If you, as a founder, don't have this level of rapport with people or you want to amplify your message and brand by tapping into someone else's presence, influencer marketing could well be the way to go. And there is no shortage of influencers to choose from.

Before social media, influencers would either be famous and notable people we felt a connection with – TV stars and personalities – or our friends and neighbours. When we like people, we tend to listen to what they say. If you're thinking of buying yourself a new product – let's say trainers – and one of your closest friends says, 'Oh – these trainers are the best, they're so comfortable . . .' – would you consider these trainers? Most people would. Speaking from experience, this is exactly how my current trainers came into my life. I was overwhelmed by all the choices; I couldn't work out what to pick, and I was then influenced by a friend.

With social media, our networks are so much wider. It doesn't have to be that friend you see every week for coffee; it can be someone you have never met in real life who lives on the other side of the world. But because of their carefully crafted social media presence and the development of their own personal brand, you feel like you know them. They've shared bits of themselves that make them relatable to you, they've built up their credibility, and when they say something is good or it works, you tend to believe them. The chances are they'll probably show the product in action too, so you get a bit more intel before you make your purchase.

Sounds perfect, doesn't it? But not all influencers are created equal. Some work hard to foster genuine connection and community and, therefore, when they speak, people listen. Others . . . not so much. Maybe they sold out early and traded integrity for money, or maybe they say everything is brilliant and move from brand to brand each day so nothing really has value any more.

Relationships matter

Lorna Andrews, aka Lorna Luxe, is a very successful influencer with over 1.5 million followers on Instagram alone.[1] She has also worked with influencers,

[1] www.instagram.com/lorna/

particularly on the launch of beauty brand 98. She knows how brands can develop good relationships with influencers that create the outcomes everyone wants. 'The sweet spot is where the influencer has already bought and liked the product, but all of my best partnerships have come about through a relationship with a PR,' says Lorna. 'All the big brands I've worked with have started with chat. The power of relationships is really important.'

So, how can businesses dipping their toe into this space start this process? 'If it were me, I'd be communicating with them on a one-on-one basis. I'd follow the people I wanted to target and strike up conversations – maybe even daily – before asking them for coffee or lunch. You should be confident in the product you're selling, you should have done your homework, and then you can win them over, and the only way to do that is through having a decent relationship and being a decent person.'

It's also about give and take. Too often, when the influencer/brand relationship doesn't work, it's because one party is taking (or the other thinks they're taking) more than the other. All too easily, people can feel exploited. But this is where the relationship matters too. Yes, money can, and often does, change hands, and in Lorna's case when she launched 98, she also gave those influencers she worked with extra reach, exposure and endorsement through her highly engaged feeds. And sometimes, it's about exchange. When a high-profile businesswoman talked about Lorna's 98 hair mask on her social media, Lorna was thrilled. Then, when Lorna received a product as a gift from the same lady, she knew exactly how to show her appreciation. 'Her range is great anyway, but she knows that there's no way I'm not sharing her product after what she did for us.' These examples could be seen as modern product placement too.

Lorna compares being an effective influencer with the film *Point Break* (the one where Keanu Reeves, to infiltrate the gang, has to become a surfer). 'What founders are realizing now is that to understand influencers and work well with them, it's best to join them. Relationships matter. No one is going to give a new brand airtime if they don't know anything about them.'

Of course, not all influencers have the same impact on the bottom line as others. With Lorna's recent launch, she says that although they had many shares, she's able to count on one hand the people who truly influenced their audiences to buy.

Beauty Pie[2] is a brand well known for its alternative approach to luxury beauty. Founded by skincare expert Marcia Kilgore, the brand works with labs, cutting out the middlemen (and the extra costs), to provide high-quality products for a lot less than you'd see a comparative item for on the shelves. Products can be bought direct or via a membership model that delivers additional benefits and savings. The company launched in 2016 and has enjoyed significant success since this time, with some sources estimating the company to be worth over £900 million.[3]

Resonance, not reach

Beauty Pie utilizes influencers to help promote the individual products as well as the concept. Shira Feuer is the chief marketing officer for Beauty Pie and shares more about the company's strategy. 'We're intentional and strategic about influencer partnerships,' says Shira. 'It's not just about reach, it's about resonance. We look for people whose values align with ours: people who champion transparency, who are passionate about quality, and most importantly, who actually use and love the products.

'We've had major celebrities who genuinely love our products and use them all the time. We also work with makeup artists who we might send products to, and they naturally start using them on their clients and sharing content on their own. We see every collaboration as a partnership, not a transaction. In terms of execution, we don't believe in a one-size-fits-all model. Some

---

[2]www.beautypie.com/

[3]https://tracxn.com/d/companies/beauty-pie/__3fipK1B5cQGpt6nNg6s7oRRLxFOkJ1-Hgsv-idSziDU#about-the-company

influencers co-create edits with us, others might be part of a campaign or host an event with us. The key is making it authentic to them so it feels credible to their audience, not scripted.

'Success for us isn't just about reach or conversions. It's about building long-term relationships that grow with the brand. When an influencer becomes a real champion of Beauty Pie, that's when we feel real impact.'

Working with influencers for the long-term benefit is definitely the better approach, but all too often brands hop from one person to the next to try and get that quick spike. Sometimes a particular person will share content and spikes will be seen, but as Shira says, the value of an influencer shouldn't always be judged on one result, and equally they shouldn't be judged on their following alone. For influencer marketing to really work, it has to go a lot deeper than this.

When Adobe wanted to reach female entrepreneurs, it identified Grace Beverley as an influencer who would be perfectly placed to work with the brand in an authentic way. 'Whether it's emerging voices or globally recognized talent, we're passionate about building those long-term relationships with creators in the right way,' says Simon Morris, VP Marketing for Adobe. 'These people have built up communities that have a lot of trust in them, and if we can tap into their audiences, that ensures that we show up in that authentic way. They know what type of content works for their audiences, and we try not to be too prescriptive in what content they produce.' There's a full case study about the brand's award-winning campaign with Grace Beverley in Chapter 6 – harnessing this approach led to huge engagement rates and some excellent content that supports its audience.

Grace is an example of an influencer with a significant following, but there are a variety of people to work with out there. Influencers can be mega or macro, all the way down to micro and nano. Although big accounts have the potential for big reach, small and niche have scope too. Or you can do something completely different, like Lastminute.com, which took a different route, opting for those the world didn't see as influencers, with great results.

Case study: Lastminute.com 2024

Social listening can be a secret weapon in marketing, as proved by this campaign from Lastminute.com. A completely organic viral VoxPop moment between an influencer and a young woman who dreamed of travelling the world and capturing its beauty through photography became a moment for the brand when she was asked: 'Why don't you ask lastminute.com to sponsor you?'. The video, entirely unscripted and unpaid, achieved more than thirteen million views.[4] And this sparked an idea. In a busy travel space, it provided an opportunity to break through a 'sea of sameness'.

'Travel content is one of the most crowded spaces online. You're not just competing with other brands but with everyone's holiday photos. We didn't want to add to the noise; we wanted to cut through it,' says Ruchika Kalra, brand director at lastminute.com.

The moment with the young woman resonated deeply because people saw themselves in her, revealing a powerful consumer insight that became the foundation for a long-term creator programme. Recognizing this, the brand decided not just to sponsor one person but to open the opportunity to fifteen creators who would travel and create content for a year.[5] Applicants shared why they should be chosen, generating a wave of user-generated content that celebrated the joy of last-minute holidays.

The company opted against using traditional travel influencers and went for 'normal' people – everyday storytellers – including a chef, a home decorator and a comedian, proving that spontaneous, last-minute joy can come from anywhere. Each creator produced authentic, entertaining content over the year, capturing the humour, energy and imperfections that make real last-minute holidays memorable.

---

[4]https://www.instagram.com/reel/CuZwYqMIOnA/

[5]https://lbbonline.com/news/how-lastminutecoms-influencer-driven-pivot-redefined-travel-marketing

'We wanted everyday influencers that our audience could see themselves in,' says Ruchika. 'That's where the trust comes from: relatability.'

The result was a steady stream of fresh, funny and relatable stories that strengthened lastminute.com's position as the home of last-minute holiday deals. The campaign delivered triple-digit growth and won industry awards, proving that entertainment, authenticity and emotional resonance can drive both connection and performance.

The campaign works for a few different reasons. The first was where the idea came from. Lastminute.com leaned into a cultural moment and then decided to spin it in a different way, moving away from travel influencers and leveraging relatability. The company also looked at nurturing long-term relationships and working with these.

Quick wins can be great, but getting an audience to engage with and follow a story is hugely powerful and undeniably creates a deeper connection to the individual creatives and the brand.

Influencer partnerships are important to the global action camera company, GoPro. Due to the presence of the brand and its reputation, the company is no doubt inundated with requests. But how does a company decide whom to work with? Not just for its own benefit, but in a way that amplifies what the audience expects from a company?

Customers as influencers

'We usually start by finding people on social that are already using our camera in unique, entertaining, and/or engaging ways and see if we can provide them with a newer model, or reach out to feature their content on social channels,' says Rick Loughery, senior vice president, Global Marketing & Digital Commerce at GoPro. 'We have a good feel about how their content would work with our audiences based on what they are already publishing on their channels.'

But how do you get it right? How do you pick people who are inspiring, aspirational, who promote your brand and open you up to new people at the same time as keeping loyal fans happy?

'I would say you want to work with influencers that understand how to authentically and creatively make content that works for your brand as well as how they will interact with your brand,' says Rick. 'This seems pretty generic because it is. But the real work comes in finding those people and fostering those relationships.'

How can you make this work for you? Key learnings . . .

- Alignment is essential.
- All influencers aren't created equal.
- Research and connect – start by following people you might like to work with, then start to engage and see where that takes you.
- Relationships really matter – put time into developing these to understand what makes the person tick, their audience and to see if they align with your brand and values.
- Often, you'll need to pay the influencer for the work they do for you – and quite rightly too – but sometimes it can be about the exchange, perhaps in terms of the opportunities you provide or products they receive.
- Briefs matter in terms of output, but be aware that being too restrictive could negatively impact the success of any campaign. Discuss your objectives with the people you're looking to work with and see what they suggest. They know their audience a lot better than you do. Once

you've worked out what you're doing, then is the time to add detail on deliverables.

- Audience is essential – yes, you might want to reach a new audience, but if you're looking at collaboration posts and actively sharing their work with your audience, it needs to sit well. You don't want to alienate your current customers in the quest to attract more.
- Be clear on whether you're playing the short game or the long game.
- Don't base your choices on vanity metrics – look at the measures that really make a difference.
- It really is about give and take. You're in this together; it's a form of partnership; everyone should benefit in some way.
- Big influencers have more reach, but micro and nano influencers can still pack a punch, particularly if supported by the brand and their following/reach too.
- Some of the best influencers could well be your customers as they already know and like your product. The perfect people could be right under your nose!

13

Endorsement and celebrity

Alignment and association

Having a well-known figure attached to your brand or campaign can give you a leg up because, essentially, the brand is borrowing credibility and reputation from that person as well as aligning itself with their values and signalling to their audience that it is connected to them.

Some companies work on a campaign-by-campaign basis, and others have long-term connections. The truth is that the right option depends on a number of factors. With Audi, the celebrities that the company works with are chosen as part of a broader campaign connected to the cars being in movies. Audi then produces additional assets itself that align with the film's content and utilizes the same actors, produced in a similar way, in close cooperation with the filmmakers, but utilized for advertising purposes. 'This was the case for several Marvel productions such as *Spider-Man: The Science Fair* (with Tom Holland and Jacob Batalon) or *The Gray Man* (with The Russo Brothers),' says Benjamin Honal, Audi Product Placement. 'These activations rank among our most successful campaigns as a brand overall – driven by strong global market adoption, outstanding fan engagement and excellent performance metrics and evaluations.'

Let's be honest, if you see Spider-Man driving a car, you're going to think about it in a positive light, aren't you? The extension of the product placement marketing strategy is also highly impactful.

Perfectly aligned

Mindy Kaling worked on 'That Place' campaign (see Chapter 21) with great effect. As Nate Able shares, Mindy was chosen because of her alignment with the brand, as well as her personality and the way she connected with the audience. 'Mindy was a great fit for several reasons,' says Nate. 'She's likeable and obviously has great comedic timing and delivery. On top of that, she was already openly a fan of McDonald's in interviews and on social media, so her involvement felt authentic rather than staged.'

Ensuring that the link between product and celebrity is strong ensures that the message feels authentic to the audience. You could get the biggest celebrity in the world with a huge following and a killer content plan to share your message, but if they've spoken about how they're not in any way interested in or even like the kind of product you sell or service you're offering, the impact will be greatly reduced.

Rachel Hardy is the director of communications for FlightStory and has extensive experience working in TV, media and directly with onscreen talent. She started her career in the beauty industry, working across designer and celebrity fragrances, so she has seen how working with the right celebrity can fast-track a brand's reach and success. It can also demonstrate what a brand stands for, communicating its values in a far quicker, clearer way than a traditional long-term brand marketing strategy.

Reputations matter

When brands are linked to celebrities in a deep way, both reputations can become intertwined from the public's point of view. This means that if one party does something 'wrong,' the other has to think about whether that association will hurt them and their brand. It sounds cut-throat, but it's simply the way of the world. You can't control the actions of those you work with, but having the ability to step away if their behaviour is in conflict with you as a brand and how the public perceives you is important. But there's still a choice there. Depending on the situation, there have been cases where a brand didn't step away from a star and vice versa. Yes, some 'fans' are appalled, and in some cases, it can be detrimental, but in other cases, it can increase awareness and profile, or reposition the brand in a positive way, bringing in new customers as news spreads and awareness increases through more press. It can be divisive, but so can a decision to work with a celebrity in the first place. 'I've worked with brands where the talent has been involved with a scandal and they've actually seen a spike in sales,' says Rachel.

New ways of working

The way in which celebrities work with brands has changed significantly in recent times. It used to be more focused on the use of the talent's image and likeness across specified assets for a set period of time. But with the evolution of social media and the talent's ability to grow their own audiences, we're seeing all different kinds of deals emerging. From commission-based deals to celebrities owning their own brands, we're now seeing famous people turn their own audiences into commercial ventures. Reese Witherspoon is a great example of this with Hello Sunshine,[1] a media company created to share women's stories in film, books and more. But you don't need to build your own empire to make commercial gains. 'We're seeing a lot more celebrities getting a share in companies they're working with,' says Rachel. 'It further cements alignment and belief in the product. It shows they're so confident in the product, they've put their cash into it. It also enables talent to become

[1]https://hello-sunshine.com/

entrepreneurs, offering them more longevity and secondary income when their public life starts to change.'

Over the last decade, the California Milk Processor Board had seen consumption trends moving from real milk to plant-based, and now, real dairy milk is coming back again. During the time when plant-based milk was gaining in popularity, many people weren't all that keen to endorse real milk. However, to help amplify the swing back to real milk, the Board brought back the incredibly iconic 'milk mustache' campaign that launched in the 1990s and featured celebrities, but with a twist. James Kulp is from GALLEGOS United, the agency of record for the California Milk Processor Board, and explains how Got Milk? evolved its approach.

'When the milk mustache campaign was launched in 1995, it didn't actually have the Got Milk? tagline,' he says. 'It was a year or so into the campaign when they switched to the Got Milk? tagline that had been gaining tremendous traction in California, and that's when the Milk Mustache campaign took off. This was like influencer marketing before influencer marketing. Celebrities sporting their ubiquitous milk mustaches were on posters, magazines, in schools, everywhere. Even now, when we're talking to influencers and celebrities, they all remember and love the milk mustache campaign and ask to be a part of it even though it's been retired for about ten years. They see it almost like a sign that they've made it – because there's so much cachet with it.'

To be clear on just how iconic this campaign was, Harrison Ford, Heidi Klum, Shaquille O'Neal, Rihanna and Hugh Jackman are just a few of the celebrities who have taken part.

Getting celebrity endorsement can help bring a product into popular culture, providing a new context for it – a different frame for people to see it through. With milk, it's seen as a commodity . . . and a rather unsexy one at that. However, if you are able to organically inject it into popular culture via celebrities, linking the product to films, TV shows and music, all of a sudden your commodity is seen in a different, interesting and very relevant way. 'Connecting with celebrities brought milk into pop culture and into the conversation, and even onto some people's bedroom walls! It created a lot of earned media – people were talking about it then and years after the campaign's conclusion, they are still talking about it!'

Choosing a celebrity who's known for a particular role, or even has a specific kind of accent, can help people connect with a brand differently and re-evaluate the ideas they had. Jamie Peate is from McCann WorldGroup and has worked on many retailer campaigns, including those for Aldi. He shares how using the right celebrities can help to realign people's thoughts about a brand. 'Sometimes, juxtaposition can be great – for example, would you expect someone who's got a really posh accent to be talking about a budget supermarket?' says Jamie. Using these key voices or people over a prolonged period of time has the additional advantage of building recognition.

Trust matters

Trust is a factor too, and when working with celebrities and looking at those endorsements, ensuring that the person you're working with has trust with the audience matters – or else their words and endorsement don't mean a lot. Another element to consider is how brand loyal they are. Celebrities can and do work with and lend their endorsement to a range of products and services, but if they're moving from competitor to competitor in a short space of time – who wins? The audience is left a little confused and could well hop around like the celebrity. The impact is far less.

Liquid Death is known for its work with celebrities. Unusually for the calibre of celebrity that the brand works with, Stephen Nilsen aka Stix (former VP Lifestyle Marketing at Liquid Death), explains that they've never paid a celebrity to work with them. 'In my time, we never paid anyone for a post,' says Stix. 'Any time you saw Liquid Death, it was because they were investors or just love the brand, and I'm talking about celebrities and rock stars.' To give you a taste of the kind of celebrities, we're talking about Martha Stewart, Tony Hawk, Ozzy Osbourne, Metallica and more.[2]

'In the case of Liquid Death, we had some of these celebrity investors, and the really smart ones knew that if they helped push it, it would help the brand's value,' says Stix. 'Mike would throw these wild ideas at them to help their own brands and to make them more relatable. Martha wasn't an investor; I knew her people, but we started throwing ideas and it worked! There has to be a deep dive there – does it fit? You can't force them into it, you have to work with them and develop it.'

Another random but amazing celebrity endorsement came from Travis Barker from the band Blink-182. Travis' band released the track Enema of the State, and Liquid Death saw an opportunity that not many others would have seen . . . a collectible enema kit.[3] Travis worked with the team on a light-hearted video promoting the kit, which also included a signed can of Liquid Death, woven in with 'customer' testimonials around their use of the kit, a fake nurse and more. Of course, the kit wasn't really an enema, but the £180 limited-edition boxed set was very real. And it sold out.

Another example of working with celebrities in a less conventional way, and what this can do, comes from Tony Hawk.

Case study: Tony Hawk Blood Board

Professional skateboarder Tony Hawk has been linked with Liquid Death across various campaigns – all unconventional, all highly effective. In some cases, they've also linked with limited-edition kits or products featuring something from Tony. One example of this was around the launch of the company's Flavoured Sparkling Waters, which contained 90 per cent less sugar

---

[2]https://liquiddeath.com/en-gb/pages/timewaster-5000
[3]https://liquiddeath.com/en-gb/pages/enema

than the top fizzy drinks in the space. So Liquid Death hired just one tenth – the head – of Tony Hawk to talk about it[4] . . . and created a competition to win a signed Tony Hawk head print. The other campaign that has to be mentioned is the Tony Hawk Blood Board.[5]

'Tony Hawk was an athlete at the first role I held, and we reconnected,' says Stix. 'The Blood Board idea came from Mike and the team, and Tony said he'd do it. This campaign broke the internet, the boards sold out immediately and it all went to charity. We didn't expect it to break the internet.'

This was a brave campaign, but Liquid Death knew it would work, that their audience would get it, and it would have an impact. Tony Hawk teamed up with the company and donated some blood, which was mixed with red paint, and used to decorate 100 skateboards. A video was shared featuring the blood being taken from Tony, and the paint being mixed. The boards cost $500 and sold out overnight, got a whole heap of earned media, and raised money for 5 Gyres, a non-profit dedicated to ending the use of plastic, and Tony's The Skatepark Project.

As per Stix's comments, sometimes celebrities share their endorsement or support simply because they get behind and believe in the project, product or cause.

This happened with the ALS Ice Bucket Campaign, transforming it from something that was gathering momentum online to something that the mainstream media were also interested in, and with the celebrities sharing, the reach surged too.

And the cost?

Working with celebrities can be very expensive – simply because of the clout they can bring to a brand and the value of that endorsement. That doesn't mean

---

[4]https://liquiddeath.com/en-gb/pages/tonyhawk

[5]www.youtube.com/watch?v=gl7MRPWSw_M (Search 'Liquid Death Puts Tony Hawk's Blood in Skateboards')

they won't deliver a return on investment, but really looking at the numbers and whether or not you're going to see a return is huge. Now, the game has changed thanks to the data, and this is great for businesses. 'When looking to work with celebrities, brands can access the backend of the talent's socials and get all that data,' says Rachel Hardy. 'Sentiment matters too, and while that can still be quite "vibe" led, the data is there to tell us how likely the talent is to convert sales. So it depends on whether a brand is looking for performance and driving direct sales or more of a brand awareness piece, and if it's the latter, this can be assessed more by sentiment and by the press attention that celebrity demands.'

It is important as a brand to spend time looking at the true connection of that person to either your brand or the core values you're passionate about. While celebrities used to be the only way to get a rubber stamp from a well-known person, the online world and the continuing rise of influencers provide numerous other options. Bear in mind that numbers under a person's name don't necessarily link to the success you're going to have. Using a celebrity that's beloved because of their starring role in a science fiction film (and has a big following of people who love sci-fi) doesn't necessarily mean that their fans are going to care about the vegan sweets you want them to promote. And if they've never mentioned anything to do with being a vegan or liking sweets before, it's a stretch. Because of the numbers involved, some people could be interested, but you'd be more likely to see a better response at a much smaller cost by working with an influencer with a smaller following and great engagement who's known for their vegan recipes and quest to find sweet treats that aren't made with animal products.

How can you make this work for you? Key learnings . . .

- Keep your ego in check. It's fine to be flattered by the idea of working with a celebrity, but look at it from a business perspective too.

- Does the celebrity have any real connection to your brand, your values and what you do? Is there any alignment there?
- What ways could you work with them that could extend beyond the expected, get superb engagement and maybe even earned media in other places? Don't just think inside the box, there's a whole world of opportunity out there!
- How will you track the impact the celebrity has had? If you're looking to see what the return on your investment is, you need to know how you're measuring success.
- Do they work with similar brands, or have they done so in the recent past? Could that negatively impact your working relationship with them? Could it dilute the impact?
- Is there a way to deepen that connection in the future?
- Can you do something with them that allows them to achieve their goals too? Support a charity they're involved with, for instance?

14

Taglines

Short and to the point

If I asked you to name the taglines of some of the biggest brands out there, could you do it? Nike? Carlsberg? Red Bull? While you might not think these subtle nods to the brand have made an impact on you, the chances are that they have. Like a logo or a specific colour palette (or if you're really geeky, the fonts a brand uses – I'm a big font fan!), a tagline is a signal that can help to reinforce a brand's presence and even what they're all about.

Coming up with a tagline isn't always easy – it's a big statement to make. With Nike, it's widely documented that Dan Wieden came up with the idea in 1988[1] and it was vague enough that it could be applied to, well, anyone. It made its debut attached to an advert of eighty-year-old Walt Stack explaining how he runs 17 miles each morning,[2] with the words that went on to become iconic at the end. Interestingly, the tagline wasn't the result of hours of brainstorming in a desperate search to create a witty one-liner – when interviewed, Dan shared that the team weren't entirely sure that they needed a tagline at all. And the inspiration? A death row inmate whose last words were 'let's do it'. The fact that someone faced with death was saying these words, to push on, stuck out

[1] www.creativereview.co.uk/just-do-it-slogan/

[2] www.youtube.com/watch?v=0yO7xLAGugQ (Search 'Nike – Just Do It 1988')

to him.[3] Obviously, a few changes happened to make it into Nike's words, but the idea came from a rather random place.[4]

Got Milk? is another well-known tagline that has survived the test of time. What's interesting about this one is that the meaning has evolved over time. The original strategy behind it was one of deprivation, developed around the fear of running out of milk and the negative impact that would have on a much-needed caffeine hit or cereal to start the day. When the campaign started in the 1990s, the competition was limited to just a handful of beverages. Today, however, that has changed with an overwhelming array of colourfully packaged beverage options promising any number of health benefits. And this has led to an evolution of the brand's strategy. As James Kulp from GALLEGOS United explains: 'We've switched from deprivation to an abundance strategy around positivity – the "Got Milk?" question now is about asking you to be a part of it. It allows for freedom and brand recognition and is connecting it all together.'

Another great example is Red Bull, the popular energy drink that's known the world over for the product, the logo, the adrenaline-fuelled events and the tagline 'Red Bull Gives You Wings'. Ruchika Kalra, now brand director at Lastminute.com, was previously global project marketing manager for Red Bull and shares her thoughts on what, at surface level at least, is a slightly random tagline for a drink. 'It's less about the tagline, it's more about the execution,' says Ruchika. 'With Red Bull, if you removed everything it would just be a bizarre tagline for an energy drink, it means nothing until you add the emotion, the activation, it gives you the energy and it lands. Understanding your audience, and the emotion you're trying to evoke in them with your product can help you come up with the tagline. But more importantly, what people need to do is stick with it. Even multi-million-dollar brands have to

---

[3] www.independent.co.uk/life-style/fashion/news/nike-s-just-do-it-slogan-was-inspired-by-a-convicted-killer-s-last-words-10117596.html

[4] www.businessinsider.com/nike-just-do-it-inspired-utah-killer-gary-gilmore-2019-7

do consistent messaging for years before people associate the tagline with the brand.'

Another iconic tagline comes from beer brand Carlsberg – although in truth, the company is known for more than one. What's interesting about Carlsberg is that, as part of a huge marketing campaign, it temporarily changed its 'Probably the best beer in the world' to 'Probably not the best beer in the world'. But with purpose and a lot of impact.

Before we dive into the case study of this specific marketing campaign, let's go back to the beginning. Carlsberg's tagline wasn't created from an idle thought on a Thursday afternoon – it comes from 1847 and was shared as a tagline in 1973. Lynsey Woods is Carlsberg's global brand director and explains why the origin story of Carlsberg links to its tagline:

'Carlsberg was founded by J.C. Jacobsen,[5] who was a big believer in science and dedicated his life to improving the brewing process and quality of beer. Known as "The People's Brewer", every decision he made was in service of that,' says Lynsey. 'Every move he made was to make beer better. He established the first beer research laboratory, employed the best scientists to work on the beer, discovered the process to purify yeast, and created the pH scale.' The company is proud of its heritage and proud of its beer, but due to its Danish DNA, it's very much a humble company, which led it to go for 'probably the best' rather than 'the best'. This approach has stood Carlsberg in good stead.

The company's 'Probably . . . ' tagline was used a little less in the early 2000s because it didn't translate as well overseas, and as a global company, this was something that mattered as there's a huge market in Asia that Carlsberg serves. In 2014, the tagline came back with a vengeance. Fast forward a few years, and it added the word 'not' into the line . . .

[5]www.carlsberggroup.com/175-years/a-history-of-brewing/

Case study: Carlsberg – probably not . . .

In 2016, the company realized it had an issue. The passion, effort, skill and science that went into each of its beers did not translate into positive comments from its customers. What people were saying as they were drinking their pints on a Friday night was not representative of what the brand was, and what it had worked hard to be. Armed with this, the team started doing more research, and dived down a rabbit hole that would change the trajectory of its brew, thanks to Twitter (now X). 'Twitter was the place where a lot of people were very vocal, but not in the best way,' says Lynsey. 'At the time, it was the only big platform that you could get on your soapbox, and when we read the tweets, as people who had looked after the brand for years, it was heartbreaking. One tweet said: "Carlsberg tastes like the rancid p*ss of Satan".'

Can you imagine being part of a company with all that heritage and seeing that written about the brand and the products you create? Carlsberg chose action. 'In China and Vietnam, Carlsberg has always been a premium brew, so there's a real contrast,' says Lynsey. 'UK consumers didn't think the same. We listened to the tweets and wanted to fundamentally shift the perception in the UK. What was really interesting was that we did the research and ran a blind taste test in the UK with 100 consumers. On the first night we got them to taste the ten biggest beers in the UK, blind. Carlsberg and Carlsberg Export were Number 1 and Number 2. The next night, we did the test but we left them branded, and we moved down the list. We knew that we didn't have an issue with the brew, we knew the issue was perception. To understand this as a marketeer was key. Coupled with our "probably the best beer in the world" tagline, it felt meaningless at this point.'

The team decided to play this to its advantage. Carlsberg reformulated based on feedback and the seed of a whole campaign was sown that would change everything. 'We got the team onside, the 600 brewers who worked so hard, and then we went public with this big campaign. We also redesigned the glasses too – we upgraded all customer touchpoints.'

Now, where this becomes genius (in my opinion at least) was what Carlsberg did next. Remember those nasty tweets? It used these to its advantage and asked permission to use them in a marketing campaign. Were those people slightly confused at Carlsberg reaching out with this request? Yes, they were!

Carlsberg promoted these nasty tweets. People thought the posts were being shared by a disgruntled employee, and they started talking online. Over a few days, this built, and then a campaign called 'Mean Tweets' was launched which included asking Carlsberg employees to read out some of these tweets, and filming their reactions. 'We didn't show them before it was done, it was really honest. We used the bird from Twitter, then we shot the bird.' Two versions of these videos were created,[6,7] which then linked to a broader, Out Of Home campaign as well as the tweaked tagline of 'probably not the best beer in the world . . . so we changed it.'[8] The company had lots of different formats that pushed the education point, to help show people that it wasn't 'just' a marketing ploy, that it had done the work and this was how and why. 'If you were on the Underground in London, you'd see ads saying "we kept this, we changed that", and there were longer form ads in different areas. People then realized what we were trying to achieve, what we were doing with the mean tweets, and everything else made sense.' This coincided with the shops being restocked with new look bottles and cans, giving the brand a visual reappraisal too.

A lot of work went on behind the scenes to ensure that the changes really did make a difference and there was a lot of sampling as well as a big drive to ensure everyone in the company understood why the changes were being made. 'We left no stone unturned,' says Lynsey. 'We needed everyone who worked at Carlsberg to get it. We needed everyone to understand why we were saying we were probably not the best beer in the world. We had to inform and update global colleagues and everyone went through a tasting as well.' The campaign concluded with a rather dark advert showing Danish actor, Mads

---

[6]www.youtube.com/watch?v=I15vSE0gQXw (Search 'Carlsberg Mean Tweets 1')
[7]www.youtube.com/watch?v=F-eqTojTzpk (Search 'Carlsberg Mean Tweets 2')
[8]https://fold7.com/work/carlsberg-probably-not

Mikkelsen rowing across a lake summarizing the issue and the solution.[9] As he gets out of his rowing boat he's greeted by a waiter standing with two glasses of beer. Mads asks if the person who was responsible for the old beer had been dealt with before the shot focuses on bubbles coming up from the lake. Mads answers, 'probably'.

The press went wild for the whole campaign. So did consumers. 'Probably not the best beer in the world' won Campaign of the Year 2019 and was nominated as the Most Contagious. The initial Mean Tweets campaigns attracted millions of views in a short space of time. This activity translated into double-digit growth. Brand awareness also doubled. This wasn't confined to the UK either, and the brand's health grew all over the world. Due to the upgrade on every element, a price increase was also put through as part of the campaign. 'Trust grew too, as when you're that honest with consumers it builds a better connection,' says Lynsey.

This isn't the only tagline that Carlsberg is known for. There's the famous 'If Carlsberg did . . . ' which has been adopted by individuals explaining how something is incredible, as well as 'That calls for a Carlsberg'. The 'If Carlsberg did . . .' tagline was last used in the 1990s and came from a series of adverts. The company decided not to use it in marketing moving forward. 'We see this as belonging to the fans now,' says Lynsey. 'It's only in the UK market for us, but we let people play with it, we love seeing it, lots of famous people use it and it's seen a lot in sport too.'

When it comes to 'That calls for a Carlsberg', that's got a slightly different story. 'A decade ago, we realized that "Probably the best . . ." didn't work as well in different places, like Asia, so we moved to the line "That calls for a Carlsberg". We still see this around, but it's another code, another recognition.'

So why do taglines make a difference? As Lynsey says, it's just another small signal that sparks a thought or aids recall. 'We get seconds of people's time in people's lives. Brands like to think we're some big part in consumers' lives,

---

[9]https://youtu.be/BNRAjMIf4bo?si=AoKbRGsnmI9qrkfr

but we're not, we have seconds in the brain, so the faster you can have that recognition and recall, the faster it connects.'

If you're reading this thinking that a tagline is what's missing from your business, there's a lot we can learn from the above.

How can you make this work for you? Key learnings . . .

- Think about who you are. With Carlsberg, it's a Danish company and this DNA means it's naturally humble and values humility. Don't push against who you are as a brand; it won't be representative.
- If you do implement a tagline, sit with it for a while. It's very important to recognize when something is failing and move on quickly, but it's also key that some elements are given time to grow.
- It doesn't have to be literal – a tagline can refer to the audience, a feeling or something else connected to a brand.
- Taglines should allow for some kind of evolution – ones that are too literal or specific can age and become irrelevant.
- Taglines can become as identifiable as logos, so consider whether or not they need to be protected as part of who you are as a business.
- Taglines are hard to create. As James Kulp from Got Milk? says, it's much easier to write a paragraph.
- The tagline alone has power, but the font and everything around it add to it in a bigger way. It's a jigsaw piece, not the whole puzzle.
- Taglines can provide another brand element in a busy world, helping brand recognition in a different way.

15

Nostalgia

Using the past to impact today

Can leaning into 'days gone by' be a good marketing strategy? If it's done well and aligns with your target audience, it can be absolutely magic. But why, you may ask, does going back in time have an impact on what's happening now? There are a few reasons.

The first is the emotional connection that it creates that aligns with positive past memories. Is it a safe bet to assume that everyone's past was positive? Clearly not everyone has great memories of time gone by, but there's a cognitive bias called rosy retrospection that can help us to remember the past in a better way. Like you're wearing rose-tinted glasses. We see examples of this in our day-to-day lives, when people recount 'the good old days' as a way to show that the world we're living in today is falling short. Sure, there may have been less reliance on technology and people weren't glued to their phones or tablets all the time, but there was also rationing and a series of events that rocked the world – surely those periods can't have been better than now? Well, if you went back in time, the chances are that they weren't, but this nifty little shortcut in the brain has made the bad times seem a lot more, well, rosy.

'Rosy retrospection emerges from our desire to be optimistic and avoid negative and self-defeating thoughts and beliefs,' says Krystine Batcho PhD, professor of psychology at Le Moyne College, Syracuse, NY. 'By focusing on the positive, we are motivated to confront challenges and overcome adversity. The favourable aspects of our past help us forgive others who regret having hurt us and allow us to forgive ourselves for mistakes we have made. Such positive thoughts and emotions can be elicited by nostalgic marketing. For example, we can be encouraged to return to a vacation or tourist location despite inconveniences of travel or disappointing weather, etc. Looking back, we can smile at the nuisances as we are reminded of the joy that was all the happier by virtue of coping with the imperfect aspects.'

How many times do we vow never to do something again – like visiting the shops on Christmas Eve, or working with a client on a specific project – only to be lured back in, safe in the knowledge that it wasn't all that bad last time? I've been there too . . .

Was the past always positive?

That's not to say that the past was bad, and many of the nostalgia levers we see map to childhood which, for most, was a relatively stress-free and enjoyable time. This emotional connection to the past can trigger positive emotions, which can be very good for brands utilizing nostalgia. Moving back to the past can also help create a sense of security as the world changes at a rapid pace, which can lead to anxiety and a feeling of uncertainty. 'Nostalgic reminiscence elicits comforting memories of simpler times when we were confident and felt loved for who we were,' says Krystine. 'Nostalgic memories keep us grounded in what truly matters. Over the successes and setbacks of our life, we had people whom we loved and who loved us. We were able to rely upon others when we needed them and also lend our support to others who needed us. Such memories comfort us by helping us realize that meaning and purpose in life come from our relationships with the people who have been important to who we have become.'

Have you ever seen a post on social media that says something like 'if you remember this, we should be friends' or 'if you remember this, you were born in the best decade' before you're presented with images depicting toys, branding, pop groups and more of days gone by? Yes, you think, that's me too – and before you know it, you're connected to that random post and perhaps others who have commented on it as well. Leveraging what are known as cultural touchstones can be a very powerful marketing tool. Imagine if a brand does the same (well, you don't need to imagine, it happens all the time!). Think of films or characters that have been brought back from a time gone by and enjoyed huge success. But more than that, brands can use objects to have a similar draw. By leveraging nostalgia in this way, the brand is clearly speaking to a specific audience and it will only truly resonate with people around at that time. This allows you to go deeper into this area and make a mark.

One example of a brand that did this incredibly well was Oreo with its Mix Tapes campaign.

Case study: Oreo Mix Tapes

'When the brief came in, the team behind Oreo's marketing were tasked with creating something that appealed to young millennials and millennial parents across Europe,' says James Whatley, a senior strategist who worked on this collaboration with Mondelez during his time at Digitas UK. 'Finding commonalities across such a breadth of targets was tricky, so we knew we had to go broad with our approach. Tapping into music, films, and video games made the most sense from a research perspective. And the team turned this into a series of strategic partnerships to tap into each of these points across Europe. 'To start, we already had a Lady Gaga partnership in the pipeline,[1] and

[1]www.mondelezinternational.com/news/lady-gaga-oreo-chromatica-collaboration/

then we had *The Batman* lined up for the next campaign . . . but then Robert Pattison got Covid. We were looking into the nostalgia side, because Lady Gaga had triggered an interest in cassette tapes, there was also a Netflix show connected to mixtapes – *13 Reasons Why*,[2] there was *Guardians of the Galaxy* . . . and I was keen to do something with Spotify too. So, we made mixtape boxes with unique Spotify codes.'[3]

When pitching the idea to Mondelez (the company that owns the Oreo brand), James and his team employed an idea he'd heard at a conference – how important it is for people to see and feel what you want to achieve, rather than just read about it. So, after a healthy dose of research, the team made the client her own mixtape, utilizing everything that would be available to customers, and she was sold.

'The brief was Robert Pattinson has Covid, *The Batman* has been delayed by a year, and we need something else,' says James. 'And that's how we ended up with Oreo Mixtapes!'

The mixtape campaign was brilliant for many reasons.[4] It showed a deep understanding of the audience, their fond memories of mixtapes and the care and effort people had put into crafting their own for loved ones in a time gone by. With everything that happened during the pandemic, many people were feeling disconnected from friendship groups because they couldn't go and see them, so why not bring back the love and feelings connected to a mixtape, but in a way that was relevant for the time?

Oreo created new packaging that looked like a cassette player. Then, using AI, special edition packs could be scanned to enter the digital experience. From here, you could create your mixtape, add a dedication to make it extra special, add stickers and then send it to a friend. To activate, they just scanned the Spotify code and they were there. And it worked. In three months, just

[2]www.netflix.com/gb/title/80117470
[3]https://oreo-mixtapes.webflow.io/
[4]www.bbc.co.uk/news/newsbeat-55476419

under 200k packs were scanned, ninety-four million impressions were gained, there was a huge brand lift and brand recall too.[5]

Oreo's Oreo + Xbox campaign relied heavily on nostalgia too – if you want to refresh your memory, you'll find that in Chapter 3.

Some brands, thanks to their longevity, can also utilize nostalgia in marketing, without really trying all that hard. The LEGO Group is a great example of this. Over the years, the company has leaned into nostalgia by bringing back much-loved sets from decades ago. Many of these sets have been updated, but the resemblance will trigger memories from those who saw them first time around. One great example of this is the Eldorado Fortress. Originally launched in 1989, when it came back in 2023 not only was the product very similar, but the packaging was too.[6]

When the company celebrated its ninetieth anniversary with the 'We Are All Builders' campaign,[7] the hero video of the piece took viewers back over ninety years of the LEGO Group by cleverly showcasing iconic moments and key styles. These included the first man on the moon, 1970s wallpaper, the building of the Empire State Building and plenty more besides. It helps us to remember that LEGO has been there for all of it.

Got Milk? is another example of a company utilizing its own IP to evoke nostalgia in an audience. The 2025 campaign brought back the iconic Milk Mustache campaign that had first launched thirty years prior[8] but had been retired for ten years. This attracted a huge amount of earned media, as well as significant audience participation. 'We took it from a celebrity-led, print legacy media-only campaign into a much more modern expression with a mobile studio travelling across California capturing 12,000 people all proudly sporting their own milk mustaches,' says James Kulp from

[5]www.publicisgroupeuk.com/who-we-are/our-work/supercharging-oreo-sales-with-a-playful-connected-experience.

[6]www.lego.com/en-us/aboutus/news/2023/june/lego-icons-eldorado-fortress-

[7]www.lego.com/en-us/aboutus/news/2022/june/new-lego-campaign-celebrates-90-years-of-rebuilding-the-world-through-play

[8]www.gotmilk.com/30years/

GALLEGOS United. 'Lots of people showed up to get their portrait taken, and walked away with a poster of themselves in a Got Milk? ad that made its way across social media in hundreds of posts. The connection to that original campaign drove tremendous engagement and excitement, as now they were the star. Having that nostalgia aspect, particularly with millennial parents, was huge.'

On top of the press and social buzz, the modern spin on the campaign connected back to its roots by selecting 140 of the images showcasing real Californians to be a part of a billboard campaign in markets across the state.

When you have a brand that has been around for a long time, the nostalgia lever seems like an obvious one to pull, but without the strategy and the theory behind it, it's all too easy to generate a 'so what' response in the people you're hoping to woo. 'Tap into the emotion of the thing that happened in the past rather than just portray it in the past,' said Phil Rumbol, ex marketing director for Cadbury. 'Saying someone was around in the 1950s doesn't really matter, it's what that brand made you feel when you were ten years old.'

Nostalgia at key times

What about key times of year? Christmas is a time when nostalgia comes into play, with many brands using this to connect to their audience. Coca-Cola with its 'Holidays Are Coming', Budweiser with its iconic Clydesdale horses and many supermarkets lean heavily on nostalgia too. As Jamie Peate from McCann WorldGroup explains, there's a good reason why: 'It's about how do you balance the old and the new, how do you capture nostalgia?' says Jamie. 'We all want it to be the Christmas we had as children, and we want our children to too, but you also want something new. It's the twist of the familiar. If you look at very successful comedy shows, you know the characters, you know the catchphrases, but they are put into different situations – there's a great familiarity. A bit of this is Christmas. How do you take all the things people are familiar with and make them news? How do we move things on without moving it off?'

With nostalgia it's not just making a point that you as a brand have been around for a long time, or that you're trying to remind people of something that happened a while ago to show you understand them. It's about how it makes them feel, particularly when the product you're selling isn't a necessity.

Past or future?

Krystine also believes that nostalgia has the power to connect us to who we want to be in the future. 'Nostalgic remembering helps us appreciate how we have changed, and how we are also different versions of who we once were,' says Krystine. 'Being able to compare aspects of who we once were and who we are now allows us to envision our future self. Do we want to continue on the trajectory we have been on? Or do we want to recapture aspects of our past self and incorporate them into our future self? For example, a person might realize that their work/life balance has shifted and that they might want to readjust it as they move forward. Or a person might gain insight into how past relationships had benefited (or suffered) by how they used to interact and then use those insights to enrich present and future relationships. Quality marketing can present powerful images that elicit nostalgic memories of our "best times" and ideal experiences. Such marketing can inspire consumers to strive to reclaim such experiences.'

There's a lot more to nostalgia than simply sharing content that takes people back. It has the ability to make people feel, remember the past and even consider the future too.

How can you make this work for you? Key learnings . . .

- It really must be meaningful and make people connect emotionally – otherwise you leave people thinking 'so what'?
- There must be a strategy in place that connects the nostalgia to the objectives of the brand in that moment.
- People look back on the past favourably thanks to rosy retrospection.
- If your brand has been around for a long time, you can leverage this. If it hasn't, you can still tap into nostalgia using past cultural moments and key events.
- Focus on how a time gone by made people feel – feelings are very important and connect us all.
- Nostalgia and focusing on something in particular can group a segment of your audience together and allow you to speak to them clearly.
- Nostalgia doesn't have to leverage situations from many, many years ago. It can be fairly recent in the grand scheme of things.
- Using nostalgia can work at any time, but key moments like anniversaries – or events like Christmas – provide a good opportunity.

16

Reacting to trends

Which to jump on, and which to avoid

Not all that long ago, being reactive when it came to marketing wasn't all that easy. When print ruled, there were usually pretty significant deadlines, and the time between idea, design, proofing, amends, re-proofing, deadline, more proofing – you get the idea. It wasn't a fast process. Of course, there were exceptions with daily publications. And all guaranteed printed inclusion came at a significant cost.

Today, reactive marketing is something that has driven huge reach, exposure and gains for many brands, and part of this is because it's so much easier. Now, more companies have in-house creative teams or social media managers that are adept at creating a relevant graphic on 'easy' graphic design software – or at least software that's not made purely for graphic designers! The places to post said content are also vast, and there's no financial commitment needed to share.

Our access to the stories that provide fuel for these reactive moments is also so much easier due to the internet – thanks to the websites that report on and post news that is mere seconds old, and the social media platforms that then share this all as quickly as they can, so they're the ones who truly break the story, gaining the advantage. All of this plays into the hands of those brands looking to use a moment in a reactive way.

More experimentation

Social media has allowed companies to post more experimental content too. The cost to play in the space is minimal, and the gains can be huge. Although brands can still use their colours, logos, fonts and other easily identifiable brand assets in this reactive content, every passing month I see a more relaxed attitude to some elements of content creation. This isn't a criticism. From a consumer point of view, it's a lot more interesting. A brand doesn't have to keep ramming corporate messages down its customers' necks to get reach, response and action that adds to the company's bottom line.

Reactive marketing can be a tricky area for any size of business. If you're a sole trader or the founder of a small company, you can be quick to respond and seize the moment, but the buck stops with you if it's just a little bit too close to the line. If you're part of a large organization that has a multi-level sign-off procedure, it doesn't matter how fast you are, the chances are that by the time it gets approval, the moment will have passed and the content is no longer relevant.

With reactive marketing, you have to be fast, but it also has to work for the brand and the audience. Many reactive pieces of content come from news reports and social media. Consider the following example.

Case study: Coldplay

In 2025, a short video from a Coldplay concert went viral. Not because of Chris Martin's amazing voice or moves, but because of two members of the audience. When the 'kisscam' spun around and landed on the couple – who looked to be having a lovely time with their arms around each other – something unusual happened. The man dropped to the floor at the same time as the lady in front turned away from the camera. Chris Martin quipped that the couple were either really shy – or having an affair.[1]

This clip, which was filmed by someone else at the concert, went viral. The couple was identified, jobs were lost, families were compromised. It wasn't good for the couple in any way – and I do sometimes think that when everyone gets excited about an 'easy' story, it's forgotten that there are real people behind the 'fun', but that's a chat for another day. The thing is, this clip didn't just stay on the internet; it was a major news item across the networks, with each new bit of the story reigniting it all over again. I was actually asked to provide a comment on the PR and optics side of this story from the company's point of view. I gave a lot of interviews over a few days, including one from a pedalo in Hyde Park, but I digress . . .

At each turn, brands got involved and some incredible reactive marketing came out of it. Funny, toe-curling, shocking, cheeky – all of it. The memes were brutal, and they just kept coming. They achieved significant reach for those brands that jumped on board. Globeair, a private jet charter company, achieved over 648k likes on a piece of content using this hook,[2] Hulu used a *Modern Family* clip to talk about jumbotrons/kisscams and achieved well over 500k likes[3] on that post and over 14.5 million views.

In an unusual turn of events, even Astronomer, the company that employed the couple connected to the viral moment, jumped on the trend too – working with Gwyneth Paltrow to use the unwanted glare of the world to help educate everyone about what the company did.[4]

---

[1]www.bbc.co.uk/news/articles/c80pnnn0gj3o

[2]www.instagram.com/reel/DMQUB-BIzSI/

[3]www.instagram.com/reel/DMRE2IiRGxb/

[4]https://youtu.be/vich2C-Tl7Q?si=q6dQNoPP6QpQjUQz (Search 'Thanks for Your Interest in Astronomer Video')

In short, newsjacking, trend jacking, adding your spin to a news item can work, and it can work really well. It can go viral in its own right, but also ride on the wave of someone else's virality too.

The downside of being reactive

Is there any danger with utilizing reactive marketing as a strategy? Well, there are a few to be aware of. Which moments should you go after? Not every story, not every trend, not every moment is suitable for all brands. There is an easy way to mitigate this risk though, and that's being clear on what your brand is and isn't, what it will go for, and what it won't. Even if a trend is taking the world by storm, if it's not right for your brand – this could be it has no real relevance, it directly conflicts with your values, or is at odds with your brand image – just leave it well alone. Some companies have core subjects that they simply don't go anywhere near. This can make the research, creation and approval of ideas and creatives a lot easier as you're already heading in the right direction.

Another key point with reactive marketing is timing. Just like a good joke, if the timing is off, it doesn't work. When it comes to reactive marketing, this can be if you share your 'moment' a day (maybe even a few hours) too late, or even if the story has changed direction with new details that change the sentiment.

'We worked out pretty early on things that we wouldn't go for – but then we said, a joke's not funny if it's told at the wrong time,' says Jamie Peate of McCann WorldGroup. 'We agreed, if there were things coming up, there would be a process to get things signed off to get content out there very quickly. One of the benefits of social media is that it builds brand meaning. Brand meaning is made up of two things – do you meet my needs, and do I like you – do I have a sense of positive emotional resonance towards you. And reactive social is a very good way of doing these things. Doing this can have a direct, positive effect, on brand meaning. This then allowed us to create a process. It's very important that it's timely or in the moment.'

As Jamie mentions above, some reactive moments can be predicted – or at least, the opportunity for a reactive moment, such as a key event. The example of the Coldplay concert couldn't, but with key events or specific times of the year, leaning into planning and then allowing the reactive side to flourish as the foundations are in place can be a great way to straddle the two.

Reactive marketing can also occur in response to a series of events that mean you have to change course and pivot. Oreo showed us a great example of this when the plans to create a campaign with Robert Pattinson went awry due to the COVID-19 pandemic, which indeed changed everyone's plans for quite some time. The ability to think and adapt, to not linger too long on what could have been and to be able to quickly regroup and change your strategy in alignment with the situation in front is vital for any marketer.

A marketing plan will serve you well, identifying the goals you want to reach in your business, but there's more than one way to reach a goal. Having clear rules around what your brand is and isn't, and having a mindset and the system to look for quick wins alongside big plans will allow your brand to capitalize on opportunities. We know it's not all about going viral and ego-boosting reach, but from a brand recognition point of view, something viral that sits perfectly alongside your goals and objectives could be magic. Being reactive can give you another route to this.

How can you make this work for you? Key learnings . . .

- Know what subjects your brand will and won't touch.
- Think about the approvals process. This isn't such a big issue for solopreneurs, but if your business has employees or freelancers, how can you streamline the process for reactive marketing opportunities?
- Timing really matters.

- The timing of some reactive marketing can be planned, around key events for example. In some cases, a fair amount of research can be done and then you're just waiting to post when that moment arrives.
- Keep an eye on how the story develops to ensure your moment/meme/creative is still appropriate.
- To utilize this strategy well, find reliable sources of news to check at key times throughout the day or set up alerts so you hear about things as and when they happen.
- Not every story will provide a reactive moment for your brand. That's fine. Don't force it. Wait for the right ones.

17

Storytelling

Telling tales is more than marketing

Once upon a time there was a brand that really wanted to connect with its audience. It wanted to show everyone what made it different and unique, and get them to be as excited about a new product as it was. But there was a problem. There was so much noise out there that an ad just saying 'Look, we make this' was likely to gain next to no traction. The company didn't have huge budgets, but what it did have was a story. It had a new product that was genuinely brilliant, and when people tried it, it would change their lives. This magical creation was developed because of a need the founder had in their daily life – a relatable moment others share. But how could the company get this point across in a way that created an emotional connection, led to brand and product recall and ultimately led to sales (and changing those people's lives)? You guessed it, through a good story.

An age-old art

Stories have been around for a long time. Most of us had our first encounter when we were read to as babies. Whether it was how Snow White dealt with her evil stepmother to shine as the fairest of them all (and avoid death), how Harry Potter defeated the Dark Lord himself so he could live a life free from constant worry and peril, or how Dorothy and her crew overcame their own personal demons (and a witch with a serious axe to grind) to reach the Emerald City, we've all grown up with and continue to be captivated by stories. More than just being captivated by them, we learn from them too, as in the case of fables that are designed to impart knowledge. Instead of saying if you lie, people won't believe you, the story of the boy who cried wolf frames that in a way that is engaging and teaches us.

Stories date back a long way – cave drawings in France depict them in an illustrated form going back around 30,000 years,[1] while Homer's *Iliad* was said to be written in 700–800 BC. Stories have been used to educate, entertain and also allow us to interact with people around shared experiences as we reveal more about ourselves.

Stories are powerful, and what's more, their power extends beyond those wanting to know what awaits at the end of the Yellow Brick Road, or where the final Horcrux is. It connects to businesses and consumers too.

A great example of storytelling was shared in Chapter 1 with the case study of the Norwich City mental health campaign. The campaign took people on a journey – just when they thought they knew what was going to happen, the script was flipped.[2] Because of the quality of the storytelling, the relatability of the characters and the authenticity of the moments, viewers were captivated, felt they knew what was going to happen and then were surprised by the outcome. This was hard-hitting and made people rethink their preconceptions. It was powerful and created a viral hit with people wanting to share the story. But it worked because it was well thought through and beautifully executed.

Dove is a brand well known for its Campaign for Real Beauty[3] and the storytelling, backed by research, around the information it shares. Like the

---

[1]https://education.nationalgeographic.org/resource/storytelling-x/

[2]www.youtube.com/watch?v=tX8TgVR33KM (Search 'Check in on those around you')

[3]www.dove.com/uk/stories/campaigns.html

Norwich City example, it isn't about the product – in fact, in the campaign detailed below, the product wasn't visible in any scene, and neither was the content linked to it. It was community-centric, exploring a shocking fact and then finding a way to show this as well as an uplifting message at the end that resonated with its target audience in this area. The campaign was called Real Beauty Sketches.[4]

Case study: Real Beauty Sketches

When you think of Dove, you might not think of the link between a well-known personal and haircare brand and a forensic artist, but that's what happened in 2013 with its Real Beauty Sketches campaign. Through a piece of research that the company conducted called 'The Real Truth About Beauty: Revisited', Dove found that just 4 per cent of women would describe themselves as beautiful. This was up 2 per cent from the initial research conducted some years previously . . . but 4 per cent still wasn't ideal.[5]

How could women see themselves as others did? How could Dove help to address this gap? Enter Gil Zamora, an FBI-trained forensic artist. He was used to drawing people from memory (and his work had reportedly helped solve around 1,000 cases during his career), so could he use the descriptions provided by women he couldn't see to create a realistic image? And could he do that again from someone else, describing the same person, to understand the disparity? Well yes, he could. He did. And the campaign was a huge success.

Twelve women were selected from San Francisco and given very little information about the project. Each woman spoke to Gil behind a curtain, so he could draw them without knowing what they looked like, based on descriptions the women provided of themselves. Gil then drew the women

[4]www.dove.com/uk/stories/campaigns/real-beauty-sketches.html
[5]www.dove.com/ca/en/stories/campaigns/inner-critic.html

again from real-life observation. When all the sketches had taken place, there was a highly emotional reveal of the two sketches side by side, and the raw reaction from the person who had been drawn. Powerful, relatable, fascinating . . . and it went viral.

The campaign's simplicity, both in concept and execution, is arguably where its magic lies, creating a story that resonated with audiences around the world. In the first twelve days following release, more than fifty million people viewed it.[6] In the month after it launched, the views generated made it (at that time) the most viewed online video of all time.[7]

John X. Carey is a Los Angeles-based writer/director who directed the film at the centre of the campaign. 'What's interesting is that this was actually the lowest-budget commercial I've ever made,' says John. 'We had a crew of five people. What made it work wasn't money; it was the strength of the idea. Credit goes to Hugo and Diego, the creatives at Ogilvy, who had the insight to bring in an FBI sketch artist. That genre mash – investigative sketch meets emotional self-esteem documentary – was such a strong conceptual device that it carried the whole piece.

'That's what brands should pay attention to: storytelling and ideas. Especially in an era where AI makes spectacle cheap and accessible, ideas matter more than ever. A single powerful image can tell a whole story – in this case, a woman standing between two sketches said everything.

'Another thing Dove did that's rare is they were bold enough to put out a clear, vulnerable opinion: "You are more beautiful than you think." Many brands avoid taking strong stances because they're afraid of controversy, and as a result, their campaigns are safe and forgettable. Dove's willingness to be bold is what made it memorable.'

The campaign went viral. John says that in 2013, viral was different and a three-minute documentary around this subject could take off. A lot was shared

[6]www.dove.com/us/en/campaigns/purpose/real-beauty-sketches.html

[7]www.prnewswire.com/news-releases/dove-real-beauty-sketches-becomes-the-most-viewed-online-video-ad-of-all-time-208124071.html

via Facebook, but after 2016, people became more sceptical towards emotional content. But why did it go viral at the time? What was the secret sauce? What captured people's imagination?

'I think it went viral because we sincerely documented people letting go of deep self-esteem issues in real time,' says John. 'The women we worked with were carrying a lot of self-criticism about how they looked. Over three days, we asked them to describe themselves to a sketch artist, then compared that to how strangers described them. Watching their reactions as they saw the two portraits side by side – and realizing how much harsher they'd been on themselves – was incredibly moving.

'That authenticity resonated with viewers, especially women who recognized their own self-doubt in those moments. And summing it all up in such a powerful visual – a woman standing in front of two versions of herself – gave us a simple, striking image that made a complex emotional idea instantly clear.'

Storytelling, as Dove Beauty Sketches illustrates, is a powerful tool, but what advice would John give about how to use this well and stand out for all the right reasons? 'Spectacle is becoming less impressive,' says John. 'I recently saw a car commercial with elaborate lighting and effects, and I couldn't even tell if it was real or AI. If I'm questioning that as a director, then the average audience will soon stop being impressed by scale or production value alone. What cuts through is story and meaning.

'The challenge is that storytelling requires time, and today's dominant platforms – TikTok, Instagram – currently reward ultra-short content. It's very hard to deliver a beginning, middle, and end in fifteen seconds. Back in 2013, YouTube was a place where people would watch a three-minute brand documentary. Right now, that space doesn't really exist. If storytelling is going to come back in a strong way, there needs to be a platform that actually gives room for exposition and narrative development.'

A lot of successful marketing campaigns have storytelling built in. Cadbury and its iconic gorilla is one example. The full case study is detailed in Chapter 20, but I wanted to cover it here as it is a masterstroke. From the time the first print ads appeared announcing the launch of something special at 9.00 pm that evening, the intrigue started to build. This was further supported when the ad started slowly, building tension as subtle brand elements came on the screen, as 'In The Air Tonight' could be heard before the gorilla came into view. Like a mute TV and its ability to stop a conversation, this slow, considered start was the perfect way to begin the story, as Phil Rumbol, marketing director for Cadbury at the time, explains. 'There tends to be a paradigm around marketing – that engagement needs to be full on from the get go, and that it needs to be heavily branded,' says Phil. 'In essence, people don't like being sold to, but they do like people telling them a story and earning their attention. It started quietly and gently and - in a sea of hard-hitting marketing - the intrigue grew and had people sucked in, asking themselves lots of questions. When the gorilla started playing the drums, it all made sense. With storytelling there needs to be some intrigue or jeopardy before resolution, and the ad fitted that. It earned attention by getting them to lean in. You're emotionally invested in him having that time. A lot of the virality early on was also connected to how it was done. We invested a fair bit of money and time on the production values because it could have been really good or really naff.'

So, in essence, people started telling their own stories around the gorilla too, further fuelling the attention that the campaign received.

Intrigue and jeopardy before resolution are key aspects of a story. Although the story arc follows a similar pattern, the creativity can be very, very different.

In 2013, PlayStation's 'Greatness Awaits' campaign started with the drop of the ad during the NBA finals. It was to tease the PlayStation 4, which was due to launch that autumn. At the time, competition was fierce with the Xbox in a strong position, and a widely documented lukewarm reception to the previous model some seven years before. The team had to make it count, and count it did, through utilizing storytelling, emotion . . . and dragons, of course!

Case study: Greatness Awaits

Nate Able was the creative director/art director on the Greatness Awaits campaign.[8] When the team was presented with the issue, they looked at the target audience of real, hardcore gamers and created a multi-layered campaign that spoke clearly to them.

'The idea really grew from the line we developed – Greatness Awaits,' says Nate. 'That phrase opened up an entire universe: the notion that greatness is waiting for you, whether as a dragon slayer, a pro athlete, or even a larger-than-life villain. We wanted to bring that empowering feeling to life through a cinematic, visual feast – a glimpse into the incredible, diverse experiences that PlayStation could offer.'

The initial ad starts with our hero in a car that's just hit a lamppost before the sharp-suited star asks us, the viewer, who are we not to be great? As he gets out of the car and starts his empowering, rousing speech around greatness, things happen behind him and people start to follow. He maintains eye contact with the camera, speaking directly to the viewer, before he walks past to the scene awaiting him filled with mythical creatures, fire, explosions . . . and plenty more besides.

'In terms of specs, those were already being covered extensively by PlayStation as well as third-party media,' says Nate. 'Even so, they don't tend to hook new customers so much as justify a purchase that hardcore gamers were already wanting to make.

'Our role with Greatness Awaits was different – we wanted to elevate the PlayStation brand beyond the hardware and create an emotional invitation into the brand's world. The goal at that level was to spark love, loyalty, and excitement – not just to sell a box of components.'

And it performed. It's reported that over seven million units were sold in five months, and has been cited as the largest video game launch in history at

---

[8]www.nate-able.com/greatness-awaits

the time.[9] More than that, the 'Greatness Awaits' concept was used for future campaigns too, such was the success and the connection to the phrase that drew serious gamers in.

Talking of serious gamers, the teaser campaign was also designed to deliver more for those hardcore fans. In one version of the ad, thirty-five 'Easter eggs' were hidden. 'Embedding Easter eggs within the Greatness Awaits launch film was really about catering to the hardcore fans,' says Nate. 'They're incredibly passionate and deeply engaged with both the brand and gaming culture overall. For them, little discoveries like hidden Easter eggs aren't just fun; they kind of fuel their passion. They love to uncover things, share them, debate them, and spread the word.

'Gamifying the teasers by making them hidden Easter eggs just plays into those behaviors they already love: searching, decoding, unlocking. And the more they engaged, the more they amplified the buzz for everyone else. It helped turn the campaign into an experience rather than just a piece of content.'

As someone who isn't a gamer, the storytelling aspect of this campaign really captured me. Not just the way the story played out visually as our hero assembled his army behind him, but his words that started with a question and led us to a conclusion. There's magic in storytelling, and Nate shares his advice here. 'The biggest tip is to always start with a human truth,' he says. 'If your idea is grounded in something your audience instantly recognizes – or a feeling that hits on a real emotional level – it's going to connect in a much deeper way.'

Nate also shared another great example of storytelling in action, which was the Axe commercial from 2012 all about Susan Glenn,[10] featuring Kiefer Sutherland's voice talking about the (fictional) object of his affections from when he was at school. While a lot of Axe's marketing had been around how its products made you more attractive to girls, this campaign was about *the*

---

[9]www.prnewswire.com/news-releases/playstation4-ps4-sales-surpass-70-million-units-worldwide-255558241.html

[10]www.nate-able.com/susan-glenn

girl, the one he remembers some years on, who he was in awe of, and yet who he never connected with.

'When my partner Peter Rosch and I were concepting on this project we started talking about first crushes,' says Nate. 'Within seconds we were both naming ours from way back in grade school . . . Susan Glenn is actually a slight tweak of the name of Peter's first crush,' says Nate. 'It's such a universal experience – everyone remembers that mix of awe and intimidation.

'So when you put someone like Kiefer Sutherland on screen, openly admitting that he too had a "Susan Glenn" that he was too nervous to approach, it instantly resonates. It takes something huge and intimidating, like a first crush, and makes it relatable in a very human way. And when the campaign launched, seeing people posting their own stories and naming their "Susan Glenns" showed just how powerful that connection was.'

Sometimes, by just sharing an awkward, emotional, painful story, it can help others feel less alone and people connect around it. It can help them feel more connected and understood to the brand too. And who doesn't want to consider a brand that gets them when they're deciding what to buy? You could say they're buying understanding too.

The fact that some campaigns from many years ago are still front of mind and that some more recent ones are forgotten in an instant could well be down to the story.

Is your weakness storytelling?

Anthony Smith, director of trailers for Diary of a CEO, is hugely passionate about storytelling when it comes to marketing. In fact, he believes that if content is failing, it's usually because of the storytelling. 'It's the biggest downfall of any asset, but it can also be the most powerful. For me, I can remember some amazing adverts, because of the story.'

Anthony references the prowess of Disney as a great example of how stories work to captivate an audience. Although DOAC and Disney are quite different in content style, the rules remain the same. 'You need that protagonist that people care about and take them on the hero's journey,' says Anthony. 'I can hear one line in an episode and know that must go into the trailer because it's relatable to so many.' Anthony believes this skill is so fundamental to effective marketing that that's where people should start their learning – storytelling techniques – alongside the psychology of humans as both of these work together. 'When you combine these skills, it's an unstoppable force,' says Anthony. 'When you have this core foundation, then you can learn the technical skills.'

Different perspectives

Storytelling doesn't just have to be from one perspective. Think of the great feature films and TV series that have defined our time, and you'll see this is a well-known and highly effective technique. It's also something that Volvo did with its incredible EX90 campaign.[11] Volvo wanted people to connect with the EX90, its flagship electric SUV, the safest car it had ever made and designed to be ahead of safety.

One of Volvo's core values is safety, but how do you make safety sell? You connect it to a powerful story. And how do you do this in the fast-paced format of today's content? You don't . . . you push against it, let the story unfold in its own time and create an experience for the viewer – something for them to lean into, which doesn't make them think 'another ad'; it makes them think of their family and what really matters to them.

---

[11] www.youtube.com/watch?v=cQX-QXxwGvA&t=2s (Search 'Meet the new Volvo EX90')

Case study: Volvo EX90

When you think of Volvo, you think of safety – and that's a core value that it has remained true to over its 100-year history. But safety isn't the most exciting attribute, is it? However, with the storytelling magic created by Volvo and agency Stendahls, it made people feel . . .

The video starts with a pregnancy announcement before the father-to-be calls his mother and tells her she's going to be a grandma. As he explains everything he hopes for his unborn child, the mother-to-be is in town, running errands. As the narrative continues, other images are shared to illustrate what he's saying. And then another thread begins showing a woman driving her Volvo in town. A distraction from her phone coincides with the mother-to-be crossing the road and the car detecting her and stopping, before a hospital corridor scene sees the father join his new family – not without a moment of suspense! The focus is safety, with the lens of family.

'Safety and technology have always been portrayed in quite an unemotional, technical way, but historically for Volvo, it's been about keeping people safe – how do we make the technology feel human, and emotional,' says Oscar Plasidus, creative director at Stendahls Agency. 'In the industry, it's about seeking out hazards, but for us, we changed the narrative – so instead of searching for hazards, it's searching for life and how to protect it, which it does at the end of the film.'

Part of this campaign was about the technology that ensured safety, and this can be hard to describe to people in a way that they feel connected to and care about. Tech can feel like something that is too complex to understand, but through storytelling, it feels very much part of the experience, which was a very deliberate choice.

My Lindstrom is head of Global Brand and Marketing at Volvo and shares her thoughts. 'The beauty of managing to describe tech for people in an engaging way is also to share how it works and what it truly adds from a value point of view,' says My. 'Our way of approaching this is that we work with our agency in a hybrid model where we have a creative team in-house that sets the foundation of everything we do and pulls out the stories, features and functions together with our engineering teams, to then get into storytelling with our partners.'

The full version is around four minutes long, but other versions showing different perspectives, including the car's,[12] also exist to show what goes into keeping the people we care about safe. Volvo did this in the style of a feature film, which is pretty unusual for a campaign today.

'If you look at marketing rules, often you hear it must be a short format, logo at the front, all about the car in the first three seconds . . . but one of our biggest KPIs on this was to get people to feel, because emotions are a global language,' says Oscar. 'You can't do this within normal marketing rules. We broke the rules. The media landscape is full of logos and fast-moving stuff, so we thought that maybe the audience wanted something else, something they could lean into.'

My explains that taking this different approach is sometimes needed to give key stories the space they need. 'It's always a bit of a gamble on letting the team produce something longer that gives that beautiful space to truly tell a story that pulls you in as a viewer,' says My. 'We knew we were onto something strong for the EX90 story and that this piece could make its place in a lot of context in our owned and earned channels. But it was truly amazing to follow how it went viral and moved so many people and still does, for the moments that matters the most.'

Volvo could have changed its approach. It could have gone along the electric/sustainable route. It could have gone after the car's looks. It could have talked about its quality interiors, or top speed, but it didn't. It stayed true to its focus and built something breathtaking around it. 'Safety can be quite boring, but

---

[12]www.youtube.com/watch?v=O9Z_vzJyToA (Search 'EX90: Designed to be the safest Volvo ever made')

it's emotional,' says Oscar. 'If you ask people, in the end, the most important thing is this.'

As with the example above, storytelling and the themes woven in need to be congruent with the values of the company, and the story then needs to be strong enough to be interesting for those who know about these values (and care!) and those who don't. 'My strong belief is that the best stories come from the core innovation of the company,' says My. 'Where passion and dedication have led to great products or services that could be brought into storytelling, so without strong story doing there is limited space for amazing storytelling.'

Storytelling can bring a brand's message to life. It can create depth around a clear focus, make people connect and feel, help them see things in a different way. Even if the execution is complicated, the core message must be simple to be impactful. And how you do that, using deeply traditional ways of sharing experiences and teaching from thousands of years ago, is still as relevant today as it ever was.

How can you make this work for you? Key learnings . . .

- Connect to something real. Do the work and get to know the audience you want to connect with, and look at their shared issues.
- Emotion plays a big role in storytelling, but it must be genuine. You can't manufacture fake emotion or get people to care about something that they really aren't that interested in.
- Authenticity matters. Storytelling doesn't have to be a high-budget production, but in order to connect in a genuine way that's going to help people understand you and your brand, authenticity is essential.
- Look to tell the story in new ways. Dove's idea of bringing in a forensic artist added a visual aspect to an internal narrative, as an example.

- Storytelling can make simple concepts a lot more powerful if you think it through.
- Stories usually need time to tell. This pushes against 'normal' marketing rules but can be hugely successful if executed well.
- Study the art of storytelling – what connects us to all great stories? It's the arc. Stories need to have them.
- Additional assets can be developed around the long-form story – such as another perspective in short-form to make it work well in other places.
- Plan it like a story you'd write, with that moment of jeopardy or intrigue before resolution.
- Consider adopting a multi-platform approach to tease if it's a key campaign. This can be as simple as a countdown on social media, or ads in traditional media if you have the budget.
- If there are additional treats you can deliver to hardcore fans without compromising the story for new fans, all the better. This can keep the conversation going in different places and extend reach too.

18

Community

When you're in it together, everyone can win

Utilization and engagement of community in marketing has always been a smart move, but with social media and the digital world we inhabit today, it's never been easier to tap into community, to grow communities – and to annoy people too.

What is community? The *Cambridge Dictionary* states that it can be people living in the same area or those sharing common interests or a social group that helps them form a unit. When it comes to brands, community can be a huge piece of the marketing puzzle and yet it's undervalued. Community isn't usually connected around a brand in the simplest of terms; it's usually connected around something bigger. It's not the pair of trainers, but it's the activities that members of the community do when wearing those trainers. It's not the make-up, but the life stages and common struggles faced by those who wear it. It might look like the community is formed around a brand or an individual, but in the vast majority of cases, it's a lot deeper.

That doesn't mean that the impact of a community can't be felt by companies. The truth is quite the opposite. Brands that respect their communities, that nurture them, that listen, can reap huge rewards that translate into sales rather than just likes, shares and other vanity metrics. Communities can also provide insights that are hard to access, support when things are going wrong and shared excitement when things go right.

The good news is that, whatever your brand, with the right motivation, you can be an integral part of creating a community that helps to support your audience at the same time as it raises brand awareness, helps people get to know more about you as a brand or individual, giving people the additional opportunities to connect with the human side of the business – you and your team!

Social proof and UGC

Part of the community side of marketing today is the utilization of these members to create social proof and user-generated content (UGC), which can be a hugely valuable tool when it comes to promoting a product or service, not just to your audience, but theirs too. When customers share content about you, it really is magic. They're influencers who have paid for the privilege of sharing your product with the world – how good is that? When influencing began – the start of what we see as influencing today – people were very sceptical about content labelled as an ad or a paid partnership, the thought being that if a brand had paid an individual, they'd have to say the product was good, right? Now, I like to think that people's opinions have moved on a little as they have developed a 'relationship' or connection with the influencer, and they appreciate that integrity and trust are a lot more valuable than a quick buck made for saying something is great when you wouldn't give it to your worst enemy for secret Santa. And let's be honest, those that actually declare that connection (as they should) are being a lot more open and honest than those that don't.

So, the point is, if you have a member of your community flag waving for you – telling their real-life friends about you, telling their online friends about you, sharing pictures of your products or singing your praises as a service provider . . . can you get a better endorsement than that? I'm not sure you can.

And this is why community is so, so valuable to any business. Whether you're developing a personal brand, a service-based model or a product-based business, community can be the difference between success and failure.

Case study: GoPro Awards

We know that community has power, we know that UGC has power, but when you combine them together, truly magical things can happen, particularly when your device is the way this incredible community captures its content. Enter GoPro, an American company founded in 2002 that is well known for its high-quality cameras that you can take literally anywhere. A lot of GoPro's community is made up of thrill seekers who use their cameras to capture breathtaking adventures, and this gave the team an idea, which developed into one of the most well-known community and UGC campaigns in the world, the GoPro Awards. Rick Loughery is senior vice president, Global Marketing and Digital Commerce at the company, and takes us through the campaigns and the learnings here. 'The awards program was born on a whiteboard about fifteen years ago when we had this idea on how we could celebrate our community and we thought up this program,' says Rick. 'It was pretty grandiose at the time, and then we realized we didn't even have a photo or video of the day, so we simply started with that and then over time added onto the program and grew it to what it is today.'

The GoPro Awards as we see today were launched in 2015.[1] The community was encouraged to submit videos and photos through the website before the

[1]https://gopro.com/en/us/news/gopro-launches-gopro-awards

awards were handed out, with the winner receiving $500 for a photo, $1000 for a raw video clip and $5000 for an edited video. The winners also enjoyed exposure through GoPro's own platforms through inclusion in social media and marketing.

In 2018, at the time of the HERO7 launch,[2] the campaign moved up a gear with the Million Dollar Challenge. This was a slightly different proposition but was a clever way to encourage sales of the new model, as to be in with a chance of receiving a piece of the $1 million prize pot, the footage needed to be captured on the HERO7. Every creator whose content was used in the video reel (created for the launch) would receive an equal portion of the money.

By 2020 – the five-year anniversary of the awards – over one million photos and videos had been received from over 180 countries.[3] In 2023, GoPro received 42,446 video submissions from 126 countries in the 10 weeks that the submission window was open, a significant jump from the fourth challenge in 2021, which received around 28,000 clips. From the 2023 campaign, fifty-five creators were included in the final three-minute-long video,[4] with them all earning just over $18,000 for their submission. At the time of writing, this video has received over 523,000 views. A great place to showcase the company's brilliant, brave, inspiring customers . . . but also a pretty spectacular way to show how GoPro accompanies people everywhere – from swimming with jellyfish and whales to snowy mountains, aeroplane wings to extreme sports, beloved pets to families having fun.

In addition to this, users with previous models can still get involved and are encouraged to share videos and images for a chance to be featured across GoPro's platforms and potentially win prizes too.

---

[2]https://gopro.com/en/us/news/hero7-black-million-dollar-challenge-video-bts

[3]https://investor.gopro.com/press-releases/press-release-details/2020/GoPro-Celebrates-Five-Year-Anniversary-of-GoPro-Awards/default.aspx

[4]https://investor.gopro.com/press-releases/press-release-details/2023/GoPros-5th-Million-Dollar-Challenge-Breaks-Records-Awards-1-Million-to-HERO11-Black--Mini-Camera-Customers-Globally/

Why is this genius? Because it encourages sales, obviously, but more than that, it celebrates the community. It helps clearly define the aspirational nature of the audience, allows people to get excited about others' achievements, inspires new journeys, celebrates customers and shows just how robust and rugged GoPro cameras are. It also really helps the team with its content creation.

'It has absolutely fostered an amazing community and is the lifeline of our social media content,' says Rick. 'We often hear from people how just being recognized is worth more than the cash rewards that we pay out. We are very grateful for this program and the community that takes such an active part.'

Using UGC is a powerful tool when it comes to social media, if done correctly. GoPro is a 'best in class' example of how to do it well, because there can be dangers with using other people's work. If members of the community feel exploited or used, any positive sentiment vanishes, but Rick has some advice here too. 'I think it's important to find what is genuine about the content and how it would relate to a brand's community. Start from there. But it also might be important to find a few champions or ambassadors to leverage them and how they see content helping that particular brand or company.'

Really, the usage of UGC must be for the benefit of the community. Whether that's pride, exposure or prizes, it has to be give and take.

Community and UGC transcend all industries and the businesses inside them – be they adrenaline-fuelled, beauty, clothing, food or drink and every other space besides.

Beauty Pie is a company that makes excellent use of user-generated content. As a beauty collective that gives customers access to high-quality products, it has an engaged community with skin care and beauty at its heart. 'UGC is one of the most powerful tools in our arsenal, both for content creation and community building,' says Shira Feuer, the company's chief marketing officer. 'When someone shares their Beauty Pie routine or excitement about a new launch, it's more than content; it's a word-of-mouth endorsement that carries more weight than any traditional campaign ever could.'

Celebrating customers

'By amplifying that content, we're not just celebrating our members – we're showing them (and others) that their voices matter,' says Shira. 'It's a way of reinforcing trust, deepening loyalty, and turning customers into active participants in the brand. They're not passive consumers; they're co-creators and advocates in a movement they believe in. From a content perspective, UGC brings an unmatched level of authenticity. It shows how our products perform on real skin, in real lighting, as part of real lives. This makes it not only relatable but incredibly persuasive. And from a community standpoint, it helps make Beauty Pie feel transparent, inclusive and grounded which are all core to who we are.'

Increase understanding

Lorna Andrews, aka Lorna Luxe, has a huge, engaged social media following[5] and is the founder of businesses 98[6] and LA Space.[7] She explains the value of community and how she's worked hard to nurture and grow hers, in real life and online. 'We do a lot of community events,' says Lorna. 'You can really understand people when you meet them – what their lives are like, what they eat and drink, what's their job, and we're trying to create clothes for that climate – that's how our next collection was created.'

Lorna comes at community from a different perspective – as an influencer first – and that means that her approach to community goes deeper than most brands who create the community as an afterthought. 'The community bought into me and my life, the priority for me is "are people enjoying my content? Am I growing?". I'm a stats girl, I study them every day.'

---

[5]www.instagram.com/lorna/
[6]https://no98beauty.com/
[7]www.laspace.co.uk/

Give and take

Community is a two-way street and is about give and take. There's a fine line that brands walk each day between engaging and supporting the community, and utilizing or leveraging it to get 'value'. If done well, these don't have to fight against each other – it can actually be very harmonious as the value provided could be feedback that can inform choices or uncover issues. This also shows the community that you are interested in their thoughts and opinions. Another area that can be hugely positive is sharing content that is shared by them about your product or service. This can show your appreciation and celebration of them, but if done incorrectly, it can feel a teeny bit like exploitation. There are other ways to work with and utilize community too, but the key has to be for everyone to win.

'I utilize my community in a few ways, but one of the main ones is one on one,' says Lorna. 'It's important because they feel heard and understood by me, and they will tell me what I'm doing right and wrong because we have that level of relationship. Those conversations grow and grow. We've got to a scale now that this can be hard to keep up with, but we also do a lot of community events where we don't try and sell anything. They can just meet me, have a natter and a glass of wine and catch up and these are so useful. We're learning. I work with the community for advice and I pay attention. I don't ask for anything back.

'A lot of people just want to be heard and have an opinion that's listened to. It's how I grew my Instagram account too. I was just taking the time to engage afterwards. For all the content we put out, we put more effort into the DMs and the nattering and asking the questions.'

Building communities one member at a time might seem like a very slow way to grow, but for businesses just starting out, it's very powerful. As your presence grows, this won't be possible at the same level, but methods can then evolve to help people continue to feel seen and appreciated.

Multiple communities

What about if you're a business that has different communities to nurture? This could be that your product range or service offering is broad, catering for different audiences who have different interests that pull them towards a community. Or it could be one product type, but marketed across different communities – or even countries – and this means that each area has to be treated differently. Carlsberg has put a lot of time into this. The company sells to around 120 different countries, and as anyone who's done any form of travelling knows, things are very different around the world. The other quandary is, how do you maintain your brand image but in different ways that make you culturally relevant, feel local enough that people connect and still create a community that matters?

Lynsey Woods, Carlsberg's global brand director, explains: 'Something we've done successfully in Asia is to have a beautiful pack designed by a local artist to celebrate Chinese New Year. They design it in keeping with the animal of the year, and the artist themselves has an interesting story too and does a pack takeover. It enables us to build a strong connection with our customers, in their world. There are some brands that will never break their codes, but our flexibility has allowed us to get closer to our audience while still protecting our distinctive brand assets, such as typeface and colour.

'Segmentation and local nuance are handled by local markets as it's difficult for our global brand team to understand it as well. It has to hold onto the DNA of Carlsberg, because you need to keep that, but combine it properly.'

Even if you don't have a team with offices all over the world, there are still plenty of ways to understand the local community. This could be as simple as connecting with customers in that area and holding online focus groups or even asking if they would help you as a guiding hand when you need it. It's hard to lead a community when you don't get the detail. Some words and situations don't translate to other countries, and the chances are that you and your customers in different areas will have very different experiences in life to you. Speaking to friends in places like America and New Zealand, the difference is very clear – and there's no language barrier here, but many other differences that guide how they spend their time. As Lynsey says, one sure-fire way to alienate a community and a customer is to assume that you all have the same human experience and, consequently, to say that your product or service is for people just like you.

'If we lose our touch with real people and what's really happening out there – pressure on consumers and consumer spend, we have a problem,' she says. 'Recently, I went out with three students from Copenhagen to just see what they did. They just talked to me about life. I think we can think, "I know what it's like to be that age", but we don't. It was so insightful. I did the same in India. It was mind-blowing. To listen to the troubles and worries and how these young people are choosing to spend their time and relax. It's something we've done for a long time, we call it consumer connections, and I believe it's the best time you can spend.'

There are other ways that we can work with our community too. I mentioned UGC and what a great source of content this can be earlier. Brands can employ strategies to ensure that this valuable marketing gold dust isn't a happy accident, and you as the brand are making it easy for people who want to get involved to do so.

A really simple way to do this is through the utilization of a hashtag on social media and encouraging customers to tag and share. This makes it easy for a brand to search too. This call to action can be added to email footers, newsletters, compliment slips – any touchpoint you have with a customer. Some brands take it to the next level and incentivize participation through a monthly prize. I've seen this be very effective when the community is big enough and, of course, cares enough.

What if you went a step further and developed assets to encourage the creation of UGC by your community? Not just a hashtag, let's say an audio that's free to use to create a big surge of relevant, inspiring content that would really get people engaged? That's exactly what Nike did for its fiftieth birthday celebration.

Case study: Nike turns 50

The campaign started off with an amazing advert, showing Nike athletes of the past along with athletes of the future. This led the team to create a TikTok campaign with characters Zimmie and Mars Blackmon, based around the line 'you think you've seen it all? You ain't seen nothing yet!'[8] Noel Yeo is a creative director and writer who worked on this mind-blowing campaign. 'For the TikTok campaign, we knew we didn't want to spend much time looking back in the past. We saw an opportunity in how the film ended, with the line "You think you've seen it all? You ain't seen nothing yet!" to be the perfect call to action for Nike's next generation of athletes on TikTok. It was so perfect, really. Felt like the obvious social campaign to do, and I mean this in a good way.'

The campaign went wild. In the first few days, Zimmie's post received sixty-one million views, generating 67,500 video responses. The audio created to allow people to show themselves in their best light on TikTok also caused a stir, beating some big-hitting artists to become the number one trending audio on the platform. The activity on social media, created by Nike's fans, triggered the traditional media who then reported on what was going on – driving more awareness and, no doubt, content too. And it also saw a commercial win in that it's reported that the campaign drove the highest traffic to the app in the company's history.

With many of the examples above, some could say that while the brand united the community, the community was already there. The skincare fans, the people who enjoy a specific drink, the athletes of the future. You could

[8]https://noelyeo.com/Nike-50th-Anniversary-TikTok

argue that the brand gave them a place to go, to find each other. For my previous book, *You've Got This*, I interviewed an incredible lady called Brie Read, the founder of Snag.[9] This company began because of an issue with tights (you know how they always roll down when you least expect it?!) but as the research and development happened, something became a whole lot more obvious. For years, tight wearers had felt – or been led to believe – that their bodies were 'wrong'. That was why tights fell down and other clothing didn't fit. What Snag did was say that no, the clothing was wrong, not the wearers and this acted like a beacon to those who felt the same. The company became (and still is) a huge force in the body positivity space. When I spoke to Brie, and I commented on the power and passion of the Snag community, she said that Snag didn't create the community, the company just gave the people a voice. And if you think about it, especially for a brand, that's a big part of what the work is, isn't it? Not dominating, not making it about the brand, but making it about the individuals that make up the community and their situations?

Interestingly, when Norwich City Football Club launched its World Mental Health Day video #youarenotalone in 2023 (see Chapter 1 for the case study), the whole objective was to support the community. 'We know we as a club over-index on males, with a 80/20 split to match day attendance,' says Gavin Beard from Norwich City. 'The data said that the age that people are most likely to die by suicide was the same as the largest group of people we see here at Carrow Road. That provided a foundation to build on.' The only objective of the campaign was to raise awareness and support the community, which it did. The content spread all over the world, but closer to home, many messages have been received that show the impact it had. 'We have had a lot of individuals reach out to say that because of the video, they sought help. Some of the stories have been very emotional, but to know we helped in a small way is incredibly humbling.'

---

[9]https://snagtights.com/

In a similar way to Norwich City, FlightStory feels responsibility for the community it serves. Although it's best known for the enormous digital communities created through its podcasts like Diary of a CEO, Georgie Holt, the CEO of FlightStory, believes that truly supporting communities connected around a cause is vital for business and humanity in general. 'We have created digital communities at scale, but now we have to build those communities to be with one another, because those communities have a shared set of values and principles about the world that they want to share and experience with people,' says Georgie. 'So whether it's a fan creating a coffee club where people can watch an episode together and discuss the topics, to running global conferences and events, you have a responsibility when you create digital communities to bring them back together in the real world. And all of our evidence shows that this is the most important piece of work we'll be doing for the next decade.'

How can you make this work for you? Key learnings . . .

- Communities aren't about the brand; they're about the values, feelings and problems that unite their customers.
- People like to be seen, heard and appreciated and the role of a brand when it comes to leading a community is to make sure people feel like this.
- Working with the community can deliver enormous benefits from so many angles and can be utilized in numerous different ways online or in real life.
- It's so important to see the value in the community, to protect that community, and to make sure that they never feel exploited or taken advantage of.

- User-generated content can be an incredible asset for any business. Look at how to utilize this correctly, so people feel special and not exploited.
- Doing the right thing by the community is a responsibility and one that should be taken seriously.
- Thinking of building a big community if you're currently at zero can feel daunting, but just focus on one person at a time.
- Engaging is a big part of community and can be achieved in a multitude of inexpensive or free ways.
- Online and in person can intertwine when it comes to communities. In person, greater depth is created between brand and fan, and fan to fan too. Online is also hugely valuable for nurturing connection, building and sharing.

19

Right place, right time

How timing plays a key part in success and failure

Timing is vital to many a marketing campaign, whether you're trying to deliver the punchline to your brand's joke, the twist that makes everyone gasp or working with people who are hyper-relevant to the time a campaign launches.

One big timing 'event' for anyone who works in retail is Christmas. Or more precisely Q4, when a lot of brands have three months of trading that can make or break their business. There's winter, there are events, there's Black Friday to Cyber Monday, there's all the Christmas hype, Boxing Day/New Year sales . . . it's a lot. But it also provides much food for thought in terms of the pacing of a campaign. When those key messages need to be released (and in what way to cut above all the noise – because Q4 is noisy from a marketing perspective!), what calls to action, how to collect data, add value, make conversions and nurture people. We know these are things we need to look at with each aspect of marketing, but when it comes to Christmas, the pressure is on to really get it right.

Jamie Peate is global head of Effectiveness and Retail at McCann WorldGroup. He's been involved in some big campaigns for retailers where Christmas really matters. More than this, one of his clients is very much part of the 'Christmas ad release' event. In the UK, the release of Christmas adverts generates a lot of hype. From customers waiting to see what magical event their favourite shop is going to dream up, to the media that is not only full of opinion and comment, but has features on these ads too. It really has become an event, which starts in early November. Although a brand needs to put out really good work, it's not a one shot – the campaign lasts in one form or another until Christmas Eve, so everything needs to be planned meticulously to ensure that the key elements are delivered at the right time, keeping people engaged and interested over a number of weeks. 'Christmas has become like the Super Bowl with people revealing ads in the UK. And it's like a marathon run at sprint pace,' says Jamie. 'You have to find ways of keeping things interesting with new news. Yes, you do your big launch, but so are a lot of other people. You can't come back with the same story over and over again because you're old news.'

In times gone by, Christmas started a lot closer to 25 December than it does today. Christmas products start appearing in a low-key way in September, with the real effort starting after Halloween, which has become a significant retail event in its own right. When November comes around, we see very festive marketing campaigns start to unfold. 'You tend to get more brand building stuff in November, and then in December, it becomes a lot more tactical and offer or product driven,' says Jamie. 'Within this, you'll see a wax and wane of other things that keep you interested, like events or reactive, for example. It's having a long view but thinking about how to keep things going over a period of time.'

Noise was something mentioned earlier, and one of the reasons for this is that even brands that don't usually advertise do so at Christmas.

Timing matters in so many aspects of life, and marketing is definitely one. If you're using humour in marketing or you're tapping into the reactive side, timing is essential, but it also matters when looking at how to pace campaigns, and even when to start them for maximum impact.

Of course, Christmas isn't the only time of year when timing matters. Consider your own industry and the key events that happen within it – perhaps specific shows, seasons or times of year when people start to take action around a specific goal. The chances are, there are lots of times throughout your year when timing matters to allow you to maximize impact and get the maximum return on any spend, time or energy put towards a subject.

A coordinated approach

Timing is also a consideration when it comes to the release and preparation of the supporting resources required to complement your campaign. There's no point getting your social media assets ready and beginning that campaign only to generate the interest and have no way of converting those people into customers – or even registering an interest. The whole system needs to be in place to capitalize on the situation too.

When Carlsberg relaunched its brew and everything else that went with it, it did so with a very bold campaign (see Chapter 14). Part of the brilliance of this was the timing of all the elements. Enough interest and attention were needed from part one, where people felt someone had taken over the account, to build interest for the big reveal at the end. Too long and people lose interest/go away believing that the company is having some kind of crisis; not enough time and you're limiting the potential reach online and in the media. Knowing when to deliver the final piece of the campaign is important.

I couldn't write a chapter about timing without sharing the brilliance of Tourism Australia's 2018 campaign. The one that everyone thought was promotion for a *Crocodile Dundee* film, and it was actually a marketing piece promoting the country itself. Let's go Down Under . . .

Case study: Dundee – The Son of a Legend Returns Home

Crocodile Dundee is one of those films that everyone knows. It remains iconic despite the fact it was made in 1986, so when people thought another instalment was coming their way, they were very excited.

In mid-January 2018, sixteen days before the Super Bowl, the first trailer was released,[1] revealing that a sequel was being made all about Crocodile Dundee's American son, Brian. The premise was that our unlikely hero was travelling to Australia to find his father who had gone missing in the Outback. People went wild. The press went wild. News started to spread. The trailer was beautifully shot with a cinematic vibe; the starring role was played by Danny McBride – what wasn't to love?

Thirteen days before the Super Bowl, the full trailer was released, followed some six days later by the star-studded cast being revealed. This included Chris Hemsworth, Margot Robbie, Hugh Jackman, Russell Crowe and more. It showed the stunning scenery of Australia in a fully integrated way. It was funny too. There was a story there that felt credible. The production quality was the same as a feature film. It had its own website, its own IMDb page.[2] It felt very legitimate.

And then, during the Super Bowl, things changed. Midway through the commercial, the dialogue takes a strange turn, focusing on Australia's incredible attributes (such as the 37,000 miles of coastline) which were oddly specific and slightly jarring, rather than the storyline of the film. A short while later, Danny McBride says to Chris Hemsworth: 'Wait, hold up, this isn't a movie?!'. And the true purpose of the trailers is revealed, to promote Australia.

Before the Super Bowl, the campaign had the most pre-Super Bowl digital engagement across related brands by some margin. Up until the June after the

---

[1]www.tourism.australia.com/en/resources/campaign-resources/past-campaigns/dundee.html#
[2]www.imdb.com/title/tt7895824/

release, the campaign had achieved over 102 million video views on social, over 14k media articles, the equivalent advertising value of $85 million, a 9.2 billion audience reach through its articles, and perhaps most importantly, a 900 per cent increase in organic booking enquiries.

This campaign was carefully planned with a high level of execution that would be out of scope for most, but there's still a lot to be learnt, whatever your level. The timing, which is very much the focus of this chapter, was excellent. If the 'joke' had been revealed too soon, the level of traction and interest wouldn't have built to the levels it did. Too much hype, or teasers that go on for too long and people get suspicious or a bit bored. Having the big reveal during the Super Bowl when so many eyes were watching – exceptional. Everything built to a crescendo delivered on a global stage.

How can you make this work for you? Key learnings . . .

- Timing is a key aspect of marketing success.
- Understand the key dates for your own business and work back from there.
- Longer campaigns, such as Christmas, require pacing to ensure budgets last, brand awareness is maintained and new interesting assets are released.
- Teaser campaigns leading up to a big reveal can help to gain intrigue before a launch, but ensure the pacing is right so people don't lose interest.

- Having key parts of the campaign planned and then infilling with reactive content can be a great way to balance engagement with content designed to convert.
- Even at key times of year and around key events, keep thinking about the value that you're providing your community. You can do this well and still sell.

20

Shock and surprise

Delivering the unexpected for impact

Brands that can deliver something shocking or surprising in their marketing can break through in crowded places, making an impact that disrupts daily life and pushes against what's expected.

Sometimes, these kinds of campaigns link to issues that are, in themselves, shocking. Hard-hitting subjects like drinking and driving, for example, have two routes to choose from: one that's designed to shock and one that isn't. While shock in marketing can have quite a galvanizing effect, with some hating it and feeling that the imagery/video/content used is 'too much', others will understand the need for it. In some cases, the shock element is supplied through reality. Seeing the aftermath of a car accident caused by a drunk driver is going to impact people. They'll be shocked at the scenes they're being served, without realizing that whilst it's harrowing to see on a TV screen, in print or on social media, the true scene surrounding the people dealing with the situation is far, far worse. It'll make people think 'what if' across the board, with the deep hope that it will educate and inspire change. Adverts that use shock hand in hand with reality are usually designed in this way. To make people stop in their tracks.

Handle with care

However, shock must be managed carefully. When ALS was looking at different options to promote the work of the non-profit, it didn't have a shortage of content that would have disrupted people's days – but it wouldn't have necessarily achieved the desired result. ALS did a lot of work with the audience, assessed the metrics and saw what worked. Previously, an ALS Chapter tested what Brian Frederick, chief marketing and communications officer for ALS, refers to as 'really dark marketing imagery' showing the real horror of the disease for those who have it. But it didn't generate the impact it needed to. 'We don't hide the truth, but we're very mindful of what moves the needle and what compels people to give,' says Brian.

Shock and surprise run closely together, with shock having, generally, more negative connotations and surprise being positive. When was the last time you went to a shock party?! Surprise can also be something that just feels leftfield for a brand that we've known to be a certain way for a long time. If done badly, the surprise can feel like a brand is losing its way, particularly when it comes with a big change of messaging or a values shift. A company dedicated to health that's then seen endorsing activities that don't contribute towards a healthy life would be shocking for the wrong reasons. It would be disruptive, but who's gaining from the disruption? Not the brand.

Surprise can also be created, like Carlsberg did with its Mean Tweets campaign as documented in Chapter 14. Here, the company 'promoted' the bad things people were saying about it to create a buzz online with people thinking those behind the social media accounts were disgruntled with the company, or that they'd been hacked. Liquid Death took this a step further when it created three albums of songs about the bad things that people had said about it online. Shining a light on the negative things people say about you can be a surprising move, but it's also one that shows transparency and honesty and can help build significant trust with an audience.

Sometimes, surprise isn't about those deep gasp moments – it can be connected to intrigue as a brand reveals a surprising campaign that isn't 'normal' for the company, industry . . . or isn't expected in any way. That is, until you know the story behind it, at which point all the dots join up and something that created surprise (and the accompanying sharing, discussion and amplification online) makes perfect sense. And what better example could we look at for this than a gorilla who'd been waiting for a life-defining moment?

Case study: Cadbury

Cadbury is known the world over for its chocolate, and most people remember it for 'that' gorilla ad too. The year was 2007, and the company needed something different. Following the 2006 salmonella scare that resulted in over a million chocolate bars being recalled, Cadbury needed something to help people remember their love for the brand. Phil Rumbol, the marketing director of Cadbury at the time, also wanted to capture a lost generation. 'When I joined, I was surprised that Cadbury wasn't front of mind for all consumers – there was a generational divide,' he says. 'If you were over the age of forty, you thought Cadbury was the best. If you were under, it was Galaxy. So the other thing we wanted to do was to recruit a lost generation of consumers, the under forties, and these people were marketing savvy and therefore it required a different approach. We couldn't just tell people it was better. It was designed to be arresting and surprising.'

Enter Juan Cabral. Juan was working for the agency Fallon at the time, working with Cadbury on the next campaign. As a new agency, the team was invited to the company to learn about the brief for the campaign but also to understand more about the brand and how it worked. What Phil didn't realize was that Juan had had an idea brewing in his mind for a while, but as yet, it didn't have a home until Phil explained what Cadbury needed.

'The brief for the campaign was to get people to emotionally connect with the brand and relate it to the generosity of the brand,' says Phil. 'This comes from various places. Most people have grown up with Cadbury and been given it at Christmas and Easter. And Cadbury as a company was one of the first purpose-driven companies. One of the founders is known for saying doing good is good for business, and this was seen in the way they looked after the people who worked for them, building factories out of the slums, healthcare, etc. We also wanted to remind people about the amazing feeling you get when you eat chocolate and link this to the generosity of the brand. And so the brief was that we didn't want to tell people something, we wanted them to feel something. To give them a moment that made people feel like they did when eating Cadbury chocolate. In one line, we wanted an ad that was as enjoyable to consume as a bar of Cadbury chocolate.'

On hearing the brief, Juan started packing up, assuring Phil he had all he needed. And he did . . .

A few months before, Juan was on set in Amsterdam and started talking about the greatest drum solo in history. His belief was that it was Phil Collins and 'In the Air Tonight', not least because something in the drumming and the focus made Juan imagine a gorilla. The idea stuck, and at 3am the next morning, he wrote it out as a short film and how he'd direct it. A short time later, Cadbury said they needed something special. And Juan knew what.

The idea on its own is, no doubt, a little random, but when you look at it in a different way, it makes a lot of sense. 'The logic that brought it all together was Glass and a Half Full Productions,'[1] says Phil. 'Having Cadbury as the purveyors of joy – the marketing wasn't a hard sell at all. This idea of a gorilla who's been waiting for this moment his whole life, in the zone, playing the drums, brought to you by Cadbury all lined up as a brilliant response to the brief.

[1]https://youtu.be/Rs2z7OA3XKI?si=v2C9hZJ5K5tyBASd (Search 'Cadbury's Gorilla Playing Drums – Advert Commercial')

'When they came to present the ideas, there were a few different ideas in the Glass and a Half Productions construct. The agency presented, we went and huddled in another room, and I remember just grinning at Lee Rolston, who headed up the Dairy Milk brand, and we were sold on the gorilla. It made sense to us.'

Juan was confident too. 'The confidence comes from an unexplainable place,' says Juan. 'It's quite hard to put into words. I reckon it comes from: I really want to make this "thing". I try to think of ideas that I would like to see, as if I was the audience. Once you envision something that excites you in your head, you know there's something powerful there. And you have to come up with charts to make proof for that, to back it up – which is sort of impossible. So you just try to transmit the excitement to other people by telling them how you imagine it and how it's going to make people feel, and hope for the best.'

Tapping into what people want to see, that makes them feel, is why this campaign worked so well at the time and continues to be referenced as one of (if not the!) best marketing campaigns of all time. 'Chocolate as a category is emotionally driven rather than logically driven so we had to do something heart-led not head,' says Phil. 'In 2007, Facebook and YouTube were less than eighteen months old, and we wanted to do something that, like the Cadbury brand, was part of popular culture. People say we lucked out with the virality, but it was by design, we wanted to create something that was emotionally engaging, surprising, that would get people talking about it and sharing.'

And talk about it they did – but again, this was by design. Cadbury treated it like a production, running ads in select newspapers to announce the launch of something special at 9pm that night on Channel 4, then there was the video, which went onto numerous different platforms; remixes were created, and new versions too.

It worked, and by some margin. The campaign won awards; there was a big jump in sales, it went viral, it got the nation talking. 'I had my laptop open watching the reaction, and by the end of that first weekend it had 250K views, which was all organic and in 2007, a time when YouTube was really just starting,' says Phil. 'This scaled to twenty million in a month and it has been growing ever since.'

Although there's not a word spoken and there's not a chocolate bar in sight (which, arguably, in itself is quite surprising!), it was obviously Cadbury from the first moment. From the Glass and a Half Full Productions branding (connecting to its well-known logo) to the specific Cadbury purple in the background, there was no doubt who was behind the ad. It worked because everything came together. Everything was considered and thought through. Surprise can be hugely effective as a marketing strategy but only if it makes sense. Without the strategy, it can appear random, disconnected . . . and not create any impact on the company like it should.

A change of direction in a story arc can create an element of surprise that can mean the campaign has more impact than it would have had. The Norwich City campaign (shared in detail in Chapter 1) did this. It used storytelling to take people on a journey, leading them in one direction so they felt confident in the outcome of the piece. In the final scenes, the script is flipped, creating surprise designed to give people more to think about and consider along with, perhaps, their bias towards how people act in certain situations.

Liquid Death is a very interesting brand, taking an everyday product that's been marketed in a very specific way, and flipping everything on its head. Not only are the specific campaigns unexpected, but the whole brand is surprising when held against the norm for the industry. Let's look at a few examples.

Case study: Liquid Death

It's actually quite hard to pull just one example of Liquid Death when looking at shock and surprise as a strategy because the whole brand was created to push against convention and share a surprising approach for the kind of product it is. Not only did this create a buzz, but it clearly signalled to its target audience that it was meant for them.

Stephen Nilsen, aka Stix, was the VP of Cult Indoctrination (at Liquid Death), but has also worked as lifestyle marketing manager for Pabst Brewing Co, and sports marketing manager for Red Bull. He says that the idea for the brand's surprising concept came from founder Mike Cessario, who identified that everything fun in marketing was the worst for you from a health point of view – as in, no one selling a product or service that was healthy was doing anything 'cool'. So he decided to change this, launching Liquid Death, a company with colours, fonts, names and brand DNA that fought against what was normal for water, creating a visual that was a lot closer to energy drinks and heavy metal. The remit to the team was to make sustainability and drinking water fifty times cooler.

In terms of shocking campaigns, a few key ones jump out. One is the Tony Hawk's 'Blood Board' mentioned in Chapter 13. The campaign saw Tony Hawk have a vial of his blood extracted, on film, before it was mixed with paint and applied to a limited run of 100 skateboards.[2] The skateboards sold out overnight.

Another occurred when Liquid Death introduced electrolytes – and didn't opt for the conventional approach. The product was called Death Dust, and the slim, black packets featuring bold colours, unusual names, and the brand's iconic skull imagery set the tone, but the pale coloured powder inside created an idea. Not one about the benefits of electrolytes to athletes. Oh no. How about an Ozzy Osbourne campaign? This great piece of work saw Ozzy appear next to two people adding Death Dust to their drink.[3] Ozzy emerges from

---

[2]https://youtu.be/gl7MRPWSw_M?si=qPn7KUN2W3WNQPf2 (Search 'Liquid Death Puts Tony Hawk's Blood in Limited Edition Skateboards')

[3]https://youtu.be/eUnBzr2oCgQ?si=74bCaPDHwmNeXmzd (Search 'Ozzy Osbourne Warns Kids Not to Snort Liquid Death')

nowhere and tells them how not to take it – as if it were drugs – before being driven away at speed laughing.

The Enema of the State kit previously discussed fits into this category too.

Or how about the Taze Test? 'The Taze Test[4] was where we put it out there for the haters,' says Stix. 'I say to my students that if you have haters, you're probably doing something right. So we said to the haters, we'll fly you to LA, and put a lot of different waters on the table, and if you can pick Liquid Death – because you say it's the worse water ever, we'll give you $1000 cash. The catch? If they didn't get the right one, they got tazed on the arm. All the brands on the table had brown bags over them. Only two people did it. It didn't work well for them.'

This – quite literally – shocking campaign created a huge buzz – no pun intended.

Liquid Death also utilized haters in another way. 'We made three albums called Greatest Hates 1, 2 and 3,[5] and all the lyrics were provided by the hate comments we received on the internet,' says Stix. 'We produced albums. And had professional musicians who were employees of Liquid Death, and investors too, to play on the albums.'

A point to note here is that delivering shocking or surprising marketing doesn't work with every product or every brand. A lot of work needs to be put in to ensure that the audience is receptive to the kind of campaign you're looking to share, or else it stands a high risk of falling flat, confusing people, or even repelling those that you really want to get it. As Stix says: 'You've got to flush the idea out. Some of these ideas might resonate with your immediate group, but if you're going to go this route, you run a huge risk of it falling flat if you haven't flushed it out with people outside your orbit, a real cross section of your audience.'

---

[4]www.youtube.com/watch?v=1xTY0hkp9Co&t=92s (Search 'Liquid Death Blind Taze Test')

[5]https://liquiddeath.com/en-gb/pages/greatesthates

How can you make this work for you? Key learnings . . .

- Some brands can do huge things using shock and surprise, and for others it's lower key. It won't work as well for everyone.
- Think of the overall objective you're aiming at – will this strategy help or hinder?
- Using shock and surprise must be well thought through when it comes to execution, or else you run the risk of people being really confused.
- Test – particularly if you're thinking about doing something really 'out there'. Maybe you're the only one who gets it. Maybe the shock is just too much?
- We know that going viral for the wrong reasons isn't a great idea – and content created to shock or surprise has this ability more than some other ideas. If it isn't aligned to your business, it's not helping your overall goal.
- Don't just create shock for the sake of it. It might be tempting to spice things up or stand out in a crowded space, but it needs to align with your core values, your audience and your campaign objectives to be a positive part of your marketing.

21

Be bold

It might seem random, but there's always a thread

The concept of random, much like beauty, can comfortably live in the eye of the beholder. Due to worldview, upbringing and the media we're exposed to, my idea of random is likely to be quite different from yours. As an example (and if my mother-in-law reads this, apologies), my mother-in-law went through a phase of showing me dead animals she found – moles, voles, moths and so on - to increase my knowledge of animals you'd see in the countryside. I should add, I didn't ask for this; it just happened one day. To her, it was the most normal thing in the world, but to me, someone retrieving a dead mole from the freezer and discussing its beauty in a normal way was incredibly random. But I guess I can now identify dead moles. So there you go . . .

But from a brand's perspective, bold and random can, and should, be less about dead, frozen animals. It could be a campaign that at surface level doesn't make a whole lot of sense. Maybe the messaging feels bold and random and pushes against convention in a way that people wonder what on earth is going on? Perhaps the way the whole brand is managed is polar opposite to the 'norm' – like Liquid Death in the shock and surprise chapter. Or maybe you decide to put someone in space . . . because that happened too!

Bold and random, to my mind at least, is the unexpected, but not in the mouth covering and deep intake way you'd expect with shock and surprise. It's when you see something unfold and can't look away because you're not entirely sure where it's leading, but you want to find out. It jars a social media feed, makes you stop and stare at a billboard, replay an advert to make sure you saw it correctly. It gets you heading to Google to find out what on earth is going on . . . and then it all makes sense.

Bold and random is a risk. Play it safe and you're neither of these things, and people aren't interested. Go too far and people assume the company has lost all sense of reason and what people thought they were isn't the case at all. Get it just right and you captivate and intrigue people, allowing them to invest time in you as the story unfolds.

Go deeper

Between me and you, these are my favourite types of marketing campaigns. Why? Because they appear bold and maybe a teeny bit random – and at a surface level they most definitely are – but when you dig just a little bit deeper, it all falls into place so beautifully. And luckily, there are some great examples we can delve into here, to help us unpick what makes a bold and somewhat random campaign work . . . and what doesn't.

One of the most iconic campaigns of all time – and one that won multiple awards – was Cadbury's Gorilla drumming to 'In The Air Tonight'. Random? Oh yes. Effective? Yes . . . and then some. The full case study is in Chapter 20 on shock and surprise, but it could have been home here too.

Keeping to the animal theme, let's take a look at Spotify's campaign all about Pet Playlists. Our pets might not be able to tell us what they'd like to listen to when we're away, but that doesn't mean that suggestions can't be made. And what better company to do this than Spotify? It might appear bold and random, but under the surface, it's really not.

Case study: Spotify Pet Playlists

According to the American Pet Products Association, 51 per cent of US households own a dog, and 37 per cent of US households own a cat.[1] In the UK, the PDSA said that in 2024, 51 per cent of adults owned a pet.[2] So the audience is there. Spotify did more research and found that of the 5,000 pet owners it surveyed, 71 per cent had played music to their pets, and 80 per cent believe that their pets liked music.[3] Noel Yeo is a creative director and was involved with the initial Pet Playlists campaign that launched in 2020.

'Pet Playlists started with an insight, or rather an observation one of our designers made, that some people would play music for their pets when they leave the house so they don't get stir-crazy,' says Noel. 'I wasn't even a pet owner then but I thought that was a remarkable fact. We initially wanted to just do a film based on this fact but there was enough interest in what we were doing that we were given what was then the crown jewel of Spotify's capabilities, the algorithmic playlist. We knew we wanted to make music for pets. After that it was a lot of figuring out exactly how animals respond to music, how different animals react differently, which pets to feature – we got some flak for leaving out rabbits!

'Most of the work went into the Pet Playlist site, and that was incredibly fun for us. We didn't want it to feel too technical and so we went with a lot of sliders (sliding buttons that allow you to place your pet's traits between two conflicting attributes, like energetic and relaxed), and kept the instructions to a minimum. We also shot three films. The guy who had to run on the treadmill alongside a hamster we felt really sorry for. Each time the hamster stopped too early, it would ruin the take, and so our guy did a lot of takes, too many, so

---

[1] https://americanpetproducts.org/news/the-american-pet-products-association-appa-releases-2025-state-of-the-industry-report

[2] www.pdsa.org.uk/what-we-do/pdsa-animal-wellbeing-report/paw-report-2024/pet-populations

[3] www.itv.com/news/2020-01-15/spotify-tunes-into-pets-with-personalised-playlists-for-furry-friends

many that we even considered changing the idea in the middle of the shoot. Everyone cheered when the hamster nailed it.

'This became naturally a social campaign thanks to those cards Spotify gives you to share your music listening data, like the sort you get on Wrapped. We knew everyone would want to share their pet's playlist, and they ended up being proud of their pet's taste because why wouldn't they, the pets would listen to what their owners listened to!'

The whole campaign extended beyond a simple 'pick your pet' concept and allowed customers to select from a dog, cat, hamster, iguana or bird. As Noel says, sliders were then used to help share more information about the pet, such as whether they were shy or friendly, before users could customize the playlist with their name and image and then get playing.[4] Of course, there was also the suggestion that the playlist card was shared on social media using #SpotifyPets.

In 2022, the campaign was re-energized[5] to give people the ability to create their own customizable playlist inside the app, combining the user's musical preference and their pet's personality. This was launched on National Pet Day in the United States.

The campaign earned lots of attention through the media and also from its own customers sharing their pet's playlists. When the campaign first launched in 2020, none other than the Prince of Darkness himself, Ozzy Osbourne, created one for his dog Rocky.[6]

Thinking about bold and random, how about telling the world that your product tastes like, and I quote, 'Satan's rancid p*ss'? Carlsberg did . . . and due to the careful management of the whole campaign (see Chapter 14), it worked very well.

But what's worse than Satan's rancid p*ss? How about calling yourself the worst hotel in the world? How about using this in your marketing and

---

[4]https://edition.cnn.com/videos/business/2020/01/15/spotify-pet-playlist-podcast-orig.cnn-business
[5]https://newsroom.spotify.com/2022-04-11/show-your-furry-or-scaly-friend-how-much-you-love-them-with-their-own-pet-playlist/
[6]https://loudwire.com/spotify-pet-playlist-ozzy-osbourne-dog/

even writing a book about it? Enter the Hans Brinker Hotel. You can read the full case study in Chapter 23, but this hotel really did take it to the next level.

But now for something less about waste(!), that was bold but in a very different way . . .

Case study: Expedia's Travel Yourself Interesting

In 2014, Expedia launched a campaign called 'Travel Yourself Interesting'. James Whatley, social media director for this campaign with Ogilvy, is particularly fond of it because, in his words, it genuinely did change the face of holiday advertising completely.

Price comparison website Expedia only has its brand to sell, so to win out over its competitors it's essential that it invests in its brand to get recognition and sales. Expedia went to Ogilvy, where James led the social media side for the campaign. The team changed the narrative away from the messages pushed out through traditional holiday advertising. 'These messages start with "I'm excited to go", and then, "I'm there"', says James. 'No one talks about afterwards because we all think of the holiday blues. We focused on an area that people didn't talk about, and in a different style too.'

At that time, all holiday ads were bright, vibrant and colourful with a focus on price, but it was hard to pick out the brands; it was hard to tell who was who. Expedia's strategy changed to, as James says, 'super slow'; the advertising was slowed down, they worked with Tom Hollander due to his voice, and the whole campaign was around the fact that you're more interesting when you've been on holiday. 'We looked at the audience and identified a new audience called believers who believed that travel was a necessity,' says James. 'Even though they didn't take up a lot of the audience, they took up around 70 per cent of the spend, so we focused on them and showcased their belief.'

The campaign[7] took people who would usually fail in social situations and showed them doing well because they'd been on holiday. It was bold and went against the grain on purpose. Expedia also laced the ads with facts, so people would become more interesting by just seeing the ad. 'In Europe, we got £11 back for every £1 that was spent, and the campaign cleaned up on awards for creativity and effectiveness,' said James. When everyone is doing the same thing, to stand out, you have to do things that are different. But, of course, it has to be a considered, thought-through move.

I couldn't write a chapter on bold marketing without covering Red Bull Stratos. This was so much more than a marketing campaign, but you can't tell me that breaking the record for the highest altitude jump, by freefalling from the stratosphere, isn't a bold move. To those who don't get it, it might even appear a little random, but trust me when I say that this wasn't random at all. It was strategic and generation-defining.

Case study: Red Bull Stratos

14 October 2012 was a day that will stay with people for a long time. It was the day that Felix Baumgartner jumped from the edge of space, becoming the first human to travel at Mach 1 (reaching 843 mph), and also the day that achieved the most concurrent views of a livestream on YouTube until 2023. Over eight million people viewed the Red Bull Stratos livestream at the same time,[8] as Felix jumped from space.

But let's go back a bit. Red Bull Stratos[9] was created to break the record for the highest altitude jump. It took years to make this happen and involved the best teams from around the world across every aspect of the event, including training and testing. It's sometimes easy to look at big events and not realize

---

[7]https://www.dandad.org/work/d-ad-awards-archive/travel-yourself-interesting
[8]https://blog.youtube/news-and-events/mission-complete-red-bull-stratos-lands/
[9]www.redbull.com/gb-en/projects/red-bull-stratos

just how much work goes in. In addition to just being 'big', this covered so much new ground, to the point that the data from Stratos has been openly disclosed to help support others and has gone on to help develop life support systems in planes and had an impact on space safety. It also paved the way for the power of live streaming. In 2012, YouTube wasn't as well known for this side of what it does and was most popular for clips of pets doing funny things. But this was a moment for YouTube too.[10]

Red Bull is known as an energy drink, but it's also known for its passion for extreme sports, its support of athletes, and creating incredible content that inspires and captivates its target audience. Instead of telling everyone its drink is really good, it goes to where its audience is and shares their love and passion, and often creates events that really tap into that. It's known for its big campaigns. The kind that cost a significant amount to pull off safely, that cause a stir, that get everyone talking – whether or not they're its typical target audience. They push the boundaries and encourage people to think outside the box. And let's be honest, Red Bull's tagline is 'Red Bull gives you wings' – 'flying' through the air from space is pretty close to that, isn't it?!

The team documented the process throughout, allowing viewers to feel part of the journey, creating an immersive, connected, and emotional experience. It didn't hang off the real risk involved, but it didn't shy away from it either, explaining how the risk had been mitigated as much as possible, down to Felix having control of the life support systems inside the capsule in case communication was cut.

To pile on a bit more pressure, there was the very real risk of it going wrong – and if it did, it could have gone wrong very badly. But Red Bull live-streamed it on YouTube from a series of cameras on Felix and the capsule. It also had seventy-seven TV channels broadcasting live.

---

[10]www.guinnessworldrecords.com/world-records/105276-most-concurrent-views-for-a-live-event-on-youtube

The initial balloon that took Felix into space wasn't Red Bull-branded – the clear plastic used had to be light, and was incredibly delicate, being around ten times thinner than a sandwich bag (according to Felix on the film about Stratos). However, the company's branding was evident – and yet not overwhelming – on Felix's suit and the capsule, ensuring brand recognition through every frame.

Did it work? Well, yes, Felix made it back safely, delivering a foot-perfect landing as his Red Bull-branded parachute helped him back to earth. The coverage was incredible, with it being reported that the landing had one hundred million playbacks[11] within the first two weeks, and over the next ten years, clocking up a billion views. It's said that the budget for Stratos was $30 million[12] (some sources report more), but what they gained was 'tens of millions' in earned media, created a legacy, won numerous awards (including an Emmy!), and many, many years later, it's still being talked about. Commercially, it's reported that there was a 7 per cent increase in sales post-event too.

Why did it work? My take is that it struck gold on every level. First up, it was something that had never been done before. It was bold, brave, and struck a chord with anyone even vaguely interested in space too – something that expands beyond Red Bull's target market.

Next, the documentation of the process. The way that the content was captured to show the struggles, the prep, the developments, the thought – it allowed people to be part of the journey from the comfort of their own homes.

The people involved. There was a huge focus on the team that created Stratos, not just Felix himself. I personally loved the pictures showing how hard everyone worked, the interviews from different team members and their reactions to it all. Their human, relatable reactions. They seemed like 'normal' people – yes, wildly talented, clever people, but also the kind of people you

---

[11]https://adventuremagazine.co.nz/ten-years-since-jaw-dropping-jump-from-space-faster-than-the-speed-of-sound/

[12]https://medium.com/better-marketing/red-bulls-30-million-marketing-stunt-almost-didn-t-happen-88d24fefdeff

could go for a drink with. And Felix himself. He was engaging, thoughtful, eloquent, relatable, humble, fun, honest in the content shared. I think if he'd been a different person, it wouldn't have struck so deeply.

And the fact that this was all shared in real time. There was a genuine concern that things could have gone wrong and the risks involved with livestreaming an event like this are significant, but part of the beauty of this is that 'we' – the world – were holding our breath at the same time. Part of something, if you will.

And for the brand? The branding was everywhere. It mapped to the brand ethos, the tagline, the target audience . . . and yet it wasn't in any way about the brand. It was about the team that made this bold and extraordinary feat happen.

If you haven't seen the ten-year anniversary video,[13] I would urge you to go and watch it.

Red Bull's bold move was well branded, but is this a fundamental part of a campaign of this nature? Or marketing in general? Well, yes, it is . . . until it's not . . .

How about a campaign that was *so* bold, it didn't actually say the company that it was about? More than that, it encouraged people to go and find out which company was being spoken about? On the surface, this seemed crazy and random, but on a slightly deeper level, it was utterly brilliant. From the first screen, the colours gave a strong hint to which brand was being discussed; the impact it had online as people searched was incredible. And the earned media? That was something else. Let's talk about That Place . . .

Case study: That Place

The first screen sees comedienne Mindy Kaling in a yellow dress on a red background saying that some people think there's a place where Coca-Cola

---

[13]www.redbull.com/us-en/theredbulletin/red-bull-stratos-history-anniversary

tastes so good.[14] She encourages people to search on Google, has some 'on hold' music, and then the ad says that that place has Coca-Cola for $1. The ad aired and it was quickly all over the news, TV and online too. People were, indeed, driven to Google the question and page after page of unpaid results appeared. A fully integrated campaign across different channels, showing different content rolled out, all unbranded – whether in print, YouTube, social, film or somewhere else. And the earned media side was enormous. In less than twenty-four hours there were nearly half a billion earned media impressions for the brand. There was an 18,400 per cent spike in search, it made its way into Google autofill . . . and it drove the most successful product trial in the brand's history.

Not bad . . . especially when the brand wasn't mentioned. But that was kind of the appeal. That's what made it so bold.

But this whole campaign could have been so different – it could have been a complete flop, as Nate Able, creative director and art director shares. 'The brief itself wasn't exactly inspiring – McDonald's wanted a campaign about $1 Cokes,' says Nate. 'Not the kind of thing that's naturally memorable. But tucked into the brief, the planners had flagged some online chatter: people saying Coke actually tastes better at McDonald's. When we dug in, we found there were real reasons behind that claim, and more importantly, it was a genuine conversation happening organically. That felt like something we could really lean into and build on.'

When you're presented with something that might not seem the most engaging, there's opportunity. 'An ad that just says "McDonald's has Coke for a buck" is wallpaper,' says Nate. 'Forgettable. But framing it as "people online are saying there's a place where Coke tastes better – and right now it's only a dollar" taps into very different behaviours. It sparks curiosity. It plays on a little FOMO, since you're suddenly out of the loop on what "that place" is. And given how often people are second-screening while watching TV, it wasn't a stretch to imagine them Googling it.'

---

[14] www.nate-able.com/that-place

The extra twist was the drama of not mentioning the brand, and making a big deal of this, saying what Mindy and the other people brought into the ad at different points weren't able to. 'It made it feel like a secret people had to uncover,' says Nate. 'And when they did search, they didn't just land on McDonald's messaging – they found articles and posts from real people saying the exact same thing. That outside validation made the whole idea more credible and more fun.'

Bold, random and highly effective.

How can you make this work for you? Key learnings . . .

- You don't need huge budgets to be bold, but you do need a clear plan.
- Bold works when there's a strategy behind it. Pushing against the norm, or harnessing your slightly random side, doesn't work if the idea stops at just being wild. Bold without strategy is just confusing.
- For this strategy to work, it needs to integrate into the brand's positioning.
- Research can be the spark behind a bold campaign. What's something that has been proven and supports your messaging that you can portray in a way that makes people stop the scroll or think again?
- Keep your brand's values and your overall goal in mind all the time. Ask if what you're doing supports that or moves you further away. The Cadbury Gorilla was bold, but the message and the idea closely aligned with the goal of inspiring joy.
- If you're going to use negativity in a campaign, make sure you know how you're bringing that back around. Carlsberg's Mean Tweets used its negative feedback to show why the company had done so much work.

- Don't be tempted to look at examples and think, 'Yeah, that's great, we'll do that.' Doing a stunt that could go horribly wrong takes investment and attention to detail that most brands simply can't afford. Be realistic and honest about your brand. You could be a brand that can utilize bold well, or it could just leave your audience wondering what on earth is going on and if you're actually all right . . .

22

Experiential

Immersion unlocks deeper opportunities

Marketing a product or service in a way that moves people 'inside' it, so they become part of its world, even if just for a short while, can be incredibly powerful. When these experiences are created well, not only can people really start to understand the DNA of a brand, but there are lots of opportunities for content to be gathered, UGC created, column inches earned and plenty more besides. In some cases, it can be hard to quantify the return on an experiential piece of marketing with conventional metrics because the return is anecdotal or qualitative and surges can be seen in sentiment, brand recognition and metrics other than money in the bank. But income is just one metric that should be considered when it comes to marketing, and real experiential marketing is a case for this – it shows clearly that other metrics matter too.

Case study: Pinterest at Coachella

Sean Goff is an Experiential Lead who worked on Pinterest's incredible 2025 Coachella installation.[1] From initial brief to development of concept,

[1]https://experiencenve.com/work/pinterest-coachella-2025/

there are so many key points that add to why Pinterest's installations are so iconic.

The main project was activation at Coachella 2025. This was the second year that Pinterest had sponsored part of the event through AEG, the company that owns Coachella. In 2024, the brand had a smaller footprint and, due to its success, it wanted to expand this time around. It was decided through discussions with all teams that a larger space would be worth exploring, along with a smaller space in the VIP section.

'The team knew they wanted a similar vibe to last year, to make it a Coachella staple, but to build on it,' says Sean. In 2024, visitors entered into the Pinterest space and got time with a makeup or fashion consultant to help with everyone's look and were styled accordingly. Some of these additions were small details, some creative – whatever the visitor's 'vibe' was, the team tried to match it. There was also a photo booth and more besides. The activation was very popular, and with success can come a bit of pressure to make something even better . . . and that's what Pinterest did!

'In 2025, we wanted to focus on collage — something you can do inside Pinterest itself, trends and how to incorporate these, remixing styles, to kind of mash up Pinterest and the individuals, and more too,' says Sean.

What some people might not be aware of is that Pinterest is known for predicting trends. At the end of the year, it looks ahead in a piece of work called 'Pinterest Predicts'[2] and creates content that's used to support these trends throughout the year. These cover fashion, party trends, food, wellness – literally every part of your life.

'Two years ago, they started predicting festival trends and we wanted to bring this with collage to help people pull together an outfit, for example. We wanted to visually represent all the things that Pinterest does,' says Sean.

For the outside of the space, Pinterest worked with a graphic designer called Ramisha Sattar, who's also Chappell Roan's creative designer. 'She does this

[2]https://business.pinterest.com/en-gb/pinterest-predicts/

really cool collage work that layers all these beautiful elements together,' says Sean. 'We needed to do a giant collage on the outside, bringing in everything that Pinterest is known for and working with AEG to help it blend in with the environment.'

The outside was an incredible combination of oversized butterflies, flowers, rainbows, cacti in beautiful colours with the installation becoming one of the most talked about brands at the event. 'As you waited in line, you were prompted to download or make sure your app was up to date, and then start a board,' says Sean. 'Inside, our brand ambassadors helped people around the trends that Ramisha created content around, and that we used on our social media too, in press releases and more. In the space, we focused on five trends – stereo punk, urban wrangler, dark ethereal, freestyle fits and main pop girl. We brought in and thought about who was at Coachella and reflected their style in the space.'

'Each of the trends was blown up in 3D, and then visitors scanned a QR code so they could see what we'd pulled together around these themes to save on their own board,' says Sean. 'We then had lockers that fitted the trends. We had TVs, amps and stereos. With some, we had a camera that showed visitors in vintage TVs. Then there was another feature where you put your head through a curtain and your giant head was in a fairy world with a working water fountain! There were stylists to help with people's make up and looks too.'

Every element linked to the trends, to Pinterest, to how people used Pinterest and the event too. Pinterest's IP was woven into the displays in a way that felt native, such as stickers on the vintage TVs, putting key phrases in specific places.

Due to the design of the stand, there were many opportunities for people to enjoy the space, to create content and to share content too. 'We knew it was all about the sharing, so we had to make sure we created the backdrop,' says Sean. There was even a space where a professional photographer took images with collage backgrounds that could then be shared with the world, further promoting Pinterest's message and, of course, people's enjoyment of engaging with the experience at Coachella. During the event, over 8,000 people went through the Pinterest activation, and the reach online was also incredible.[3]

These kinds of events, on this scale, take a long time to come together, as well as an extensive team. The strategy work started in September (Coachella is in April), and the previous success and the company's reputation meant it had a lot to live up to. It had to mirror the company's values of positivity too. Nothing inside the feature cost anyone who entered anything. What it generated in terms of social media and PR blew all the goals out of the water.

'People are craving that interaction, so when you show up and you do it right, it gets remembered,' says Sean. 'The digital world is incredible, but that face-to-face, human connection, that is different. When you can create experiences for your company and feel taken care of, it's different. There's so much power in just showing up. Even if someone just walked past and took a picture, it had an impact on them and it made them think about the brand.'

Another great example of experiential marketing in action was the launch of *The Marvellous Mrs Maisel*, Season 2. This Amazon Prime Original follows Mrs Maisel, a New York housewife and mother from the 1950s who, following the breakdown of her marriage, starts a career in stand-up comedy. It all begins in a location called The Gaslight Café, where a set delivered in her nightgown following the split gets her arrested.

What was interesting about this was that the big launch didn't happen for Season 1. It was the second season that saw the big launch. This is unusual, but the data and insight gathered around the first season identified an opportunity for growth. Charlene Charity, vice president of integrated strategy and brand experience at Digitas, and ex-head of Brand Marketing for Amazon Europe (where she was working at the time of the launch) explains . . .

---

[3]https://experiencenve.com/work/pinterest-coachella-2025/

Case study: The Marvellous Mrs Maisel

To launch Season 2, Amazon created a fully immersive 1950s style event, taking in three key areas that were seen in the show, including The Gaslight Café.[4] The experience started pre-event, where guests stepped out of a New York style taxi before being immersed in the 1950s. In the department store area, guests could accessorize for the evening in 1950s pieces and admire the displays designed to emulate the 1950s vibe. In the salon space, makeup artists and stylists were there to change their looks to fit the scene, alongside hood dryers and copies of *Stylist* magazine (check out Chapter 11 for how Mrs Maisel, Amazon and *Stylist* worked together), and then people were offered a selection of 1950s cocktails before moving through to Gaslight Café where they enjoyed a brass band and acts from three fabulous female comedians.

'The interesting thing about this launch was that the big budget launch was for Season 2. The data available showed that the people who watched it completed the whole series, showing that if you were able to target the right audience, people would watch it,' says Charlene. 'This made me think it didn't get a solid Season 1 launch. With the data and the insight that I'd seen, I went back to the business and asked for budget. The information online also showed it had a cult-like fan base.'

The launch took a lot of work, and when experiential marketing is done well, it does take considerable resources and creativity. But Charlene has some thoughts on this too. 'It is a lot of work, but if you work with good providers (we worked with a great experiential agency called Experience12) and if it's done properly, an immersive event can enable deeper connection. The follow-up is there too – you are bringing people back to you. Essentially, it needs to feel authentic to the brand and deepen the connection.'

Experiential can't reach the same numbers as a standard ad, but the connection can be much deeper. And it's not just the people who actually

[4]https://experience12.com/projects/prime-marvellous/

attend who are part of the experience. With the right follow-up, there's a lot that can be done. 'It needs to be looked at as part of the whole – if you do it in the right way and stay true to the brand and the consumer, there's a halo effect,' says Charlene. 'With Maisel, we did a lot of pre-event work – we worked with *Stylist*, we ran a competition, we created lots of content working up to the event. We had the event, and there was a massive waiting list, and we followed up with clips and freebies, and we all know the power of FOMO too. Post-event we had lots of communication with people, encouraging them to watch the show, there was lots of video content, social, hashtags. You can create a real groundswell around it to keep the message and the story going.'

Experiential marketing isn't just putting your logo on a stand and inviting people into your world. It needs to have a clear goal in mind if it's to feel cohesive and achieve its objectives. This starts with a broad view, but then goes down to the detail, and it can be those finishing touches that help improve people's sentiment towards a brand, their retention, and even how much they spend if that's the purpose of the event. 'It's going to mean a lot to people if you do little things for them really well,' says Sean. 'Having gluten-free options if people are gluten-free, or having really cool mocktails for those who don't drink. It's all strategic. If it's a sales event, you need to make the salesperson's job easier; you're giving people everything that they need so that they can do their job well. When you give people an event that's memorable, they'll come back to you before you go to them. All of these little things matter and add up.'

As mentioned, done well, experiential isn't cheap, but when done properly, an experiential piece of marketing can create and nurture super fans, create huge amounts of content, and get people genuinely interested in what is going on – even for people that aren't there. But do it without the detail, and it won't land the right way. Best case, people won't feel a connection and wonder why they're there, and worst case it can even hurt brand sentiment. 'I think we've all been to events where it's fallen a bit short where it doesn't feel completely relevant and I don't feel absorbed,' says Charlene. 'With Maisel, from the moment you walked in you were transformed. There were make up artists and goody bags – it comes down to the detail. No detail or decision had been left. It created complete immersion.'

Experiential doesn't have to be at a big event. Small acts can also make a difference and can be used as a powerful way of extending a social or digital campaign, allowing people to experience and appreciate the messages in a personal way. Norwich City's viral campaign (see Chapter 1) caught the attention of millions of people, but the team wanted to bring it to life in the stadium too, so in 2024, it did something else – football's first-ever 'Minute Unsilenced'.[5] 'This meant that both teams came together and we had a minute where we had some prompts on the screen and it generated conversation between the fans as well as the players,' says Gavin Beard. The idea was a simple one, but further supported mental health awareness and the importance of speaking and interaction. Due to the nature of football and the rules that govern it, a lot of people had to approve the concept before it could happen, but the club didn't have any problems getting people on side, and a hugely powerful moment was created.

'We didn't want to deliver one thing once a year then disappear,' says Gavin. 'We had digital activations and physical activations too. We have 27,000 fans that turn up every week, so it was the perfect opportunity there.'

Another great example of experiential that wasn't one big event came from Got Milk? which had a tour all around California and beyond to celebrate the tagline's thirtieth anniversary.[6] The tour went from city to city, inviting people to come and get their very own milk moustache which would then be printed in the style of the original ads as a poster for them to take home. The response to this was wildly positive and saw a surge in UGC shared across social media as people proudly displayed their very own customized posters.

---

[5]www.canaries.co.uk/content/minute-unsilenced-before-hull-city-fixture

[6]www.gotmilk.com/30years/

How can you make this work for you? Key learnings . . .

- Know how your brand should show up.
- Know what works for your audience and what doesn't – always keep them in mind. Understand what they're looking for.
- Don't be afraid to seek outside help – experiential marketing can be more like a theatre production, so getting someone who has that level of experience can be really useful to create something extra special.
- Work with the goal – what are you trying to achieve, and how can you make that come to life?
- Ask people for their ideas and allow them to express their ideas freely. Some will be wild and won't work, but there will be some gold there.
- Costs can really add up, so be aware of how much things cost when you're creating your space.
- Have your IP woven into what you're doing, but not in a way that slaps people around the face.
- Weave in moments of joy, surprise and delight. People will have a better time and they'll remember your brand and the experience.
- Create moments that truly immerse people – if you're using experiential marketing, really make it an experience.
- Look to create memories in what you do.
- Provide opportunities for those involved to create and share content too, to further the impact beyond the immediate audience. This could be areas designed for content creation, or even working with professional photographers to capture moments for people.

- Experiential marketing works with a small audience segment but goes deep. These people can become huge advocates that amplify your message and brand.

23

Authenticity and relatability

Why telling the whole truth can inspire connection

Authenticity might be the most overused word in the modern world, but when it comes to marketing, some brands really nail it, and their audience love them for it. I can't think of a brand that shouldn't be authentic. Authenticity is – according to the *Cambridge Dictionary* – the quality of being real or true. A possible reason it's become one of the most overused and, possibly, hated words is because people and brands use it when they're not being 'true' at all. Or maybe they think they are, and they're declaring they are . . . so does this mean they're fibbing the rest of the time?! The overuse of the word, unnecessary use and incorrect usage has diluted its true meaning, causing many an eye roll. There are filters, smoke screens, mirrors, spin, maybe straight-out lies that are designed to improve the perception of a brand or product, but perhaps a tiny scratch of the surface and not all's as it seems. One area that's seen this backfire in horrible ways is sustainability when people dress up their own sustainable efforts as being market leading when they're actually the bare minimum. A name has been given to this particular line of inauthenticity – greenwashing. You know it's bad when there's a whole new name, don't you?

With the example above, the truly authentic approach would be to say, 'This is what we're doing and we're trying to be better.' Then, share the journey, the learnings and the new initiatives through words and imagery that depict the reality of the situation. Wild, right!?

Many companies don't opt for this, because they want the world to see them as superior in some way. But the thing is, reality has a habit of biting hard. It could be via a disgruntled employee or a fan innocently stumbling across your secret. But when your 'secret' is uncovered, it has the potential to cause huge reputational damage in a very short space of time. The thing to remember is that making big claims is great – *if* you can back them up. The consequences of not doing this can range from customers losing faith in you to a complete business disaster as your status slips away.

Due to the digital world, it's never been easier to create stories about you as a brand online, and share them, even when they're not accurate. It's much harder to look someone in the eye and tell them an untruth. Social media is made up of users (businesses and individuals) who work hard to project themselves as something that they're not because of the belief that this will lead to other opportunities in one way or another. When this started to become common knowledge, it created a huge amount of distrust in content seen online. And this is before we even look at how editing, AI and other tools have impacted the trust people have in each other in digital spaces.

True authenticity extends beyond the obvious

To be authentic, you just need to tell the truth – the *whole* truth. For example, if there's a surge in a subject and someone thinks, 'Well, we kind of do that so can get in on the buzz,' that's not the whole truth. If the words 'kind of' enter your mind, please reconsider. Getting in on the buzz might be nice, but if you get found out, the damage can be pretty significant.

Authenticity extends beyond the actions of the company as a body and includes the leaders of the company, employees and sponsored people/ambassadors/collaborators too. There have been plenty of occasions when a company's values have been called into question because of its extended network. It seems harsh, but it's the truth, and that's why some companies have clauses in contracts that talk about what happens if the company is brought into disrepute from actions taken by others.

Authenticity breeds authenticity

Do the right thing when it comes to being authentic, and allow this to be the example to people in your network, connected to your company. Don't ask them to be inauthentic on your behalf. If they don't feel aligned to a product or service you want them to promote, please just move on. Ask them why for your own research but don't push people into compromising their integrity. No one wins.

Radical honesty

But let's take this to another level – and I'm going to call this radical honesty. Authenticity at the highest level. This takes bravery, but if handled well and carefully thought through, the payoffs can be huge.

When we are looking at radical honesty, it often starts in an uncomfortable place and, in some cases, we start to tiptoe into crisis management. When things start to go wrong, brands can either bury their heads and just hope that no one notices, lie and insist nothing is wrong (even though everyone can see it is!) or take a deep breath and address the audience.

For something minor that can be fixed with ease, keeping quiet as you resolve the issue is not always a bad thing. You shouldn't be holding your hands up and running a full campaign for every little misstep as people will just think you're incompetent. Things happen every day in business that are less than ideal – and many can be resolved with relative ease or the minority of people being impacted. But when something big happens, that can be the time when radical honesty is the only real answer. A brilliant example of this was when fast food giant KFC ran out of . . . chicken.

Case study: KFC to FCK

February 2018 could have been truly disastrous for KFC in the UK, but through using radical honesty, brand sentiment soared, and so did market share.

The problem was chicken, or a lack of it. A distribution issue meant that hundreds of stores across the UK had to close because they didn't have any chicken to serve. Some reports say that over 90 per cent of outlets were closed at one time.

When something this big happens, burying your head in the sand isn't really an option. Twitter was going mad, hashtags were flying, and people even *called the police* about the problem. Of course, the media were all over it with news reports alongside social media talking about the situation. The noise around this issue was huge – and why wouldn't it be, it was an amusing story with the jokes almost writing themselves.

So, what can a brand do when it finds itself in this situation? Many would have pushed the blame onto someone else, but KFC didn't. One of the most brilliant marketing campaigns of all time (in my opinion at least) was created. FCK. On the side of an empty bucket. On full-page ads in newspapers.

Initially, it was thought that the problem impacted just a few restaurants, but over the course of a few days, the full scale of the issue became evident, and a lot of outlets were affected, resulting in widespread shutdowns. KFC worked hard to address the issue, and although the marketing and advertising side was not an immediate priority, it became more important as the stories started to come online around the crisis.

As mentioned above, the press caught hold of it, some customers were furious, some thought it funny, but what was clear was that KFC and its problem were everywhere. The brand was in all the places, for all the wrong reasons. And when that happens, action must follow. To start, most people saw the situation as amusing with endless chicken-related puns filling the online space, but the truth of the matter was that there are around 26,000 people working with KFC in the UK, plus about forty independent franchise partners. Whatever the brand did, it needed to balance these two very different viewpoints.

KFC had recently started working with Mother, an agency based in London known for some truly iconic campaigns. The company was brought on board to help get KFC's best work out there as part of a broader company objective connected to modernizing the way the company worked. But this was quite a different proposition. Mother jumped into action and addressed what can be one of the biggest missteps in crisis communication – the vacuum. When there's no information, people fill in the gaps and the work to undo all this is vast and can further damage a brand's reputation. It can feel bold to hold your hands up, but when a situation is so public, it really is the only option for longer-term benefit.

'In situations like this you need to let people know what's happening and with this story, the press were digging for more to add to the narrative, and none of this put KFC in a good light,' said the executive creative director from Mother at the time. 'We wanted to shift their attention to something positive – that KFC was doing everything it could to sort the situation out and was sorry for letting down customers and team members. So we took ourselves away and developed the ad at the agency. When it came to presenting it to the team, we were conscious that advertising was the last thing on their mind – they had much more pressing issues to deal with.'

The ad was simple but highly effective.[1] The visual of the empty FCK bucket was powerful, but so were the words: 'A chicken restaurant without any chicken. It's not ideal . . ..' The copy apologized to customers, thanked team

[1]www.bbc.co.uk/news/newsbeat-43169625

members and franchisees before ending with more honesty: 'It's been a hell of a week, but we're making progress . . . thank you for bearing with us.'

Going from a crisis to a version of the F word is a pretty big leap, by any stretch, and yet KFC went for it because it captured the sentiment perfectly. The vulnerable apology to everyone inside KFC and customers too showed the power of radical honesty, of being human, and of vulnerability.

The campaign started in print because of the gravitas connected to it, and the time it would be 'live' as daily newspapers have a very short shelf life. *The Sun* and *Metro* were selected because they'd gone hard on the coverage of the issue, and the boldness of the ad meant it got shared organically by people. In fact, the FCK content wasn't shared on KFC's official channels at all. The campaign extended to social, to a microsite, all using the honest tone. And it worked, not just on customers, but on the people working at the outlets too as the way customers treated them changed; they empathized with them.

More than people feeling empathetic towards KFC, the brand bounced back stronger than before with positive brand sentiment and a market share increase the following year.

But radical honesty doesn't have to be reserved for a crisis. It can be a key pillar of a marketing plan too . . .

Case study: Hans Brinker

Most hotels look for five-star reviews and promote all the features that will make people opt for them over others. Not Hans Brinker. No, this hotel took a very different approach, marketing itself as the worst hotel in the world[2] and putting together lots of examples why. There wasn't a twist at the end. Hans Brinker meant it!

---

[2]www.kesselskramer.com/project/hans-brinker-budget-hotel

The campaign was created by KesselsKramer, an agency that started working with Hans Brinker in 1996. The hotel increased the number of beds it had, increased its prices, and needed to get attention. It also knew its audience – young backpackers who frequented hostels that were less than ideal but did the job. The accommodation that backpackers tend to visit along their trips is cheap, and due to the cheapness, a lot of things slide. There is many a story in circulation about how awful particular hostels and hotels are, but most hotels don't want people talking about this. Hans Brinker leaned in. It was never going to be the world's best hotel – but the worst? Well, maybe not, but it could use honesty, humour, and bold marketing to grab people's attention . . . and what's quite funny is when you read some of the reviews, people share that the accommodation is, in fact, not that bad!

Matthijs de Jongh is from the agency KesselsKramer and worked on the campaign. He explained that, when it comes to honesty in marketing, you must start from the ground up and really understand what you're dealing with. 'David Ogilvy taught to closely study the product before you make advertising for it,' says Matthijs. 'He emphasized that advertisers must be knowledgeable and honest about the products to persuade consumers and avoid misleading them. He drove a Rolls Royce while writing the famous line "At 60 miles per hour the loudest noise in this new Rolls Royce comes from the electric clock".[3] When we took on the Hans Brinker Budget Hotel, we spent a night there, which was dreadful: rude staff, noise, uncomfortable beds. You wouldn't recommend your worst enemies to stay in the Brinker. Clearly, Brinker wasn't luxurious. Instead of lying about its shortcomings, we made honesty its ultimate luxury.'

How did they do this? They really went for it. Posters saying that there's now a bed in every room, that there's more noise than ever, and that there's 'now even more dog sh*t in the main entrance' (that's an actual quote from a poster!). How about putting flags in lumps of dog faeces with messages too?

---

[3]www.latimes.com/archives/la-xpm-1987-12-08-fi-27459-story.html

They did that. Instead of soap and other things you'd expect in a hotel room, the Hans Brinker Hotel provided a piece of paper with shapes labelled to symbolize what you'd expect in a room. Guests could then cut out their soap, shampoo, hair dryer, etc. They were made of paper and had zero use, but that didn't stop this being used for marketing! It shared imagery of luxurious rooms with asterisks all over the picture, before the bottom of the image showed that '*' meant 'not included'. It created videos showing someone bouncing off people's doors down the corridor, explaining that this was the wake-up call. It had images of check-in versus check-out, with the guest checking out looking exhausted and dishevelled to further illustrate the bad situation. The agency even wrote a book about it![4]

Did it work? Yes. It got people talking (and still does to this day) – in fact it's been said to be the most talked-about hotel brand ever. From a business perspective, it saw a 42 per cent increase in occupancy.[5] But more than that, this radically honest approach, being authentic, attracted a lot of earned media, with the flags in the dog faeces outside bringing CNN to the hotel.

Why did it work? The Hans Brinker Hotel fully committed to the message and that carried through to every touchpoint it had with the customer. It used humour in its bold approach, and it was really, really bold. For the wrong brand, this would have been a business-ending piece of marketing, but Hans Brinker was honest with itself. It knew what it was providing, it knew its customers, it knew what it was doing. And it worked. Whatever the budget was for the campaign, the earned media, the commentary and the exposure would be worth significantly more. Being radically honest, even about your faults, can work. If you know what you're doing.

Matthijs has an interesting take on how brands can stay honest while still creating engaging and interesting campaigns that align with core values. For

---

[4]www.amazon.co.uk/Worst-Hotel-World-Brinker-Amsterdam/dp/1861543115
[5]https://rohitbhargava.com/the-worst-hotel-in-the-world/

him, it's not always about reality, but integrity. 'All we know is that most brands don't know where to draw the line,' says Matthijs. 'Brands often overpromise, exaggerate and end up sounding clichéd. The hotel business is notorious for showing rooms, reception, sauna, restaurant and gyms much better than they really are. You don't have to stick to reality, but you do need integrity. Not per se to "do good", but to connect with people. And if you can, make it fun.'

An unexpected side effect of honesty is the management of customer expectations. If you say your product or service does things it doesn't, you're going to have disappointed, maybe even angry, people banging on your door or flooding your inbox. Through being honest, you can decrease customer complaints too, something that Matthijs says the Hans Brinker Hotel saw.

Relatability

While some campaigns utilize futuristic, aspirational or even impossible scenarios, there's huge power in using relatability in campaigns. The trend for this continues to grow. Recognition of the highly edited versus 'normal' life can be seen by the social media trend 'Instagram versus reality'. Extending beyond social media, relatable campaigns that allow people to see themselves in your narrative and story, and the pain point your product solves, can be an easy and highly effective way of showing people how what you do or sell can really help them and their lives. 'Let the Song Play', an incredible piece of marketing by Spotify, taps into that relatable moment when your favourite song is playing but you've just arrived at your destination. For anyone who's sat in a car to let a song finish, or felt aggrieved that an appointment has cut their enjoyment short, the campaign instantly connected.

Case study: Spotify's Let the Song Play

Although the campaign was US-based,[6] it's relatable everywhere, stemming from the fact that most music listening happens in cars – or on the move. Taking this simple, relatable insight, Spotify wanted to get people to decide to stream from Spotify rather than putting on the radio when they were travelling. Noel Yeo, creative director of the campaign, says, 'Music is such an emotional thing, and so we thought we needed something sticky, something you'd remember, and so we were searching and stumbled upon this random fact from a tyre company, buried at the bottom of this chart, almost like a footnote that said something like 63 per cent of people have stayed in their car to let a song play out after arriving at their destination. Something very dry, but it felt universal and relatable, and 100 per cent a music-based insight, and so we knew we had to do that. After that it was just lining up scenarios to get our point across, and making sure the takeaway from our audience is, yeah, I've done that.'

The longer video shows people in a range of different situations as they pull up to a destination, but the track they're listening to, and love, hasn't ended. This included a pizza delivery, a sports game, a party . . . with people waiting to receive the person, or product, and them remaining in the car. 'Staying in the car to listen to a song play out, it's easy to over-act here, so a lot of work went into the casting, more so than usual, just to find folks who could pull it off without the whole thing feeling slapstick,' says Noel. 'Just that first scene alone, when the valet tries to open the car door and the driver just ignores him? That was so incredibly hard to nail. Our driver initially auditioned as the valet before we realized he was actually the perfect driver. Made us laugh by doing very little. We got lucky with our cast.'

Sia's Elastic Heart was the track chosen for the campaign. Interestingly, this song was released in 2013, but Let the Song Play wasn't released until 2019. To maintain relatability, the song also needed to strike the right chord with a

[6]https://noelyeo.com/Spotify-Let-the-Song-Play

diverse audience. 'This was much harder than we anticipated,' says Noel. 'There were a few songs we knew everyone would first think of, maybe a Whitney Houston or Celine Dion song, but they were also kind of old or too retro, which meant there was a chance it had already been parodied in popular culture. We were also Spotify and so knew we wanted to showcase a more current song, something that felt more now. That Sia track, especially a less known version of it, felt believable that someone would stay in the car for, know the words enough to sing along, and let it play out.'

Although the longer film (sixty seconds being long these days!) was one piece of the campaign, a number of fifteen-second clips were made following different individuals in the film and their stories.[7] It was also part of a larger campaign with the content being shared through digital assets and on boards in prominent places, to emphasize the message. 'Our "enemy", so to speak, was the radio,' says Noel. 'We didn't want to get into why music streaming was better than radio in the film, we wanted that to be emotional, but felt we could call out radio on the billboards.'

Relatability can also work well from a founder-led perspective – and even big brands can leverage this through sharing the founder's content, or tapping into stories from customers happy to share their real-world struggles and situations, and team members too. The more threads of relatability that can be shared, the greater the audience connection is. And this can reap big rewards for those brands that use it.

Being human

Being relatable shows a human side to the brand – that the people behind it really do understand you as they're humans themselves (surprise!). This can help to deepen the connection that is felt to a brand.

---

[7]https://noelyeo.com/Spotify-Let-the-Song-Play

Sometimes, being relatable can also show a vulnerable side – or a perceived vulnerability. Some products and services are created from vulnerabilities when people find a solution to an issue in their own life. Being vulnerable as part of a marketing campaign is brave, but get it right (and you can do the research to make sure you're really not alone in your thoughts), and it can give you the opportunity to find a place in people's hearts.

Can vulnerability = weakness?

Some worry that vulnerability can show weakness and – perhaps controversially – I think it can, when that vulnerable moment is made into the whole story rather than just a part of it. Let's run through an example. You as the founder have had a very bad day and you're crying. You feel like everything is too much, things have gone wrong, you're mentally and physically exhausted – you're just done. And you decide to film yourself being very upset. This is relatable, and people will engage with this vulnerability, but put your PR hat on – what does this say about the current situation? And your ability to fulfil the function you need to? The better option would be to share this *when* you've reached the solution, as a part of the story. This helps to show growth, it's deeply relatable, it engenders trust because you've been open, but also shows you and your business in a highly professional way. It's still relatable. It's still vulnerable. But it also helps to elevate your brand and you as a thought leader/expert in your space. You don't have to compromise professionalism for relatability.

An interesting example of the power and pushback of vulnerability came from Braden Wallake in 2022. He shared a LinkedIn post[8] with an image of him crying following layoffs in his company. He became known as the 'Crying CEO'. He did it to show the human behind the decisions, and I absolutely

---

[8] www.linkedin.com/posts/bradenwallake_this-will-be-the-most-vulnerable-thing-ill-activity-6962886723617910784-_L4w/

get that, and so did some others – but many didn't. The fact that Braden was branded the 'Crying CEO' shows that, doesn't it? However, if you read this post with a critical eye, something big is missing which, in my opinion, would have reduced a lot of the backlash . . . celebrating the people he had to let go. By name (obviously with their permission). Helping them find their next role. Sharing his vulnerability but for a reason that was bigger than what many interpreted as 'I've had a bad day'.

Or he could have waited a while, shared a post where he wasn't crying, and explained hard decisions in a way that shared knowledge. But would this have got the same reaction? No, because vulnerability does get reach – whether you like it or not. What's interesting is how this post would have been received if Braden were female. But that's a subject for another day . . .

How can you make this work for you? Key learnings . . .

- Being authentic should be at the foundation of all you do. If you're not being authentic, why not?
- Honesty is a powerful marketing tool, but that doesn't mean you have to share everything about every aspect of your business! Honesty, to my mind at least, is all about telling the truth in what you decide to share.
- You can have some fun with it. By critically assessing your brand and business and finding its quirks, you can lean into these and use them as part of your messaging.
- Authenticity and honesty aren't just about the brand; they're also about employees, influencers and ambassadors – everyone connected to the brand has the potential to amplify or damage the messaging. Don't oversell yourself when you're on shaky ground – there should always be truth behind what you say and imply. Don't say you're a green company

if you only recycle your plastic water cups! It's not correct, and it could damage your brand if you get found out. Saying you're making small steps in the right direction is more accurate. Don't spin and fabricate – be better.

- Relatability can be a brilliant strategy, encouraging people to see themselves in your campaigns.
- You can show relatability in many different ways – this could be in humour, life moments, you name it.
- Showing vulnerability – authentic vulnerability – can provide a lot of engagement, but ensure it doesn't compromise your brand's reputation when it comes to being professional.
- Sharing vulnerability needs to be carefully considered. It's often better as part of a story arc when the solution has been found that created the vulnerable moment.
- Although big campaigns can be around relatability, so can moments in day-to-day life, which can be used in scrappy, temporary content.

24

Visual effects

Utilizing AI and CGI for the right reasons, not just to cut corners

Although Artificial Intelligence (AI) and Computer Generated Imagery (CGI) have been married up in this chapter, do not be under any illusion that they're the same. They're really not.

When we look at the visual side of marketing, both have a part to play, and both are used frequently. You're much more likely to see and be able to access AI to help you create visuals than CGI – simply because AI creates things from a prompt, whereas CGI requires numerous elements to be carefully woven together to create the output. There are many other uses when it comes to AI in marketing too, but we're starting from the visual side because we can look at the different roles each plays here.

Let's begin with AI. Not all that long ago, AI felt new and terrifying, with many people sure it would take over the planet, or at the very least their jobs. The truth is, when 'we' got hold of AI and it started to be presented to us in usable forms, it had already been around and helping us for years.

Now, the usage of AI for marketing is a lot more mainstream. Although it's easy to ask whatever engine you use to create something for you, it doesn't mean what it creates is any good. I think we've all seen examples of companies experimenting with AI and getting it horribly wrong. One that stands out to me is seeing a five-legged horse trying to jump a fence, and not only did it have the extra leg, but the fence was somehow in the middle of its body. The stuff of nightmares. While it's kind of funny, if your brand has legions of fans passionate about a subject, and you share an image the equivalent of a five-legged horse, what does it say about you? Most of us, and most brands, spend a huge amount of time getting the correct colour for the logo, have brand guidelines, have invested in the tone and the customer journey to ensure that customers feel seen, cared for and understood. All of this means that the company is seen as professional – maybe even an expert in the field – who's careful and considered. What does a five-legged horse say in this situation? This, alongside the vast quantity of rather shoddy work created using AI flooding our social media feeds, is what Martin Pagh Ludvigsen, creative director of AI and creative tech at Goodby, Silverstein and Partners (GS&P), refers to as 'AI slop', a phrase we will increasingly see in the future.

But before we bash AI too much, let's look at some of its uses in the creative, visual side of marketing that have been utterly game-changing.

A helping hand

'We use generative AI in conjunction with more traditional methods,' says Martin. 'AI is one more source we can get imagery from. Generative AI opens up possibilities for us, to create shots and sequences much faster than before, with multiple iterations. So when we're working on something, the creation of the AI sequences still goes through the same processes, before they are put together in editorial. It's another instrument we can play in the great symphony of creativity, and it has expanded out creative possibilities and allowed us to do things that weren't possible at all or within the timeline or budget available.'

One of the uses for AI is helping to demonstrate an idea, allowing it to be shared in some format beyond the creator's head. This can make it a lot easier to explain a concept, a flow, or a story to the team. As GS&P has clients to consider, it can save considerable time, allow for more iterations to be tested, and ensure that everyone is on the same page when it comes to the idea. 'Previously, we'd use tools to try and create the best-looking image of the sequence of events we want to happen in a film along with a script for whatever we were trying to achieve,' says Martin. 'But there's a limit to how many of these that can be produced in the time allowed, within budgets. Imagine if you're presenting four ideas – you know three won't make the cut, but the work still needs to be done. Generative AI has unlocked so much in that respect. It's saving creatives a lot of time, allowing them to present the idea better. It's opened up so much to allow us to show some of the wild ideas we have – it is truly wonderful for us.'

In most cases, AI won't be used in the final piece of work, but that doesn't mean it isn't useful.

AI can be used particularly effectively in cases where real life wouldn't permit the idea. One example would be making an animal look like another type of animal by dressing it up, where it would be unethical to do this in real life. Another example is using AI to make it more affordable and safer to achieve other dangerous feats – such as stunts, for example.

Counterculture

And there's another way that AI can be used . . . and that's as counter culture. Martin worked on a campaign for BMW called Real, For Real,[1] which focused on the market for certified pre-owned cars. Purchasing second-hand

[1]https://youtu.be/6OU2f0FBg3k?si=oPIkHfP2pNmUTH27 (Search 'BMW Certified Reality Check Video')

vehicles can make people worry they have no idea if what they're being sold is as good as it seems. BMW harnessed this belief and AI in a very different way. 'We've reached the point in the use of generative AI in marketing that we've started to see counter culture evolve,' says Martin. 'We used generative AI to show that in a world where it's difficult to know who to trust, you can trust the BMW certification programme. We have these spots that start with videos of AI-generated things, like pigeons riding skateboards. One person in the ad is saying, 'Have you seen this!' and the other is saying, 'No, it's AI', and that leads them to ask, 'What can you really trust in the world we live today?'

Effective, fun, and a way to use AI that is authentic to the brand.

Not all brands should utilize AI in their end product because it could jar against their audience, values, product or service. If you're a premium brand using AI for the final images or video you're sharing, will that resonate with your customers? If you're using an AI-generated version of your product, would that inspire trust in the people you really want to buy it? Showing an artificial version can sow the seeds of doubt in people's heads. You need to consider your audience too. While a younger generation might be more accepting of AI elements, older customers might not be. True fanatics connected to a product or service could also put up more resistance because, as Martin says, with generative AI, the quality isn't there yet. And the little details matter, particularly to an audience that really do love the detail.

Case study: Speak to Dali, through AI

The Dali Museum in St Petersburg, Florida, is dedicated to Salvador Dali – not just his paintings, but his other work too. To showcase his brilliance, the museum works with GS&P to find ways to use emerging, cutting-edge technology to bring Dali to the next generation of museumgoers. This was the scene for one of Martin's first generative AI projects, in 2018.

'We used a predecessor to the current ways of generating images, which meant we could only generate one type of image and you'd need to train the model on lots of similar images, whereas now you can create anything,' says Martin. 'We used the system to shoot a performance of an actor and then used a generative adversarial network (GAN) to put Salvador Dali's face on top of the actor's. This was called Dali Lives[2] and you could go up to a kiosk and have a limited interaction with him. It's an interactive video experience that has videos that play in different sequences.'

For the time, this was incredible, and a brilliant way to bring art and the person behind it to life. But as technology developed, so did GS&P's ideas as to what it could do to further the museum's mission. In 2024, the company used generative AI to create something that wasn't possible before – Ask Dali[3] – which allowed people to have discussions with him, around whatever subject they wanted through an iconic Dali-inspired lobster telephone. 'You pick up the phone, and you can have a conversation with him,' says Martin. 'You can ask him anything, and people will take these conversations to amazing places. They ask him about his art, controversial topics, celebrities he's met, or people even use him as a therapist. It's possible by combining a few generative AI tools.'

Martin and his team managed to recreate Dali's voice in English using snippets found from interviews on British and US TV channels. To make it sound even more Dali-like, the tool was also trained for tone. 'He was a prolific writer, so all the information on his written work has been fed into the tool, allowing him to use the words that he really would,' says Martin. 'This has been a smash hit for the museum. People get really engaged in the conversation. This would not have been possible to do without generative AI.'

---

[2]https://thedali.org/exhibit/dali-lives/

[3]https://thedali.org/exhibit/ask-dali/

In 2025, the museum and agency extended the project's reach to celebrate Dali's birthday by providing a number that would allow people to call and speak to Dali from anywhere.[4]

But you don't have to be a big agency to utilize AI, and you don't need to have huge goals for creating something like the above. There's a lot of power in utilizing AI to help make your creative work better, supporting you in creating materials that help you move the needle in your business. Our demand for visuals has never been greater, but neither has the opportunity to create them at scale and at speed. Adobe has integrated AI into its products, one key example being Adobe Express, which is a quick and easy tool for anyone to create standout content. 'We view AI as augmented intelligence, it's something to enhance human creativity and not replace it,' says Simon Morris, VP Marketing at Adobe. 'We see people who have a clear creative vision using AI to reduce or eliminate those tedious and time-consuming tasks, freeing up more time to spend on the deeply creative high-value work. For business professionals and marketers, who might not identify as a "creative professional", AI can be the spark to overcome the fear of the blank page, using prompts to get some ideas. What's important to remember is that AI is in the service of the human and not the other way around.'

Other uses of AI in marketing

AI might feel space age and like it's beyond the grasp of most, but it's really not. The key is to think about what AI can bring to the party and how that can help you streamline and improve your processes and enhance your customer experience. Here are a few common uses for AI in marketing that could change your business in a positive way . . .

---

[4]https://thedali.org/dial-dali/

Personalization

Some companies have effectively used AI to provide a personalized approach, at scale, to their customers. Whether this is allowing people to input their information and create a bespoke skincare routine, or try on different hair colours or outfits, utilizing AI in this way can provide instant, tailored advice that makes people feel seen and special. Connect this to an email nurture sequence for those who don't buy instantly and you're likely to gain more sales (and loyalty) as a result.

Personalization can also be used effectively in online ads – a great way to stop the scroll when people are served something that feels written and made for them, versus a broad ad that's desperately trying to target everyone.

Support in creative

Ever seen a blank page and wondered what on earth you were going to do? AI can be a brainstorming 'buddy' to help get creative juices flowing, suggest ideas and help bring those together in front of you. Using AI in this way, as a keen, creative assistant, can support better ideas, the iteration of these, and the exploration of new concepts too. To utilize this, you need to work on your prompts to ensure you're giving your helper the best chance of being useful.

Digital marketing testing and iterating

When you have a million ideas but don't know which to choose, you can use AI to help refine and test, record results and iterate based on this organized feedback. Whether this is done through something as simple as a split test (when you test two versions of an advert at the same time and assess the results before rolling out a full campaign), or personalized ads that constantly adjust to create a bespoke experience, the list is endless.

Chatbots

Utilizing chatbots to help address people's frequently asked questions, guide them to the right information, help them decide what to buy, or point them towards the right department can be a highly effective way to reduce man hours and customer annoyance at the same time as ensuring you don't need to be sat at your computer all hours trying to keep people happy. Bots can be a great way to keep customers content, enhance retention and drive conversions – because if your brilliant marketing is driving people to a place, you need to make sure they're being cared for when they arrive.

Automations and sequences

These two little beauties can change the email marketing game. By utilizing AI inside many of the email marketing software options available, you can design automated sequences that take people from lead magnet to being nurtured through offers and information, all the way through to making sales. Lists can also be segmented to improve open rates and click-throughs, so people feel like you really are speaking to them. And the beauty of all this is if you put the work in at the start, constant management isn't required, giving opportunities to scale.

Automation can also be a highly effective strategy on social media. There are an increasing number of services that, when triggered by a word in the comments, set off a chain of events that deliver what you ask them to, such as specific links and sign-up forms, instantly.

And this really is just the tip of the iceberg.

CGI

CGI is a very different animal but one that many big brands use to bring an extra dimension to their marketing.

It is the case that, for most small businesses, CGI isn't a consideration. It's an expensive process that takes a team of people with considerable skill to do well. And if you're not going to do it well, it's best to do something entirely different. Essentially, CGI is based on reality, but gives the creatives enhanced control and the ability to combine scenarios and situations that wouldn't be possible in normal life.

One example of this, provided by Martin at GS&P, comes from Mountain Dew's Super Bowl campaign, featuring the legendary singer, Seal, as a seal. Singing an adaptation of his hit 'Kissed By A Rose'[5] but with a beverage-appropriate twist. While people thought this was created using AI, it was actually made through CGI. 'We shot on a green screen and then there was a whole process with Seal laying on one side in the pose of a seal, singing his song,' says Martin. 'It starts in a place of culture, it's been a meme for ages, turning Seal into a seal. And the seals around him were added with CGI too. There was a lot of facial tracking involved because Seal has a very expressive face, and that's what allows the CGI to really work well because that's what makes the seal really recognizable as Seal.'

So why opt to use CGI? As Martin explains, it gives an element of creative control that can't be matched in real life. It can also save money in certain situations and reduce the time taken to create specific scenarios. 'You really can plan every single camera move the right way,' says Martin. 'In CGI, cameras can do things that they can't do in real life. You're not limited by physical capabilities. You can go inside objects, for example. A long time ago, I shot a car campaign that was a full spin around the car, above the car, and then the camera went into the car and looked around the cabin and around

[5]www.youtube.com/watch?v=eVkms228VGo (Search 'Mountain Dew Super Bowl Commercial 2025')

the back. We had to remove the roof of the car. It was a really expensive shoot. The size of the camera crane we needed to do it was incredible! If CGI had been at a quality level that would have worked in 2017, it would have been a much cheaper shoot and we could have planned everything in advance, every camera motion.'

How can you make this work for you? Key learnings . . .

- There are many tools out there that you can try for free or not very much money at all. Explore as many as you can. You might find you like different tools for different activities.
- Check what you create. Don't expect AI to be perfect – it isn't. It's as good as the prompt, and as good as what it's been trained on. And even if both of these are good, you're not guaranteed something perfect. Check over anything created using AI, and be aware that sometimes you can be too close to the work, so don't be afraid to seek expert help.
- Don't fear it. AI can be incredibly useful when you see it as an assistant rather than something trying to replace you.
- Push against the temptation to add to 'AI slop'. Just because you *can* create loads of content doesn't mean you should! What you do create, even if you use AI, should still be high quality in all the ways it needs to be.
- AI can be a great way to bring an idea to life in next to no time. This can be useful if you're trying to show someone your idea and you're struggling to articulate it. It can also be used in tandem with graphic designers, helping you develop much better briefs for work.

- There are lots of ways that AI can be used behind the scenes to streamline, enhance, test and personalize your marketing. These can lead to big changes in engagement, retention and conversion.
- AI is becoming an integrated part of many of the other marketing tools used in business – design software, email marketing, social media and more. Explore these options – their purpose is to make your life easier and your business better. A change in mindset could change the trajectory of your business.
- CGI is expensive to do well, so don't try and scrimp and save. If you can't dedicate the proper budget, change the plan.
- CGI can be used to save money on complex shoots and gives creators a high degree of control.
- People get AI and CGI confused, but the processes are very different, as is the quality of the output at this time.

25

Data

How to tap into the core metrics that influence the creative

While data might not be the most exciting side of marketing, it's an essential piece of the puzzle. It can show whether something is working at the level you want it to – not just from vanity metrics or anecdotally but whether those conversions are happening.

But it can be overwhelming. There's a huge amount of data available now, thanks to the digital world, and while interpreting every element of every campaign could well become a full-time job, understanding the parts you need to help you move the needle in the right direction by iterating ideas is essential for success.

We've already met Lorna Andrews – an influencer and founder of brands LA Space and 98 Beauty. She uses data to understand more about how her community is responding to the content she's creating, and that then fuels her next moves. 'I look at the data and see what they're interested in,' says Lorna. 'As a business, we sometimes see spikes and we need to see where that comes from as it's important and sometimes not obvious. How can you scale when you don't know what works? For me, data is really important, it's not the be-all and end-all, but from the business perspective I receive a report every Monday that says what I need to share to maintain the trajectory we have got.'

LA Space,[1] Lorna's fashion brand, is at an exciting point where it is taking on wholesale partners, and she is using their data to inform her choices. 'It was their stats that won me over; it wasn't their marketing as a retailer, it was the potential of who they could put us in front of.'

Of course, the data isn't always going to show what you want to see, but it's more important than the information that strokes your ego – if you have the right mindset to accept it and take on what's being shown to you as a challenge. 'Even if it annoys me, it'll trigger me to be reactive,' says Lorna. 'The whole reason I've been able to stay relevant on Instagram is by being reactive and not being scared. Because there's a point when the old stuff doesn't work anymore.'

Get started

Martin Huntbach from Jammy Digital, and the person behind entrepreneur and author Daniel Priestley's online success, explains that data is hugely valuable, but the most important step is to start. While research is important, the only way you're going to get usable data that relates to your audience is to get cracking. 'We look at where we're posting, how often, what are people resonating with – is it a particular concept, for example,' says Martin. 'Look at the data but don't let it dictate everything. It's like a news broadcast that only looks at things that will get engagement. Think of fame and fortune. It's not just the views, it's the comments, the words in the comments, the amount of copy in those comments, how many people click, where did these clicks come from, how many leads did it generate, how many people purchased. We like the full width of data.'

The vanity argument can really sway data here, and particularly on social media, where vanity metrics stroke the ego, but it's the conversions that pay the

[1] www.laspace.co.uk/

bills. That's why finding the bits of data that actually matter and extracting this from everything you're able to access is essential.

Three hats

Anthony Smith, director of trailers for Diary of a CEO with Steven Bartlett, views how data integrates with marketing in a very visual way. 'I have an analogy of the three hats,' says Anthony. 'There's the top hat, which is the storytelling hat. This is the hat you need to wear when crafting a narrative and the edit itself, learning from your failures and successes, the years of knowledge you've gained, the experience you've earned. With this hat you understand how story structures work, what music is perfect for that exact moment, how to create a hero. Then, there's the baseball cap, which is the marketer's hat. This is the hat you need to wear to constantly remind yourself about the goal of that content, which is usually to sell a service or a product or to lead your audience to another place. This hat is there to ensure the work you craft through your experience and knowledge aligns with your role as a marketer/brand builder, and it does that by pulling out the playbook of human psychology. And then you have the hard hat, or the data hat. The hard hat is there to, ultimately, protect your work and the brand, by using data and experimentation to ensure that the work you're producing has the best possible chance of achieving its goal and reaching its audience. It's very often thought of in the creative industries that data restricts freedom of expression and constricts art, but that is a challenge every content creator, video editor, graphic designer, or copy writer needs to overcome and realize that it is not the case.'

Anthony says that you can't wear all the hats together as it can cloud judgement, hinder progress and even create anxiety. They need to be put on and taken off to allow all the viewpoints to assess the work independently to ensure the marketing activity is going to work.

Even with this three-hats strategy, that doesn't mean you can dispense with testing and iterating. However, understanding how the parts work together allows you to create the best first drafts you can and facilitates learning and improvement. 'With the trailers [for the podcast], we know whether we should start on the guest or Steven, we know what type of music works, we know what hooks land better, we know the cliffhanger works,' says Anthony. 'Even now, we test hundreds of thumbnails, and we track the interest across them all. When we get the data back, I know that's what the audience want to know, so that's what my hook becomes. That's why understanding and using the data is so important.'

More than your own data, there are also other sources available, like search volumes, that you can access around specific subjects, further informing your strategy at different points. There's no excuse not to make decisions with the help of data. We all want our marketing to be as effective as it can be and achieve whatever success metric it has been designed for. Data helps us do this, by providing markers to help us create, try, test and then go again. You don't need to worry about all the data that is available, but to be effective and better than you were on your last campaign, you need to learn what bits matter.

How can you make this work for you? Key learnings . . .

- Data is your friend as a marketer – not your enemy. Get comfortable with it, and change your perspective on it – it's there to help you be even more effective.
- Understand the metrics that really matter. These won't be vanity metrics; they'll be the ones that drive the results that count.

- Test, test and then test some more. Seeing the information that comes back as useful information rather than success or failure can transform your relationship.
- Understand that art and data can work together; it's not a case of one or the other!
- To get good data, you have to start something! Start off with your best 'guess' and then review the data to inform your next step. But the key is, you *have* to start!
- You can look at other sources of data too – not everything has to come from you and you alone. Sometimes these other sources can provide a good base to start your own experimentation.
- Think about the three hats in your marketing – particularly if you learn in a visual way. This is a really useful way to think about balancing three core aspects and how they work together for maximum benefit.

Conclusion

It has been a huge privilege to be able to share these real-life examples with you – to decipher the DNA and share the code that these incredible companies have used to reach success in their respective areas. I've tried to bring together a range of products, a range of services, a range of people, to give a real 360 view to help enhance understanding of what can be done, how to do it, how to know if it's right for you . . . and what success could look like.

The world of marketing continues to evolve at an alarming pace, and although that can feel scary, I am really hoping that this book has opened your eyes to what's available, and how exciting that is. Not all that long ago, utilizing AI for campaigns in any format would have been beyond most people, and now the vast majority of businesses use some form of AI in their work, and in their marketing too . . . even if they don't see it as AI! The access we have to data has also increased so much, to allow us to more effectively try, test and track what we're doing, to allow us to iterate and improve at a rate never seen before.

What hasn't changed is the human – your – ability to know your business inside and out, and find creative ways to engage, inspire, educate and excite your audience with your marketing. Turning someone with a passing interest into a dedicated customer and cheerleader with the right nurturing is magic . . . and the way you do this is the same as it's always been. You find that way to connect with them and tell the story that connects to the product, service or passion in a way that resonates with them. Whatever technology comes into the marketing arena in the future, you are still connecting to a human. Tools help you do this, but they don't replace you.

This book should help you to think about how you're going to improve the way you market your brand. To connect with your customer. To lean into what makes you and your business special and unique. To get those creative juices flowing. To think of things differently. To step away from what everyone else is doing 'just because' and start to evolve and adapt your marketing in a way that works for you and your clients. Stay in your lane. Don't get distracted by what others are doing and be swayed off course. To be great, you need to have that obsession in your business at every level. To do amazing things, you need to focus. You need a strategy that allows you to make consistently good choices that drive you closer to your goal. Screw what everyone else is doing. Utilizing the data, you'll have confidence in it.

You might think that some of the campaigns you've read about only apply to the big players. And yes, on a surface level, it's going to be tricky to pull off some of these feats with less budget. But the ideas behind them can work regardless of budget. Whether you decide to lean on humour or shock, influencers or product placement, there are so many opportunities out there to improve what you do. Perfect it and you'll grow your brand and business. Borrow the proven strategies used by the big boys, and apply them to your brilliant brand or business.

There's also the mindset you need to adopt. I've been lucky enough to speak to – in my opinion – the best of the best when writing this book and have had a glimpse into what makes them tick. Why their campaigns succeed when others fail – even when their budgets are small. It's a relentless pursuit to deliver excellence. To try, test, fail and learn. It's never giving up. As Georgie Holt, CEO of FlightStory, said when I spoke to her, it's an obsession. And it really is.

Even if people have bigger budgets than you do – and there will be loads of them – no one is you. You can make the choice to study your craft better than competitors. To dedicate yourself to that learning and testing. To push boundaries. To embrace the new. To become obsessed. Businesses don't succeed because of budgets, they succeed because of ideas. A bad idea is still a bad idea with a budget – it's just an expensive bad idea. It still won't generate the impact.

When I started writing this book, I was excited to really get under the skin of some of the campaigns that I've admired for a long time, and I am so, so grateful to all the brilliant people and brands who have come on board and shared their time and experience.

Now it's up to you. How are you going to apply the learnings from this book to amplify your message? I'd advise focusing on one bit at a time, treating it as an experiment, and looking at what you can learn and improve at each stage. I can't wait to see what you achieve. If you'd like to tell me, I would love to hear from you at book@rheafreemanpr.co.uk.

Thanks so much for being part of this journey – now it's time for you to shine.

ACKNOWLEDGEMENTS

I have a lot of thank yous for this book – because writing this much and wanting to weave best-in-class examples in, and share knowledge from the best of the best – well, it's been character building, let me tell you that. Some people have been delightful and really gone above and beyond in unexpected ways (and you'll find those thanked below!). Some brands and the people behind them have been, well . . . I guess the less said about that, the better.

Let's start with the people who let me interrogate them. A huge thank you to Martin Huntbach, Dr Jonah Berger, Gavin Beard, Phil Rumbol, John X. Carey, Ruchika Kalra, Monica Earle, Robin Dunbar, Jamie Peate, Noel Yeo, Rick Loughery, Lorna Andrews, James Whatley, Bob Burg, Georgie Holt, Stephen Nilsen (Stix), Rachel Hardy, Anthony Smith, Simon Morris, Oscar Plasidius, Karin Hedberg, Brian Frederick, Sadira Furlow, Sabrina Hall, My Lindstrom, Johnny Burn, Benjamin Honal, The LEGO Group, Victoria Carfantan, Luca Lorenzini, Amy Mansell, Lucy Frosdick, Charlene Charity, Nate Able, Shira Feuer, James Kulp, Lynsey Woods, Krystine Batcho, Brie Read, Matthijs de Jongh, Tom Wong, Sean Goff, Martin Pagh Ludvigsen and Tourism Australia.

I'd like to thank my brilliant publishers Bloomsbury – to Alex, Ian and Amy. You've been a joy to work with . . . and I still have to pinch myself when I say you're my publishers.

I'd also like to thank my family – although they don't really understand what I'm doing most of the time and why I get so excited about the work I do, they still support me. My sons, Charlie and Oscar, have tried, really hard, to understand more about what I do, celebrating word counts reached, chipping in with 'wisdom' when they can – they even did some proofreading during a half-term break. It's amazing what insights ten-year-olds bring to marketing.

My long-suffering husband, in-laws (my mother-in-law even approved the dead mole mention) and my father.

My long-suffering friends – again, I don't know where I'd be without them. Nicola and Woody (the dog), who accompany me and my four-legged friend Indy on walks while listening to me, trying to untangle chapters, Ruth – the queen of the emoji – who sends me more eye roll pics when I'm getting worried about things (mainly things being rubbish or landing badly!), Donna, who's always there with a voicenote or proofreading eyes, Emily, who's always in my corner, and Claire and Agy, who are forever cheerleading – I'm very lucky to have such a great group of people in my life. I don't think I'd keep throwing myself into these opportunities without them.

And to you. For reading. Without the support for my last book, *You've Got This*, this book might never have happened. If you got to here, and you liked what you read, can I ask you one last favour? If you could share some nice words as a review wherever you bought the book, it would be a *huge* help. Reviews really do help authors, and I'd be very grateful.

INDEX